D1071783

Juries and Justice

Books by Marcus Gleisser:

Juries and Justice
The World of Cyrus Eaton

Juries and Justice

Marcus Gleisser

340
G

South Brunswick and New York : A. S. Barnes and Company
London : Thomas Yoseloff Ltd

to

my father,
the late Ben Gleisser,
and my mother,
Riva Gleisser

Acknowledgments

The author expresses his gratitude to the many fine publications which have granted him permission to quote from various articles and books.

Special permission was given by the *Journal of Criminal Law, Criminology and Police Science* (Northwestern University School of Law) for "The Grand Jury Under Attack" by Professor Richard D. Younger; by the *Law Journal of Ohio State University* to quote from various articles in the spring, 1958, issue; by the *Wall Street Journal* for its article of May 23, 1961; by Harper & Row, Inc., to quote from *The American Legal System* by Professor Lewis Mayers, and by the *Journal of the American Judicature Society*.

Other excerpts came from such sources as the *Cleveland Bar Association Journal; Some Old Scots Judges* by W. Forbes Gray (Constable & Co., Ltd.); *The Law Times of Lincoln's Inn,* London; *Journal of the Law Society of Scotland;* the *University of Chicago Law Review; Nebraska Law Review; Anatomy of a Murder* by Robert Traver (New York: Saint Martin's Press); *North Carolina Law Review; Harper's Magazine; Columbia Law Review; Illinois Law Review; University of Kansas Law Review; Cleveland-Marshall Law Review;* Princeton University Press.

Preface

It is time for a good hard look at what has long been the sacred cow of justice and regarded by many as fundamental in a democracy—the American system of trial by jury. Too many persons regard it as an inviolate institution, a sovereign never to be questioned, something not to be disturbed.

Unfortunately for those who take such views, democratic systems invite challenge and thrive on questions. Invasion of the darkest corner is welcomed. Long-standing idols may be examined to see if they deserve continued respect or if they have been left behind by changing times.

It is with such a spirit that this book is undertaken: the spirit of inquiry and exposure. The subject is of major interest to all concerned with a basic problem of society: *equal justice for all*. Growing numbers of civil rights cases in the middle sixties emphasized the problem.

To the reader, I issue two invitations: The first, to take a trip through a number of courts and contrasting trials by means of this volume. In this way I hope you will receive a broad, panoramic view of your system of justice. And, in truth, it is *your* system of justice. You elect legislators to make laws and you vote for judges to administer them. Your neighbors and you are the jurors summoned from the outside to add your touch to justice.

You may someday stand before the bar of justice as an accuser — or as one accused.

The second invitation is for you to take a trip to your nearest court for a personal look at how it operates. Pay particular attention to the jury and its role in modern justice. In doing this, you will have a small idea of what was before me in compiling this volume. As I was, you may be impressed with both the grandeur and the importance of law in our lives. You will be impressed, too, with the necessity of seeking paths to improved administration of justice, to raise it to an ever-higher status.

In short, this book is surely not directed to the purpose of decrying our system of seeking justice, but to improving it; not to spotlighting weaknesses for the purpose of hurting courts, but to illuminate flaws with the hope it may lead to sorely needed corrections. This report is not the result of a brief moment's inspiration; it comes from lengthy study and deep thought as both a lawyer and a long-time newspaper reporter. It reflects the feelings of many persons whose daily tasks take them often into the heart of the arena where justice is molded.

It should be made very clear that this questioning of the present jury system is hardly revolutionary or original. Many academic leaders of the law have previously addressed themselves to this subject. Many practitioners have opposed the flaws of the jury system by complaining of its deficiencies and problems.

Take, for example, the situation in a single case in Cleveland, Ohio. It may have appeared insignificant in relation to other great problems, but for the participants, it was of the utmost urgency. It was, indeed, in microcosm, the epitome of a major legal problem now in existence across the country.

The case was based on lawsuits involving some $300,000

in investments that had collapsed. There was a broad hint of skulduggery; a lawyer was being sued for malpractice because he induced his clients to invest. By the time these events took place, the case had been in the court's files some three and one-half years, and one of the very important defendants had died. In addition, several witnesses had moved out of the city.

Handling the case was Samuel H. Silbert, the chief justice of Common Pleas Court at the time, and a veteran of more than 40 years on the bench. He suggested a solution : submit the case to three arbitrators, one chosen by the plaintiffs, one by the defendants, and one by the court — *and waive a jury trial*. Or waive a jury and have an out-of-town judge assigned to hear the case.

The chief justice, who had seen more than his share of jury trials, told the participants : "No jury in the world, without pencil and paper, will be able to follow this case. The jury will have to guess on the case and it will take six months. I don't want to take away your rights if you think you want a jury. In my opinion, you are just wasting your time. Presenting the case to a jury is a ridiculous thing because that jury can never get the facts."

As added reason to waive a jury, Chief Justice Silbert said that if the lawyers insisted on a jury despite obvious difficulties, he would have to postpone the case for another two years because "we simply feel we cannot spare the time to take your case and choke up the whole docket. There are so many more important matters. We haven't the facilities to take it up at this time. We have to bear in mind that when certain cases tie up the docket we have to defer them for a while in the interest of justice because there are other people who require attention." (This, too, pointed up another problem brought by juries — that of delay.)

What was the response of the attorney to the entreaty of a long-time veteran of the courts who could see the problems clearly? "I think the jury is the only answer." Asked by Chief Justice Silbert "If the jury is the only answer, what if the jury errs?" The attorney replied: "I will abide by the jury's decision."

Here is the view that too often confronts those who in all sincerity seek to raise the level of justice and expedite its administration. It is a view born of the fear of changes needed by society and founded upon some vague thought of the miracle expected from a dozen well-meaning but uninformed citizens selected at random from the general community.

It may be that the lawyers expected an advantage from persons who would not understand the complexities of finance but would feel an unreasoning kinship with others who had lost hard-earned money in an unfortunate investment. It would seem evident that a jury, far from the realm of finance, could feel a resentment of those mysteries that would not rise in experts.

In any event, the incident brought into focus the jury problem: the desire of the disinterested, objective veteran to skirt it, and the hope of a participant to capture some expected advantage from it no matter what difficulties it presented to the administration of justice. Interestingly enough, when this case finally came to trial, the judge eventually ruled the plaintiff did not have enough facts to support his contentions and dismissed the case at midpoint. This decision came only after several valuable weeks had been consumed in selecting a jury and going through the tedious presentation of complicated evidence.

In view of the many problems inherent in the jury question, this book is written not only for those who are directly involved in the courts—the judges and lawyers—but also for those who have been, or someday unwittingly will become, enmeshed in the tangle as litigants. It is also for those many, many good citizens who have sat baffled through a complicated trial and then found themselves with the almost impossible burden of trying to decide who was right and for how much money — the jurors.

The zeal with which this volume is written may raise question in the minds of some, while others may feel it does not go far enough. So it is with any controversial subject. Whatever the reaction, however, it should be borne in mind that I have striven in large measure to be objective in the basic areas. I have attempted to show the arguments of both the plaintiff's counsel and his adversary, the attorney for the defendant. Above all, I have tried to give the casual reader, the lay person to whom our courts are in large measure foreign grounds, somewhat of an insight into the operation of our system of justice.

Admittedly, it is difficult in a panoramic book to explore all the infinite details of each section. The highly specialized legal technician will have to forgive me for that. Deliberately left out were such procedures as directed verdicts, additures and remittitures, and other such academic "safeguards" against juries found in law books but rare to the courtroom. Instead, the purpose here was to give the impact of the problem in its entirety rather than to debate *ad infinitum* the ramifications and their many tributaries. Not only would such debate carry limited interest, but it would destroy the effect of the entire picture by needlessly portraying each blade of grass.

Hopefully, this book may start a few mental brush fires to join with others already burning on the same subject in widely separated areas; or it may set off some discussion and questioning; or it may start some thinking about, and a greater interest in, the public state courts and their methods of operation; or it may do nothing more than throw a little light into what thus far has been a dark and almost forgotten corner of our democratic system.

If it does any of this it will be well worth the effort it took in the writing. A little bestirring and questioning is good for all of us once in a while.

MARCUS GLEISSER

Cleveland, Ohio.

Contents

Juries and Justice

"We have a jury system which is superior to any in the world; and its efficiency is only marred by the difficulty of finding twelve men everyday who don't know anything and can't read."

—MARK TWAIN
Sketches New and Old.

PART I

How It All Started

1

The Grim Gamble

ON A WARM JUNE EVENING, I STOOD IN A COURTROOM IN Cleveland, Ohio, and watched as a poker-faced jury filed quietly into its box and, almost casually, handed in a verdict that rocked the state. News of this trial swept across almost every court in the country. It touched the medical profession too. The figure written on the printed form etched a new chapter in the history of personal injury damages. It gave $625,000, tax-free, to a fifty-eight-year-old former laborer who was previously earning about $5,000 a year. It placed him in the millionaire class with a single sweep.

A swirl of memories from the trial just concluded went through my mind. I had covered the two-week hearings with an eye to the drama, as a long-time news reporter who had handled thousands of trials both civil and criminal. I paid special attention to the details, and to the techniques of the attorneys because I, too, was a lawyer.

I recalled the man, both legs amputated, lying, pitifully wan,

on a crisp white-covered stretcher staring, staring, staring into
the eyes of the jurors. His actual testimony had been comparatively brief but, as I had written for my newspaper, packed
with punch. After completing his testimony, he simply lay mute
through the rest of the evidence—in full view of the jury for
hour after hour. It was planned that way: when the jurors
went out for a brief recess, they had to walk around his legless
body; when they came back from lunch, he was there, silently
staring.

I remembered how his attorney, A. H. Dudnik (who died
before the case was finally decided on appeal), a colorful grey-
haired man of middle years with a remarkable reputation for
victories with juries, had told me he had a choice of bringing
this suit in a federal or state court and for tactical reasons had
chosen the latter. His reason was that here he would be allowed
to "put on a better show for the jury, and my client is entitled
to as good a performance as he can get." Not good justice,
but a good show.

The jury had come back with the surprisingly high verdict
against the Baltimore and Ohio Railroad in a case built around
an insect bite. It was an insect no one ever saw: a bug which
the man without legs claimed came from a pool of stagnant
water near which the railroad track ran.[1]

The victim claimed that on a day in August—he was not
sure exactly which day—he had just come to work as a foreman for the railroad. He was standing near a pool of water
which had collected in the city's industrial valley from the
rain when he felt a sharp sting on his left leg. He said he
reached down and pinched what he thought was an insect and
felt something tumble down inside his trouser leg. Just then
the railroad cars he was to handle came along and he swung
aboard, never pausing to look at the "insect." From this, he
charged, an infection began which spread through his body

[1] This case is discussed in detail in the Appendix.

and caused first one leg and then the other to be amputated. "The insect's poison literally ate his legs away," was the more dramatic way his lawyer put it. He brought the case to life in a way an inexperienced jury could understand — and feel.

For this unknown and unseen insect, supposed to have come from an infested pool on railroad property (although this was never definitely proven) the jury was asked to make the railroad pay $750,000 for its negligence in allowing the pool to remain there. Some members of the jury later said several of their fellow members were ready to give the full amount. What is more, the lowest amount suggested in the jury's deliberations was $300,000. Evidently the final decision was a compromise of sorts. Presuming the man had a normal life expectancy of twenty-five more years (as it happened, he died two years after the trial), the $625,000 verdict, because it was free of income taxes, came out to a yearly income of about $88,000. If the victim had had to pay normal taxes on this latter hypothetical income, he would have had $25,000 clear after taxes.

To earn that net amount in a single year, tax experts have figured he would have to earn a staggering $2,200,000 or more.[2]

As the jury broke up after returning its verdict, and after it had been politely thanked by the judge, my mind turned back to another case I had covered in that same building a few months earlier. It was just before Christmas and an attractive young widow had come to Cleveland from her New York home for a trial that involved a $250,000 suit over the death of her husband in an automobile accident. She had hired adequate counsel, but they were lawyers known more for their bookish interest in the law than in their dramatic skills before

[2] A couple of years later a waiter at a restaurant where the jurors ate claimed he had been paid to bribe a juror in this case with $200. He later said his claim was a hoax and was convicted of trying to blackmail the lawyer.

a jury. The widow constrained herself admirably. There was
no weeping spell in front of the jury. When she broke down,
it was delicately : out of the jurors' sight. Drama was kept at a
minimum; this may have been her big mistake, as she should
have known a jury wanted to see her cry and, if possible,
faint, too.

Then, too, the defendant was not a large railroad or corporation with lots of money. He was only one of her husband's
co-workers. He was a balding, meek-looking man : another
working engineer-salesman, as her husband had been. His
attorney, a lawyer for an insurance company, had made several
settlement offers to the widow and her two young children.
The youngsters were not present at court sessions, and this cut
the drama even more.

The last offer—unknown to the jury—was $52,500. (The
defense attorney whispered to me that if the jury came in with
a verdict anywhere near $50,000, he would consider it a real
victory for himself.) The widow turned it down. Surely, a
healthy young thirty-three-year-old husband was worth more
than that. He should have had a long life ahead of him, and
he was already earning about $12,000 a year.

It was nearing time for the Christmas holidays when the
eight-day trial ended. The jury went up to deliberate. But in
less than an hour it was down again. There had hardly been
enough time to elect a foreman and discuss the merits of the
case. Its decision left the young widow ashen-faced and
stunned : She had been given nothing.

Even the defense attorney and the judge were shocked. Yet
there it was, secretly arrived at; and this jury, too, was politely
thanked and sent on its way. Why that conclusion? No one
would ever know. The grim gamble was completed. The roll
of dice was over. Justice was believed done, and the decision
was recorded.

There are many, many other examples of unexpected, unexplained actions by jurors. In criminal law, there was the Dr. R. Bernard Finch murder case in California. It had been climaxed by undignified bickering while two lives hung in the balance. Then there was the Cleveland case in which one jury had condemned a young man to the electric chair and a later jury found the same man (on the same facts) to be innocent and freed him. There were the two juries which I observed closely in the world-famous Sam Sheppard murder case, the first finding the osteopathic surgeon guilty of second-degree murder in December, 1954, for the bludgeon-slaying of his wife Marilyn and the second finding him innocent in November, 1966, after he had spent a decade in prison. And there was the murder case where a juror reluctantly agreed to a verdict simply because she was hungry and wanted to go home. Also, let us not forget the civil rights cases of 1965, in which a shocked nation watched as white jurors freed suspect after suspect alleged to have slain civil rights workers.

The two civil cases illustrated to me, by their contrast, the hoyden-like nature of our juries. The innocent, well-meaning jurors were the second sorriest sight in a court where justice is supposed to be weighed with fundamental equality to all mankind. Jurors, elevated briefly in their box above the level of the litigants, are the second sorriest sight because, in truth, the sorriest sights are the plaintiff and the defendant. One must either put on a worthwhile show or lose his case. The other has his life savings hanging on a split-second accident and the dramatic powers of his lawyer. They are the victims of this situation.

H. L. Mencken, the journalistic sage of Baltimore, once said : "The penalty for laughing in a courtroom is six months in jail; if it were not for this penalty, the jury would never hear the evidence." In fact, today's jury trials might indeed be vastly amusing for their errors were it not for their grim effects. Before their whimsy tumbles legal precedent, equality is made mockery, and law, the basis for organized society, becomes the most disorganized and unpredictable of professions.

By the middle of 1966, Harvard Law School's Dean Erwin N. Griswold was saying:[3]

[Discrimination] is found in juries, where, by one device or another, Negroes are rarely—often never—found seated on a jury which actually hears a case with racial aspects. It is found in the fact that a Negro convicted of rape is usually given a death sentence, while this is rarely the fate of a white man convicted of this offense.

Looming in the background of all this, is the fact, well known to Negroes, that a white man who harms them will rarely, if ever, be severely punished. The murderers of Mack Charles Parker, though known, have never been indicted. No one has ever been charged by the State of Mississippi with the murder of three civil rights workers in 1964. The trials of persons charged with the murder of Lemuel A. Penn and of Jonathan Daniels resulted in acquittals.

The measure of progress in this area, and our present lamentable situation, is indicated by the fact that a person was actually charged with the murder of Medgar Evers, and was brought to trial, resulting in a hung jury; he was retried, with the jury hung again. Here the prosecuting officers and the judge did their duty—all credit to them—but juries are a part of our system of administration of justice, too. The trial of one of the persons charged with the murder of Mrs. Viola G. Liuzzo likewise resulted in a hung jury. A re-trial led to an acquittal.

Jurymen take an oath to administer justice fairly and impartially, according to the evidence produced before them in open court. Until they do so, can it be surprising that Negroes have little confidence in the administration of justice in southern courts?"

[3] *Cleveland Bar Association Journal,* May, 1966; p. 147.

From the heart of the battle zone came the voice of the man who had faced its fire. Alabama's liberal attorney general, Richmond M. Flowers, told me when we met in Cleveland's Hotel Statler Hilton on May 19, 1966, that "basic jury reform is something which requires action on a national scale including action by Congress and through the powers of the federal courts." Flowers, just defeated in his race for governor against Mrs. Lurleen Wallace, had had the courage to denounce acquittal of a white man by a jury in a civil rights murder as a triumph of bigotry. And he had challenged another jury, filled with openly avowed white supremacists, all the way up to the Alabama Supreme Court—and lost.

Tall, red-haired, soft-spoken, and unsmiling, Flowers emphasized that in his opinion juries in all sections of the country frequently leave something to be desired. He said:

"The integrity of the jury system in Lowndes County, Alabama, brings into question the integrity of the jury system in Queens County, New York, and in Los Angeles County, California." He had earlier said this publicly in a speech before the trial section of the New York State Bar Association. Meanwhile, in Washington, President Lyndon B. Johnson called for jury reforms to prevent continuing injustice.

It should be made clear that the jury dilemma is not always the fault of the citizens who sit as judges of the facts and appliers of the law. They are simply caught in a system which accepts change only with great effort. Juries at one time had value: they marked emergence from a more primitive way of seeking justice. They met a need of early, uncomplicated times. Their history shows a growth stemming from necessity. Unfortunately, the jury system became solidified in America, and as a result has resisted the changes needed in the twentieth century.

The beginning of today's jury problems can be found in the jury's history.

2

Where it Started: History of the Jury

AN ANONYMOUS WRITER ONCE MADE AN INTERESTING ANALOGY between the early American jury trial and a baseball game: both were a form of melodrama, in his opinion, down to the final unpredictable decision. Here is how he saw it:[1]

Baseball is not a recreation, but a form of drama. It is, in fact, America's native contribution to the oldest of the arts. It has all the aspects of the drama. Especially has it one great basic factor of drama—the combat between good and evil; good, represented by the home team, evil represented by the visiting team. In a successful staging of this primitive drama, the forces of good and evil alternately prevail, but good is somehow expected to triumph in the ninth inning.

Roscoe Pound, in one of his illuminating analyses of judicial procedure, has pointed out that for a long time the only drama that a goodly share of the American people witnessed was the jury trial. Court is in session in the typical county seat town.

[1] *Journal of the American Judicature Society,* February, 1940.

The "rigs" lined up around the courthouse square testify to the presence of people from every village and township. Some are present as actors (O beautific role) and some as spectators only. For days and days the drama unfolds. Good and evil are represented now by one set of actors, now by another. The play has many acts, like a Chinese melodrama. It has the unity of time, place, and persons which baseball has; and it has a dark, gripping hatred as a foil to virtue's fearsome adventure. Neighbor is struggling against neighbor, kinsman against kinsman. The stakes are high, for fortune may change hands on the word of a witness or the artful machination of forensic orators. Hearts may be broken by the vote of the jury. Families may be disrupted, neighborhoods involved in feuds, or—perhaps most horrible and most seductive of all dramas—a fellow being may be condemned to die.

There is no doubt that very generally throughout the country, for several generations, trials at law satisfied the natural human craving for melodrama. At least jury trials did. Nobody ever saw the courtroom crowded during a chancery hearing [where there is no jury]. In the jury trial, everything was brought down to the intelligence level of the ordinary half-educated, idle spectator. It was good drama for it was realistic. The actors were no mere marionettes. They exulted when they won verdicts and they suffered genuinely when they lost.

It's a cold and dispassionate opinion that sees in all this "a training in citizenship." The jury trial has been a sad fiasco if its function has been to train citizens in civic duty and legal rights and obligations. But as a source of amusement when other thrillers are scarce, it has been a great success.

A gratification of the instinct for drama and entertainment is a part of every complete social environment. Fortunately, other devices than trials at law have been found to meet this natural craving. But the jury trial has come to occupy so large a part in trial procedure that it persists through its own inertia. Seen as a form of drama, one comes to understand better the nice balancing of procedural rights which were worked out, the rules tending to make it an all-star cast, the alternation of the forces of good and evil, and the exquisite prolongation of suspense.

While this anonymous writer interestingly described the beginnings of the jury system in early American life, it had by then grown from roots buried in Europe and England. When it first became known, it was far different than it is now. This fact offers hope for the present situation, for it shows that change does come and that the administration of justice can be made to adjust to the changed tempo and deeper understanding of a new era, albeit very slowly and with great effort.

TRIAL BY "ORDEALS"

The trial by jury was recorded to have originated with early Frankish kings. While its advocates now see the jury as an institution for the protection of poor, humble citizens, a barrier against the will of persons who are tyrannical and powerful, it really began as a form of royal inquisition. It was used to pry facts out of citizens who were believed to be holding back what they knew.

In early juries, it was customary for the members to be fully informed about the matters on which they sat. They were literally witnesses. For example, the king in the twelfth century might need to ferret out property for taxation; but neighbors would refuse to spy on each other, so an inquisition had to be set up. A hundred neighbors would be called by a royal officer of each county and ordered to reveal what the king needed to know; they faced a stiff penalty if they failed. Those summoned might also have been used to check on the behavior of servants or to tell of the misdeeds of the subjects.

Before this budding jury system was introduced into England by the Norman conquerors, three ancient methods of trials were in use there. They were being defended as vehemently against inroads by the then-new jury system as those who now favor juries are protesting new attempts at modification.

The first of these three methods was the wager of law. In this, the establishing of fact called simply for the taking of oaths. The solemnity of an oath evidently was completely believed in by the Anglo-Saxons. When the accused was a person of known standing, his own oath would be enough to clear him. But if the accusation against him was supported by the oaths of others, he was required to bring along his friends to support his oath. These supporters, called "compurgators," had to be eleven in number and would swear to the credibility of the twelfth, who was accused. A trial by compurgation is described in this way by Blackstone in his famous *Commentaries:*

Hear this, ye Justice, that I do not owe unto Richard Jones the sum of two pounds, nor any penny thereof in any manner and form as the said Richard hath declared against me, so help me God. Thereupon, his eleven neighbors or "compurgators" shall avow their oaths that they believe in their consciences that he saith truth. His credit in court depended upon the opinion his neighbors had of his veracity. This gradually led to the practice of allowing the other side to select witnesses from which the defendant must choose his eleven and if he failed he would suffer the "ordeal" to save himself. The "compurgators" who were so unfortunate as to support a losing cause were punished as perjurers, and one hand was cut off, although later, the law allowed the redemption of the hand by the payment of a fine.

The oath helpers were not required to be witnesses speaking from knowledge of the facts. They simply swore that they believed the principal's oath was true. The privilege of one who had been accused of crime to exonerate himself by this method was a valued privilege of Englishmen. It was a common method of trial until the sixteenth century and was not wholly abolished until 1833.

If this were not the accused's first offense, however, or if his compurgators did not agree to make the necessary oath, he was put to the "ordeal," or God's judgment of fire or water. Of these judgments the ordeal of fire or hot iron was applied to noblemen and freemen as being the more honorable and more easy. The ordeal of water was reserved for persons under the rank of the freeman. Despite its application to justice, the ordeal was really regarded as a religious procedure. The priests in the parish church conducted it, and the intervention of Providence was assumed to be secured on behalf of the innocent. This was the normal procedure: The accused was handed over to the church to be prepared by prayer and fasting for the trial he must face. He was brought into the church after three days' preparation. There he faced the accuser, each party being accompanied by not more than twelve friends. The intercession of Heaven in behalf of the innocent was sought by prayers. If the ordeal was by hot water, the accused plunged his naked hand or arm into a bowl of boiling water, searched for and picked out a ring which was suspended therein. If the gravity of his alleged offense was not so severe, the ring was hung to the depth of a man's hand. If the charge were more serious, it was placed to the depth of a cubit and the accused had to plunge his entire bare arm into the boiling water. If his hand or arm came out uninjured, it was assumed that Heaven had worked a miracle to declare his innocence. If, however, his hand or arm was injured, he was held to be guilty.

Another ordeal was by cold water. Here the accused again went through the three days of fasting and preparation by prayers. The pond of cold water itself was admonished before the ordeal. An elaborate formula of words was addressed to it. This was supposed to make the water so pure that it would not receive into itself anyone stained with crime. The priest addressed the stream — abjuring it in the name of the Almighty who first created the water, the baptism of Christ in the waters of Jordan, by His walking on the water, by the Holy Trinity, by whose will the Israelites passed dry-footed over the Red Seas, and at whose invocation Elisha caused the axe to swim — not to receive the accused if he were guilty, but to make him swim upon it. The accused was then tied with his hands in back of his knees and thrown into the cold pond. If he sank, he was innocent. But if he floated, he was guilty and must be hanged. Apparently the accused was in trouble either way. His choice was of drowning — or at the least a bad dunking — or being hanged.

In still another form of the ordeal, the accused was prepared the same way and fire was brought into the church. No one was allowed to enter but the priest and the accused. Nine feet was then measured from the fire to a mark. An iron, weighing from one to three pounds, depending on whether it was a single or triple ordeal, was laid on the embers. It remained there while the mass of judgment was performed. The hand of the accused was sprinkled with holy water and he took the hot iron. With his case well in hand, one might say, he walked the prescribed nine feet and threw down the iron. He went to the altar where his hand was bound up by the priest. The bandage was removed after three days in the presence of all parties and his guilt or innocence depended upon how the hand looked. If he was innocent, the wound was clean, but if he was guilty it would be impure. The idea was that a divine protection would shield the innocent from harm. How many times the simple laws of bacteriology convicted an innocent man no one could say.

In another type of ordeal, the accused walked between red-hot ploughshares. Another trial saw him given a piece of bread from the altar. He was safe if he swallowed it, but quite obviously guilty if it stuck in his throat. In still another method, the accused was blindfolded and made to choose from between two pieces of wood, one being plain and the other marked with a cross. He was obviously innocent if he by chance chose the one marked with the cross, and clearly guilty if he happened to pick the other.

In any case, trial by ordeal was frowned upon by the church and began to lose its popularity in the thirteenth century.

Still another form of trial was by battle. The theory here was that heaven would favor the truthful and make him prevail. It was in essence a duel, and a party to the lawsuit, or a witness, could be challenged and thus have to defend himself; the weapons here were specified in great detail. But if anyone was suspected and nobody would undertake to be the accuser, twelve of his neighbors would be called and they would consign him to the ordeal which they felt was a decisive test of innocence or guilt.

JURY TRIALS TAKE OVER

By a slow and gradual process, the jury began to displace these ancient methods of trial. A great advance was being made but the "progressives" who favored it had a hard battle ahead of them. As was noted, when the jury system first came to England it was an inquest: a royal tool for prying into the affairs of common people. Its character gradually changed and it came to be used as a means to determine facts in civil and criminal trials. It was an innovation, and for a long time it did not replace the ancient methods of trial. Especially difficult was the introduction of juries for criminal cases, when the accused would still stand on his rights as an Englishman and demand a trial by one of the old methods.

It was not until the ordeal system was finally abolished that the new method of trial by jury began to take its present form.

But it was important that jurors spoke only from their own knowledge. In other words, jurors also carried the role of witnesses, since they could rule only upon incidents which they themselves knew about or had seen. It was the complete opposite of today's system where jurors are carefully screened to be certain that they know absolutely nothing about the matter under consideration.

Even up to the time of the "English Justinian," King Edward I, a personal knowledge of the facts was still the major qualification to hold office as a juror. This did not change until many years later. The details of the process by which the jury came, in the course of two centuries or more, to lose its functions as a body of witnesses, and to assume in its place the job of judges, is still not very clear. It is clear, however, that in criminal cases the substitution of jury trials for compurgation, trial by ordeal, or battle proceeded much more slowly than did the similar displacement of ancient methods of proof in civil suits.

In this same period, historians find that the process of "attaint" came into existence. Attaint was the ancient system of a superior group of jurors punishing trial jurors for any misconduct. This included the rendering of a false verdict. The punishment came on the theory that the original jurors had perjured themselves, since they were still looked upon as witnesses; and for a long time the punishment by attaint was the only way of remedying a false verdict. The juror who was thus convicted lost all his movable goods to the king, was imprisoned for at least a year, and since his oath would never be accepted on another case, he would never serve on another jury. This attaint, in full force in the fourteenth century, often also saw the jurors' wives and children turned out of doors and their lands taken. Attaint finally began to fade away with the introduction of new trials when juries found against the evidence presented to them, and it was finally abolished altogether in 1625.

About the same time that the attaint trial was at the height of its popularity, however, a new element came into the trial system. Attorneys began to make statements of facts and offered to support them by bringing witnesses into court. Through this the practice of witnesses appearing in court crept into the system. Even though the bringing of witnesses developed, the jurors continued to remain the fact-finding bodies; the judges continued in ignorance of the basis for verdicts, but gradually they began to require more and more that they be fully informed of the facts upon which the jury made its findings.

Throughout this period of growth, jurors were still chosen because they knew a great deal about the matters being brought before them. In those situations where the information came from several different counties or vicinities, jurors were also summoned from the several panels in the various areas. The reason for the change to today's method is interesting : witnesses began to be required to appear in open court, rather than just before the jurors, so that both the judge and the jury learned what facts they had to offer. With this came the gradual change from witness-jurors to a jury whose members acted purely as judges of the facts given by witnesses.

Thus came the change from the early juries, which attempted to seek the truth without the legal restrictions and controls that have since sprung up. The jurors at that time sought verdicts on the basis of their own information and from a personal view of the facts and situation rather than upon the dramatic performance and oratory of an impassioned attorney.

It is obvious that dramatically shouted arguments and the deft shading of evidence were not even considered at the birth of the jury system.

In early criminal cases, jurors were called before the Star

Chamber. There they were fined for what the court thought were "wrong" verdicts of one type or another. With the downfall of the Stuarts, the Star Chamber also disappeared, and with it the view that jurors could be held punishable for conscientious action.

In medieval England there was a great deal of perjury, and the jury system turned out to be an exceedingly slender reed upon which to rest personal safety during the time of Kings James II and Charles II. To understand this situation, it must be remembered that judges were completely under the control of the king, and even went to the point of practically repealing the laws which they were appointed to administer if the king should happen to wish that. It was the period of such men as the Lord Chief Justice of England, Jeffreys, better known as the "bloody" judge and Lord Braxfield of the Scottish Court. Activities of Lord Braxfield were described as : "It is impossible to condemn his conduct as a criminal judge too gravely or too severely; it was a disgrace to the age. A dexterous and practical trier of ordinary cases, he was harsh to prisoners, even in his jocularity, and to every counsel whom he chose to dislike. It may be doubted if he was ever so much in his element as when tauntingly repelling the last despairing claim of a wretched culprit, and sending him to the gallows with an insulting jest."[2] Such men needed juries as a barrier against them, but even here the juries failed.

By the sixteenth century, the doctrine was well established that the jurors were to render their verdicts exclusively upon the basis of evidence. In the reign of the Tudors, the jury in criminal cases came increasingly to be seen as a protection to the subject against the oppression of the officers of the Crown. This was particularly so because the several extraordinary tribunals created during the Tudor years for the suppression

[2] Gray, W. Forbes, *Some Old Scots Judges* (London : Constable and Co., Ltd.) pp. 107–108.

of treason and heresy all operated without juries. These included the Court of High Commission, the Court of the Star Chamber, and the Council of the North.

Under the Stuarts, the jury became established as the sole tribunal for criminal cases except the crimes on the high seas, and certain other crimes connected with navigation, which were tried without a jury in the admiralty courts.

In the Bill of Rights, enacted in 1688 and embodied in the settlement which brought William and Mary to the throne, the right to trial by jury in criminal cases was apparently for the first time declared in statutory form, in the provision that jurors ought to be duly impaneled and returned; and thus a part of the body of basic English constitutional doctrine was formally restated.

In describing the birth of juries in England, Prof. Lewis Mayers states in *The American Legal System*[3] that:

In the struggle to establish the right to jury trial in criminal cases as a fundamental right of the Englishman, the alleged antiquity of the right was of course much stressed; and much was made of the provision in the Magna Carta that "we will not set forth against him (any freeman) nor send against him unless by the lawful judgment of his peers." This provision (on whose precise interpretation scholars are still not agreed) demonstrated, it was alleged, that the English freeman was entitled to jury trial even as early as the thirteenth century. From what has been said, however, it will be apparent that at that time trial by jury as we understand it was unknown. Historical learning in this matter was still fragmentary in the Tudor and Stuart times, and the mistaken belief that the phrase in Magna Carta referred to trial by jury tended to give that institution, at a time when its importance as a shield against the oppression of the Crown was being recognized, the appearance of a venerable antiquity that it did not in fact possess — so much so that by the seventeenth century

[3] *The American Legal System* (New York: Harper and Row), p. 113.

it had already become customary to refer to it as an "immemorial right."

It would seem evident that the major function of early juries was to protect ordinary persons from the great power of the early classes. That need has long disappeared, since, in a democracy, the ruling group reaches power by votes of the people and remains there only at the will of those voters. Misuse of power can be set right at the next election. Here is a strength early citizens lacked.

Despite the belief that early juries were to protect against tyranny and unjust use of power, that protection was not always certain with juries even at that time. A good example, in more recent history, was seen in the trials of Captain Alfred Dreyfus's supporters in the French courts. In one, the well-known French writer, Emile Zola, who fought for the wrongfully accused captain, had a full jury sworn in to protect his rights. It soon became clear that this jury's only function was to register the edict of the government, the army, and the press—and to echo mob views. All demanded a conviction. In this atmosphere, all efforts at a show of justice became impossible. Invective from court, prosecutor, and witnesses took the place of evidence and argument. At the end of two weeks the innocent Zola was convicted and sentenced in 35 minutes. So did a jury serve to "protect" equal justice for all even before modern times. It took some time before a court composed of judges alone cleared up the Dreyfus mess.

The value of juries, even in their early years when they were most needed as a buffer against tyranny, can now be questioned in light of what they accomplished. It was evident too many times, during the reign of King James II and such judges as the terrible Jeffreys, that trial by jury was in reality a mere form. Jurors who ventured to bring in a verdict against the wishes of the Crown met with severe and summary punish-

ment. At one time, for example, when a court was dissatisfied
with the verdict, it at first committed the jury to prison and
later sentenced the foreman and another to pay £2,000 apiece
within two weeks, and the other six £1,000 each, and sent
them all back to prison until the money should be paid. This
attitude resulted in frightening completely those who had no
great desire to be martyrs to their own consciences, and it is
recorded that many jurors who first returned verdicts of not
guilty were practically ordered to reverse them. Upon retiring,
the jurors were locked up without food or drink, and were
allowed no communication with the world outside until they
returned with the desired verdict.

Thus it can be seen that the jury system during the time of
the Tudors and the Stuarts in England, although it existed
even then in the same character as it does today, was but a very
poor safeguard for the personal liberty of the British subjects.

It has been recorded that trial by jury was introduced into
America with the landing of the Pilgrims. That period also
saw acceptance of the body of the common law and many
of the British statutes. The American colonies, one by one,
adopted the system in their constitutions. They did not all,
however, adopt it at first, and even those who did so adopted
only a modified form. No instructions in the law were given to
the jurors, and the defeated party had the privilege of review.
That is, he could have a new trial before another jury but if
he lost at the second hearing, that was the end of him. On the
other hand, if he won at the second trial, the other side could
then demand a third hearing and that verdict would be
regarded as the deciding one.

A guarantee of the right to jury trial, in criminal cases, was
placed into most of the state constitutions adopted during the
American Revolution. It was also adopted in the constitutions
of all the states later created, and that guarantee, in one form
or another, is now found in every state's constitution. Although

during colonial times it would appear that a fairly uniform pattern for jury trial was prevalent. It was modeled on that which was then in vogue in England. This pattern provided for jury trial even in misdemeanors. Since then in various states, however, the right to jury trial in misdemeanors has been altered more or less. However, during all this time, the right to jury trials in felonies has remained untouched by law in every state. There it is guaranteed by the provisions of the state constitutions. The only times this provision has been invaded in any practical sense has been by the increasing frequency of waiving of jury trials in felonies. There, unless they are specifically denied the right to waive, ever-greater numbers of defendants are eluding the emotional, time-honored and outmoded method of rule by juries.

It is pretty largely because of state constitutions that the right of jury trial continues in state courts. Many lawyers feel that the provision in the Fourteenth Amendment to the U.S. Constitution, which prohibits a state from depriving any person of life, liberty, or property without due process of law, does not require the state to provide a jury trial even in felony cases.

The right to a jury trial in criminal cases in the federal courts was included in the Constitution. The form of the guarantee in the Constitution, however, was long opposed as being defective, and amendments adopted in 1791 attempted to clarify it by holding that the jury should be "of the state and district wherein the crime shall have been committed, which district shall have previously been ascertained by law."

One of the most prominent opponents of jury trial in civil actions was Alexander Hamilton. (See the *Federalist Papers,* Number 83.) Due in large part to his opposition, the Federal Constitution as originally drafted contained no provision at all guaranteeing the right to trial by jury in civil actions. This provision was finally adopted much later as the Constitution's Seventh Amendment. Hamilton's comment in his paper was that "the best judges of the matter will be the least anxious for a constitutional establishment of the trial by jury in civil cases, and will be the most ready to admit that the changes which are continually happening in the affairs of society may render a different mode of determining questions of property preferable in many cases in which that mode of trial now prevails."

Close study of early American history shows that these were not the views of Hamilton alone, but represented also the opinions of a great many men who were present in the constitutional convention in Philadelphia. Those views were held at a time filled with hopes and ambitions of a people wary after a great fight for liberty and freedom. In a time that fairly bristled with a demand for liberties and rights, any hint of curtailing them would have set off an emotional explosion. How then, under such circumstances, could they actually ratify a constitution which contained no guarantee of trial by jury in civil cases? Since this was not brought about until later amendment, it is obvious that they did, and without any fuss on the matter.

From this it is evident that those who originally set forth the Constitution, the document to guarantee and guard the nation's liberties, had no conception of jury trials—in civil cases, at least—as necessary for such ideals. They came from an area in which jury trials flourished, and in which many property rights were disposed of by judges alone without any contact with juries. This was England. They came fully aware of the values, especially at that slow-paced and uncomplicated time, of jury trials, yet they did not see fit to shout demands for its inclusion in the original Constitution.

This provides small comfort for those who point the historical finger at the great role of the jury trial in the country since its founding. The civil jury, began here with obvious weakness, was added to the Constitution as an afterthought, and over the years has steadily declined almost in direct ratio to the country's development in an increasingly complicated world of commerce and personal interactions.

3

Decline of Juries Abroad

THOSE STILL FAVORING THE JURY SYSTEM TELL HOW IT flourished in Europe and England during its long and proud history. That is all quite true. But to make the story complete, it must also be told that juries have all but vanished in England, where once they held the most power, that they have been greatly modified in France and Germany, that a great move has been under way to eliminate them in Scotland, that disgust at their operation has caused them to be wiped out in India, and that such progressive democracies as Israel have never had them at all.

Reasons for the decline of juries abroad are many. For the most part, they follow the troubles with juries discussed in this volume. The decline, however, was far from easy. There were many who still wished to adhere to the system with which they had been familiar for so long that it appeared almost sacrilegious to speak of doing away with it. In deference to them, the changes usually have not been swift or dramatic but have come about through slow and gradual evolution. The fact remains, however, that the changes have come and that they have, to a large extent, been forced by the exigencies of the times.

DYING OUT IN ENGLAND

In a speech by a member of the English bar it was once declared in characteristic British understatement that "in England it would appear that the jury trial has largely lost favor." The speaker then went on to reveal that in the Queen's and King's Bench actions, the percentage of cases involving juries in 1875 was 95, whereas in 1950, the percentage was less than five. Thus is shown the startling change that has come over the country where, more than 200 years ago, Blackstone wrote in his book on *Civil Wrongs:* "Trial by jury has ever been, and I trust ever will be, looked upon as a glory of English law."

Two centuries later, not only did the jury no longer hold the role it once did in Britain's legal process but, in civil matters especially, the jury led a rather desultory existence. Special juries, which had been gradually falling into disuse for some 40 years, were virtually abandoned by the Juries Act of 1949. The British grand jury had disappeared in 1933. With the vast extension of summary trial, well above 95 per cent of criminal prosecutions are now disposed of without juries.

A candid view of the British attitude toward its juries can be seen in this quote from *The Law Times,* published at Lincoln's Inn, London (March 9, 1956):

In the limited field that remains, the blessings of jury trial may no longer appear wholly unmixed. If the jury is still regarded as an essential part of our legal system, fulfilling a valuable function in trials for serious crime, it is so despite recognised shortcomings

and in the face of its admittedly unfortunate effect on our rules
of evidence.

As times go on, the arguments against the jury in the old
form appear to become stronger; criticism has grown of late and
reform is being urged here and there. Mr. Claude Mullins, who
used to express the opinion 'I am convinced that often the
reasons behind a jury's verdict are fantastic,' has lately been
joined by Dr. Granville Williams who, in his Hamlyn Lectures
for 1955, has examined possible alternatives.

Thus, little by little, are objections raised to juries and, in
that same degree, the system is being eroded away. The litigant
in England today does not have an absolute right to a jury.
This former right, in effect, finally disappeared with the passing
of the Administration of Justice Act in 1933. English thought
that preceded and finally brought about the abolition of long-
held rights to juries is interesting. The English Business of
Courts Committee Report, published in 1933, read :

We have no doubt that the present system [of juries] leads to
an increasing expenditure of time in the trial of civil actions, and
to the imposition upon jurors of a considerable burden.

It has also been argued with much force that the result of a
trial with a jury is more uncertain than that of a trial by a judge
alone . . . that there is serious risk of disagreement which may
lead to a new trial entailing heavy expenses. There is also the
risk that the judge may misdirect the jury, in which case, after
an appeal with its attendant cost, there is a new trial.

It should be remembered that this opposition to juries in
Britain developed even though the system there had many more
strengths in its favor than does its American counterpart. For
example, the judge had far greater control of his courtroom
and the selection of his juries. It was the judge who questioned
the jurors and selected them in a brief time and without inter-

ference from the barristers. The British judge, too, had the power to evaluate for confused jurors what weight should be given to different witnesses and other evidence. Despite all these powers, which, if put into operation here, could in themselves bring about a vast improvement in America's state courts, the British felt even then that juries did not help their administration of justice enough to make them worthwhile.

It should be made clear, however, that there is a very small group of cases in which it is still possible to have a jury in England. These include such matters as a charge of fraud against the party seeking the jury, or a claim in respect of libel, slander, malicious prosecution, false imprisonment, seduction, or breach of promise of marriage. These may be ordered to be tried with a jury unless the judge is of the opinion that the trial of such a case would require a prolonged examination of documents, accounts, or any scientific or local investigation that cannot conveniently be made with a jury; in such a situation it would then be tried by a judge alone. But even where the latter is not true, the decision of whether or not to have a jury is within the discretion of the court alone and is not a matter of absolute right to the parties.

It is interesting to note that the types of cases which could have a jury conspicuously do not include actions of damages for personal injuries. That is the type of court action which is jamming up the American courts and often delaying justice up to five or six years. There are no comparable delays in British courts and judges there have expressed shock and dismay at the situation in America.

Obviously, bringing the new British attitude here would do much to remedy that situation. Americans, however, appear eager only to hold on to the antiquities of British justice and refuse to cast an eye at the modernizations being conducted by their former teachers.

CHANGES IN FRANCE

The trend toward reform of the jury has been much more marked in France than even in England. During the seventeeth and eighteenth centuries, the jury had achieved a high reputation as a "democratic institution" because it drew the direct participation of the ordinary citizen into the administration of law. This led leaders of the French Revolution to borrow the idea of jury trials—but only for criminal cases—from England, with a few modifications after 1789.

Since the idea of the jury was associated with the fall of despots, it spread gradually from France over the whole of Europe. For example, it was adopted by Austria after the 1848 revolution; Italy took it after the liberation in 1860; the German Empire took to it, after it had been in use in many of the German states, after unification in 1877.

In a number of countries, such as Holland and in some Scandinavian lands, it never really caught on and, in other areas of the European continent, it seemed never to be at home. It was described by the *Law Times* (London) March 9, 1956, as appearing like a "somewhat alien and anomalous institution transplanted into unsuitable soil, and never perfectly understood."

According to the *London Law Times,* those countries which did take over the jury, more or less on the English model, soon found themselves faced with the need for alterations somewhat radical in nature. The French system began as an imperfect imitation of the English jury trial at that time, but without some of its distinctive features, such as cross-examination. The unanimity rule, never quite so absolute as in England, was abandoned after the first few years in favor of a two-thirds majority and later, about 1853, a simple majority of votes was enough.

Before too long, it became apparent that jurors, although

they were supposed to be restricted only to the question of guilt, proved themselves greatly preoccupied with the punishment likely to be inflicted by the court. This was a situation similar to that of many American courts. In France it was found that many acquittals were due, not to the jury's conclusion of the innocence of the accused, but rather to distrust of the court and fear of subsequent imposition of too unduly harsh a sentence. As early as 1832, therefore, the French juries were enabled to give, in addition to their verdict of guilty or innocent, a decision on the existence of aggravating or mitigating circumstances. This allowed jurors, somewhat indirectly, to influence the penalty. This was brought into focus a hundred years later when, by a law of March 5, 1932, the jury was authorized, after it had found and announced its verdict, to meet the court of three judges for direct consultation and decision about the penalty to be inflicted. This was then reached by a simple majority vote.

An interesting series of pendulum swings began in 1880 when the judge's final summation before the jury retired was eliminated. The theory was that it carried too much weight with French jurors and thus, in their minds, overrode the evidence they had previously heard; but after this summation was removed, the situation became even worse: it was felt that, with the judge's guidance gone, the naïve jurors were figuratively placed into the hands of the dramatic lawyers.

Since then, the pendulum has swung back again because, as the *Law Times* put it: "It is, of course, the common experience of all countries which have known jury trial that jurors can be swayed by competent counsel, especially in the direction of acquittal, and there can be no doubt that the verdicts so obtained by persuasion against the weight of the evidence are the pride of successful counsel for the defense. But it is equally true that this makes for haphazard and capricious justice and it is stretching the desire for 'fairness' far that one accused should stand a good chance to get away with an acquittal where another—less fortunate in his choice of counsel—would certainly be convicted and sentenced to imprisonment."

It was the notorious "scandalous acquittals" of France, in increasing frequency, which finally led to a great change in the jury system. As time went by, it became increasingly apparent that the accused were being particularly favored only in certain types of cases. Those given the favored treatment included such crimes as drunkenness or serious traffic offenses. Others, which always received particularly harsh treatment, included such crimes as arson and burglary. The reason for this division soon became obvious in the fact that most jurors were drawn from the lower middle class, which particularly feared those types of crimes. These acquittals, plus other problems, such as the highly complicated technical questions that were increasingly being placed in the jury's hands, brought much criticism and dispute.

Finally, new laws were passed to make the complete change from the regular type of jury known in America. This change, which should be most interesting in view of our country's jury problems, was based upon the major innovation of no longer allowing the jurors to deliberate alone; they must now consider the case together with the judges.

What had brought about this significant change?

Direct participation of citizens in the administration of justice, the French argued, must be made to fit in with the overriding consideration that justice should be administered in the best way possible. The French were convinced that sole responsibility of the jury for the question of guilt had not proved to be the best way. As a result of being faced with these important jury problems, the French created juries which consisted of seven citizens drawn by lot from a list of local inhabitants. Their qualifications included being over thirty

years of age and ability to read and write. They deliberated
with the three professional judges, and together they considered
both the questions of guilt and the punishment. The decisions
on both of these were reached by the judges and jury together
and required only a majority agreement. This arrangement
gives the professional judges a chance to make their views
known, and their legal advice is fully felt by the laymen. At the
same time, however, the judges are not able to outvote the
laymen. In this system, too, there is no need for a foreman
of the jury because the president of the assize court takes over
the chairmanship for the deliberations.

It is this type of procedure which eliminates one of the great
dangers inherent in American juries — that some very vocal
jurymen, who are not usually the most discerning or the most
scrupulous, will seize control over their more gullible com-
panions and, in the seclusion of their jury room, pressure them
into an unjust or a prejudiced verdict.

European legal experts have noted it has sometimes been
suggested that the French system now has departed so far from
the original conception of the jury trial that it almost would
be more accurate to describe the French jurors as "assessors."
This term, however, does not altogether fit laymen, selected by
lot, as jurymen are, and sitting only for one trial, as is done
in France. Actually, the expression "assessor courts" could
better be supplied to those criminal courts which have lay
members appointed to serve continuously and over a long
period of time. These courts, which are made up of professional
judges, sitting with a varying number of lay assessors, belong
to the continental legal tradition inherited from the Middle
Ages and form an historic national institution there much as
juries do in England.

Indeed, after the somewhat unsuccessful importation of the
jury in the English tradition, most of the continental countries
have in the last half century or so been returning to the many

variations of what has been known as the assessor system. Germany did it in 1924. Italy turned in 1931. Many cantons of Switzerland have it. This system is now once again considered to be more modern and capable of successfully handling legal complexities than the regular jury system.

GERMANY MODERNIZES ITS JURIES

Germany went so far as to split its systems to achieve greater flexibility in the handling of various types of cases. The jury courts, known as *Schwurgericht,* still perform limited tasks and are a modified version of what the English-speaking lands have. They deal with the most serious crimes. They are of the reformed type, consisting of six laymen who form one bench with the three professional judges. This court, through joint deliberation and by simple majority vote, passes both upon the guilt or innocence of the accused and also decides upon the sentence to be given to those convicted. These jurors, the *geschworene,* serve for one sitting only and then are replaced for the next trial.

Serving side-by-side with these jury courts are the assessor courts proper, the *Schoeffengerichte,* which handle the great majority of non-summary offenses which take place in West Germany. Their very interesting mode of operation consists of one professional judge who sits at cases with the two lay assessors. The lay assessors are specially nominated. They are appointed for two years to serve regularly, though in a part-time honorary capacity.

In its practical application, the comparatively small number of lay jurors, as well as the method of selections, makes it possible to take real account of quality rather than quantity in the picking of this "lay jury." This is a factor of some importance, it has been said, in view of the fact that in Germany qualifications for jury service have not changed since 1823, and have an exceedingly broad base.

The assessor system has been gaining ground in many areas of Europe. It appears preferable even to the reformed jury. With the long-time service of the assessors, rather than the one-shot arrangement of jurors as known in America, the lay assessors have more time to gain real insight into some of the complexities of trials — both criminal and civil — and have more chance to develop the capacity of forming independent and well-reasoned opinions. In theory, at least, the assessor system enlarges the jury's power at the expense of the judges since the former possess a majority of votes and can, through unified action, insist on making their views prevail. But in actual practice, it has been found to be a successful fusion of abilities of professional judges and laymen. It succeeds in bringing together the respective contributions that each has to make.

Thus, it can easily be seen, such cooperation can preserve the fundamental principles of the jury system, the close association of the ordinary citizen with the administration of justice, yet at the same time bring about needed improvements. From this it is evident that the old methods of jury trials have been tried in Europe and found wanting and have been corrected.

An interesting comment often made by advocates of juries as they now exist in America is that foreign judges command much greater confidence from both the public and the legal profession than do their American counterparts. They point to the big role played by politics in the selection of our judges as compared, for example, with the lifetime appointment of foreign judges on the basis of merit and training.

To a large degree, this argument carries a great deal of persuasion. In our federal courts, with lifetime judicial appointments and more careful selection of jurors, much less question can be raised as to the conducting of trials. At the same time, however, it can be seen that if a tyrant is placed in power in such a court he can do much greater damage to the cause of justice. It would be difficult to remove such a person if he were taken away from the control of voters.

MOVE FOR CHANGE IN SCOTLAND

Pressures have been building up in great degree to abolish juries in Scotland because of the injustices which they bring to the law. Voices are raised in criticism of British powers for having pushed a jury system here where it was not wanted and for having used influence to retain it. In the *Journal of the Law Society of Scotland,* periodical of an organization made up of all the solicitors practising in Scotland, it was stated bluntly that a very large majority of the Council appointed to study the matter were of the opinion that jury trials should be abolished. The report of this majority stressed that, in its opinion, it was wrong to suggest, as had been done in some quarters, that the jury should be preserved because it effected a softening of the full force of precise application of the law. On this phase, the report said :

This exemplifies clearly the confusion between a question of principle and one of procedure which can easily arise when this subject [of juries] is discussed. The law, whatever it is, should be certain. If it requires alteration, it should be by the development in an ascertainable way of existing or new principles by the judiciary or the legislature, not by a loose and unpredictable applicaton of the existing principles.

It has also been said in support of jury trials that, *by and large,* they do justice. [That, too, is one of the more kindly answers given in America.] It is submitted that this also is an altogether wrong approach. It must be of small comfort to a pursuer awarded inadequate damages, or unsuccessful in his litigation, that another pursuer was awarded too much, or succeeded where he should have failed.

So it is that strong criticism is raised to the comment that juries "average out" favorably in justice over the long run. This averaging really means a compounding of injustice — it is as unfair to the overpaid litigant as to the one who loses when he should have won.

The report in Scotland then went on to point out briefly its particular opposition to the jury system. It was not too surprising that the criticisms sounded like an echo to those here. The troubles with juries are an intrinsic part of the system wherever it may be. Here is what the committee, appointed by the secretary of state of Scotland, found:

1) A jury does not have the experience or the training and does not normally have the knowledge to sift and assess a mass of contradictory evidence, frequently on technical subjects, or with an industrial background, or to evaluate its relevance.

This is not to criticize the intelligence of jurors. It is merely a recognition of the difficulty of persons trying to visualize a set of circumstances, usually completely strange to them, from their recollection of verbal evidence seldom noted down and given over two or three days, and at the end of the evidence trying to say what it would have been reasonable to do in such circumstances.

2) The jury's task already difficult becomes even more so where the question of apportionment of fault and of damages arises. There have been illustrations known to solicitors in Court, and by no means always reported, where juries have manifestly become confused in endeavouring to fulfill this responsibility.

Such confusion does not always result in a transparently mistaken award, although there have been several outstanding instances of that kind, but does cause lesser errors and most importantly saps the confidence of those who witness the confusion, including the litigants, their advisers, and the members of the public who may be present, in the efficiency of the system.

3) The fact that juries do not give reasons for their decisions prevents the growth of a body of law which may guide parties in the conduct of their affairs . . . it should therefore be one of the functions of the courts to build up a body of law which will afford a guide to disputants and their advisers and which will facilitate the resolving of the dispute without resort to Court action. It is submitted that so long as the jury system survives, this function is not properly fulfilled and the public suffers.

So it is that the same troubles which have beset American juries have been found in equal number in other lands which have them.

FAILURE IN INDIA

One of the most rapidly developing countries in the world is India, stretching forth its growth in freedom from England. Its background is entirely British: a strong residue remains from those who ruled it for long and instilled in it the British methods and procedures. Yet even India, in its first faltering years, has been strongly opposing the jury system it inherited from England. It is one of the very few things it learned from England that it is finding cannot be fitted into, or used to help mold, the growing government and its functions. India's dramatic decision to eliminate juries as a failure broke into American headlines in May, 1961, with an Associated Press dispatch from New Delhi. Here is what the world learned:

Trial by jury, one of the most sacred concepts of British and American law, is being abandoned in India as a failure. Only two of the 16 Indian states still use juries. These two are now considering turning legal decisions over to the judges alone.

Trial by jury always has been limited in India to some areas and particular types of cases. Even within these restrictions, the results have not always been satisfactory. Some legal experts complained that juries too often produced miscarriages of justice.

"I have known juries finding prisoners guilty in the face of no evidence," Mohandas K. Gandhi, the father of Indian independence, wrote in 1931. "We must not slavishly copy all that is English."

The jury system originated in England as protection from decisions by judges who might be under the thumb of the king. The constitution of independent India guarantees to citizens "procedures established by law." Unlike the American Constitution, it does not specify that everyone is entitled to trial by jury. There have been few public complaints when trial by jury was eliminated by state legislatures.

In Uttar Pradesh, India's most populous state, an investigating committee was told that jurors were generally "open to approach" and did not give a fair verdict. A Bihar state committee found that "a number of persons have made it almost a profession to get themselves chosen as jurors for the sake of the remuneration and also the illegal gratification which some of them expect to get."

Indian society is split by caste and religious antagonisms which can weigh more heavily in most men's minds than legal evidence. The educational level is extremely low. States can ill afford the money for jurors' fees. These reasons are cited against the use of juries.

LAST STRONGHOLD OF JURIES : AMERICA

The last major nation to staunchly defend the value of juries and to oppose reforms in selecting jurors, or the types of cases they may handle, is America. It is here, strangely enough, that most of the emphasis is placed upon difficulties with judges rather than turning the spotlight on inadequacies of the jurors. Even the smallest efforts at reform bring objections. For example, New York has what has been called the "blue-ribbon" jury. These are special juries selected on the basis of intelligence, profession, or property held. They are called for especially difficult trials. Yet in one case a dissenting justice said : "The vice lies in the very concept of 'blue ribbon' panels — the systematic exclusion of all but the 'best' or most learned or intelligent of the general jurors. Such panels are completely at war with the democratic theory of our jury system, a theory formulated out of the experience of generations."

It appears evident to many, however, that if the jury system is to be retained in America, some changes must be brought about, either by selection of better jurors in general, or by changing the methods by which jurors sit briefly and are dismissed before they can learn even the bare essentials of their assignment. That, however, is exactly what those who claim that juries are important as a symbol of democracy in action oppose the most strenuously.

As Prof. Mayers said in his book, *The American Legal System:*[1]

No improvement in methods of jury selection will produce a jury really competent to pass upon some of the more complicated and technical issues of facts which some present-day civil litigations present. However, a vast improvement of the quality of the juror can unquestionably be affected in many jurisdictions by unremitting efforts to improve the selection procedure.

In such efforts, it is important to have clearly in mind that the need is for jurors of intelligence, probity and understanding; that that need can be met only by a process of fairly strict elimination not only of those lacking in native intelligence but

[1] P. 403.

also of those lacking in that type of intelligence which comes from a reasonable amount of education, whether acquired by schooling or by self-instruction. This criterion encounters, however, the opposition of those to whom the jury is not primarily an agency of justice, but rather a safeguard of democratic institutions. Though it is not considered to be repugnant to the nature of a democratic society to insist that its public officials generally should be of a high order of intelligence, jurors, who after all are discharging a public office of the gravest importance, are in this view in a special category.

That the more modern view would eliminate use of juries is shown in the experience of newly independent countries seeking the best of the old order as the foundation for their new. Even as American colonials took from their mother country, England, the best of the jury system at that time as the most effective method for handling their needs in the slower-paced era, so are the new countries of today seeking the best procedures for justice. With the recognition of the greater complexities of modern times, they are evading the pitfalls of the older countries. So it is that India discarded the juries with all their faults and followed the new path of Britain toward better justice.

And so it is that Israel, on its emergence from the British control, never even set up a jury system. Israel is a nation composed largely of people who have sought desperately for justice over many centuries. The Jews, persecuted beyond belief throughout the world, were the first to demand the greatest assurance of justice in their own land. So it was that when they set up their network of courts no mention was even made of jurors. This even though the history of their former "guardians," the British, was filled with the jury tradition.

This stood out prominently in the world-famous trial of Adolph Eichmann, the former Nazi officer accused of murdering millions of Jews. In the searing spotlight of world opinion, three highly capable judges patiently conducted a five-month trial. Such strain would have worn thin the nerves of a citizen jury and could have brought a verdict based on revenge no matter what the evidence. But the panel of judges, highly trained, coldly intellectual and clinical in its approach to the evaluation of evidence, gained the respect of all those who followed the proceedings.

Throughout the lengthy hearings, sometimes charged with emotion and at other times monotonous in continued repetition, not a word was heard of any lack of democracy by the failure to have a citizen jury. Instead, there was much praise for the judicial dignity apparent throughout the sessions. Try to imagine a jury judging Eichmann like the first one in the Los Angeles murder trial of Dr. R. Bernard Finch and Carol Tregoff, a jury of mash-note passers and angry arguers (see pp. 155). Such a farce would have made Israel look foolish in the eyes of the world and the country could never afford that in a case as serious as Eichmann's.

Yet who can say that any case in which a man's life is at stake is any less important, even though the accused is not a world-wide figure and the publicity stops at the county line. In this contrast can be seen the great importance of proper conduct of a trial no matter what the offense. That is why the troubles with juries are a matter of public concern whenever they create another act of injustice.

And this is why leaders throughout the world have long urged modification of the strange reverence for juries. Yet even though many in the foreground of the legal profession have hesitated to make any changes for the better, the general citizens and their legislators, the businessmen and the professional men, have taken matters into their own hands in many instances to minimize use of juries wherever they could do so, as will be described in detail later. To this degree they have been able to reduce injustice and to speed up redress of their wrongs while the old jury box still stands in the control of those reluctant to change, a phenomenon peculiar to America.

PART II

Problems of Today

4

Personal Injury: "Big Business"

JURIES IN THE UNITED STATES ARE IN TROUBLE IN MANY AREAS. The main area is also the most widespread, affecting millions of individuals each year. It is almost certain to touch every person at one time or another: the one who drives an automobile, or slips on an icy sidewalk, or trips over a case of food in a supermarket.

It is the field of personal injuries.

There is probably no aspect of law which has developed as rapidly in recent years as that having to do with physical hurt. There is no part of law that is so precariously close to slipping across that very faint border from profession to business — and a very big business it is — as that of getting money out of accidents. There have been times when even large and powerful law firms have made that slip and found themselves in the "business."

Payment is often good, the flow of clients is plentiful, and the field of battle is exciting. It is difficult to find remorse among the overflowing coffers. It is in this field that we find growing criticism over many aspects of a multi-million-dollar-a-year business, from the contingency contracts which often stimulate suits to a question of fraud where persons in "deep pain" suddenly toss aside leg braces and crutches once a verdict has been reached.

A contributing factor found at the heart of this problem is the citizen jury, innocently caught among the great pressures generated when a lot of money is at stake. Interestingly enough, this is one area of litigation that was never even imagined in its present status when civil juries were established in state courts. High-powered automobiles and trucks, which could bring vicious injuries in split seconds, were unknown when juries were hit upon as a means of settling differences between parties. The eight-lane superhighway, which brought high-speed travel, as well as sudden death or maiming, did not appear in anyone's wildest dreams.

Yet this is an area in which juries now play their biggest roles every day. Here they face contradictory and highly complicated medical testimony; here they have the literally impossible task of determining the dollar value of a person's backache, stiffened leg, or lost arm. Jurors would be amazed if they knew how often a trial judge has said: "I'm certainly glad the jury has to decide the value of damages. I know I never could in this case—and I can't imagine how they can."

The answer is often all too obvious. It is here that the juror takes over the job of the legislator and makes his own elusive law. It goes without question that the law of damages is jury-made law—and it is just as unequal, unpredictable, and unjust as one might suppose of such "legislation." It rests on no foundation and is tied to no guide; it surely has no control. It is the "jackpot"—or the tragedy—of the law, without reason or logic. It is not found in law books and can never be pre-

dicted with any accuracy, yet it is the basis of negotiations by insurance claims adjustors.

It is naïve to state that personal injury cases are a big business which often brings great rewards to a venturesome and ambitious group of lawyers and their clients. A glance at any state court's civil docket will show it heavily laden with automobile accident cases. The whiplash pain, where the neck is snapped forward and back in a rear-end crash; the collision cases, where the ones bringing suit are "thrown about the interior of their automobiles," are so numerous as to be commonplace and not worthy of publication in a newspaper.

It has often been said that if courts across the country could rid themselves of automobile accident cases, as they once did of industrial accident compensation, through setting up state boards, most of the publicized delay and backlog in our courts would begin to evaporate.

Along with the growth of the burden in courts from these cases has come an interesting burgeoning of law firms which specialize in such matters. These firms work as office teams. A typical office, for example, will have several good trial lawyers — men expert at appealing to the juries and most capable of describing great pain — who have become completely at home with lengthy medical terms over which even doctors sometimes stumble. Their knowledge of the human anatomy often tops even their specialized store of legal information. These men are usually backed up by a team of investigators who hurry out immediately to gather up witnesses, photograph scenes of accidents, and contact their regular physicians and surgeons to make X-rays and prepare diagnostic reports. In the meantime, back at the office, the inside men are already at work on the case, looking up the law, putting together an

impressive file, contacting the insurance claims agent with whom they are by now long-time friends.

A grinning skull and a dangling skeleton are as much a part of these highly specialized law firms as are the more routine sets of law books. A client who might innocently walk off the street into one of these offices in hopes of having a simple will drawn would be greeted by the lawyers with open-mouthed amazement. This is not their field and they usually want no part of such legal endeavors.

To stay in business, these personal injury firms need a constant flow of new clients; it is not too often that any person becomes a regular client with repeat work in accidents. In view of this, these law firms have devised many ways of bringing clients through their doors while still remaining within the borders of legal ethics. One such is the taking of referrals with fee-splitting arrangements. Where a general practitioner, or one specializing in another phase of law, gets a difficult personal injury case, it is sent to the expert, the lawyer with the dangling skeleton and the office team. Subsequent fees are divided between the referring attorney and the one who actually handles the case. This is perfectly proper in law and, in fact, often guarantees the best legal care for the injured.

Another way of holding clients is the contingency contract. Here a person does not have to pay a large legal fee to the attorney until some results have been shown in the case. These contracts may give the lawyer from one-fourth to one-third of the money collected in a simple settlement, and up to 40 per cent of the amount won if the case goes to trial. Thus the client has everything to gain and little to lose by going ahead with his law suit. If the lawyer wins no money, he gets no fee. Only the preliminary medical examination and court costs run into money. The attorney takes most of the risk in this and, in doing so, he encourages the client to proceed with litigation. The public value in this is that it provides a legitimate client

who might not otherwise be able to afford it a means of getting into court.

It is not all easy for the client, however, according to Dr. Walter C. Alvarez, emeritus consultant in medicine at the famed Mayo Clinic. He claims that many a person with a minor injury can get himself so entangled in the legal labyrinth that his anxieties over this can heighten his original pains. In his nationally syndicated column, Dr. Alvarez has said: "One of the common complaints today is of pain in the neck and perhaps back of the head—pain which follows a so-called whiplash injury sustained by someone in a car when it was rammed from behind by another car. One of the sad features of this type of injury is that it has become such a football of attorneys in court." The doctor noted that there was no question but that many sensible people with a whiplash injury and no law suit to worry them sick keep suffering severely for months. But there is no question also, he emphasized, that many a person who, after the accident gets terribly worried about his law suit, gets such an aggravation of symptoms, and perhaps even so much hysteria, that he becomes a very sick man.

In hundreds of cases, it is hard for even expert orthopedists and neurologists to guess how much of a man's pain is due to the injury and how much is due to his grave anxiety over how his law suit is going to come out. His medical and his incidental preliminary legal expenses have climbed so high —and he may have turned down a settlement offer—that now he says that unless he wins his suit, he will be left a pauper. His wife will reveal that he is now walking the floor at night.

Most significantly, in view of the task of the jurors in this type of a situation, Dr. Alvarez says: "What impresses me and my fellow physicians is that if we, who have been trained all our lives to see our way through such difficult problems cannot decide how much of the man's pain is due to physical injury and how much to anxiety, how on earth can a jury made up of good people who have absolutely no knowledge of medicine be expected to make the correct estimate? Why should we expect them to be sure when an old physician like me would hate to hazard a guess?"

At another point Dr. Alvarez observed : "What we doctors know is that often such a man — whose honesty we did not question — got well the day his law suit was settled in his favor. Another fact that we doctors know is that often a man we can see with X-rays has a severe injury to his neck and who should have terrible pain does not complain at all. This may be because he is an insensitive person who cannot feel much pain or he is the type of person who can't be bothered to fuss about his health. Many a time I have easily talked one of my old friends and patients out of suing for a slight injury after an auto accident. My argument was that he was such a worrisome person that prolonged litigation over his health might easily throw him into a miserable state of ill health. The man and his wife agreed entirely with me and did not go to law."

CRITICISM OF PERSONAL INJURY LITIGATION

Personal injury suits have been the target of growing criticism both from within the legal profession as well as from the general public. For example, Robert S. Marx, of the Cincinnati law firm of Nichols, Wood, Marx & Ginter, wrote in the *Ohio State Law Journal* (Spring, 1958) :

I criticize [personal injury litigation] because it is not fair. It works with tremendous inequality. It forces the personal injury claimant to assume risks that he never knew existed. He assumes the risk of uncertainty in the law, the difficulty of proving negligence, of the choice of proper counsel, or being coerced to settle because he cannot afford the long delay until he might get his case heard, and the risk that the defendant might not be able to pay any judgment he may eventually obtain. The defendant in the personal injury case must also assume some of these same risks and, in addition, he must assume the risk that he may be called upon to pay many times the economic loss of the claimant, and the risk that the plaintiff's lawyer will be able to convince the jury that the pain and suffering of the plaintiff should have a remarkably high value. The defendant has no methods, because of the wide variation in jury verdicts, by which he can standard- ize his exposure. Nor does the availability of insurance aid the defendant as much as would be first supposed. Insurance costs money and in these days of rising jury verdicts it is not unusual to find that a defendant, who assumed that he was amply covered by insurance, is faced with a verdict far exceeding his policy coverage. Liability insurance is not, in any event, universal. No more than 75 per cent of the automobiles on the road today are covered by liability insurance and the percentage is much smaller in those personal injury cases which do not involve automobiles.

It is clear that the arena of personal injury litigation is one filled with much emotional heat from both sides of the trial table and I go into it with the knowledge that it will bestir cries of anguish from one side or the other. The objective is to favor neither, however, but to present the problem in relation to difficulties of our jurors summoned from their homes to decide on these matters.

George L. De Lacy, one critic of this problem asks:[1] "How long will the public tolerate the continual upward spiral of jury verdicts in personal injury cases? You are familiar with reports in the newspapers of tremendous verdicts growing out of the operation of railroads and automobile traffic. Think of a ver- dict, tax free, of $400,000 to a forty-four-year-old waiter for brain injuries and injuries to his legs, of $250,000 for a brain

[1] DeLacy, George L., "Jury Trials of Auto Injury Claims Threatened," Volume 35, *Nebraska Law Review,* p. 389.

injury sustained by a forty-eight-year-old freight agent, of $100,000 for an eye, of $240,000 for the loss of a leg. These enormous figures have acted as stimulus for many spurious claims, and a tremendous amount of litigation that has little or no merit has been instituted."

Criticism of the constant drive to raise these verdicts comes from defense attorneys and insurance companies. As far back as October 18, 1957, the *Journal of Commerce* carried an article in which the insurance industry assailed the National Association of Claimants Compensation Attorneys, now known as the American Trial Lawyers' Association, as an "unvarnished pressure group" whose campaign to increase the frequency and size of damage awards could bankrupt insurance companies.

To this comes answer from the plaintiff lawyers. For too many years, they claim, the insurance companies dominated the field. They could afford to hire experts and scientists to build up powerful defenses. They even now have almost limitless funds at their disposal to knock down the case of the poor claimant. They point to the delay in law, with civil cases running three to six years behind in state courts, as a tremendous handicap to overcome. Witnesses tend to get lost, original pain begins to evaporate, and scars to heal. Thus their cases are much weakened by the time they come to trial. Many times, claimants in dire need of money cannot afford to wait out that time and must accept settlement for much less than the case is worth in order to get their funds immediately so that economic pressures can be relieved.

The plaintiff's attorney asks what would you accept in return for your arm, or an eye, or being condemned to a wheel chair for the rest of your life because of someone's misconduct or negligence? It is evident that they present a powerful case for their side. And it is equally clear that the powerful pull from each side in this lucrative personal injury field exercises exceedingly strong pressures on those twelve willing, but woefully unprepared, citizens called upon to decide who was at fault in the particular incident and to assess the amount of damages to be paid to the victim. Sympathy for the victim, placed together with knowledge that too great freedom with insurance funds can raise premiums for all the insured, makes this pressure even stronger.

A GROWING — AND IMPORTANT — PROBLEM

This is a problem that cannot be passed over lightly. It is of the utmost importance to everyone now, not only the litigants presently involved and their attorneys and insurance companies, but also those who will face it in the future. It is a problem that is constantly growing in importance. In December, 1951, for example, newspapers made mention of the fact that the one millionth American war fatality took place in Korea at the same general time that the one millionth automobile fatality happened in the United States. Thus the automobile, in its 50-odd years of existence, had become as great a killer as all the wars in America's entire existence had been. Add to this the additional 1,300,000 individual disabling bodily injuries that take place yearly, bring into the picture higher and higher jury bodily injury awards, and it can be seen that we are in the ascent of a spiral of indeterminable consequences.

Obviously, when juries were introduced to this problem they were not confronted with the perils of present-day society where the average man by simply leaving his home is faced with a potent daily opportunity to ruin life and property of others at the great risk of his own personal liability. Previously the common man was by and large circumstantially unable to risk civily his meager aggregation of worldly possessions.

The problem of jurors lost in the mazes of personal injuries charges and counter-charges by hosts of conflicting experts has long raised questions as to the desirability of this system. As far back as 1953, in his *Report on Justice,* Judge John W. Peck—the former presiding justice of the Appellate Division of the New York Court, First Department—suggested that the jury be dispensed with in negligence cases. For one thing, he criticized the slowness of such jury cases, which contributed greatly to the delay in court and brought about the problems complained of by plaintiff lawyers. He stated somewhat bluntly: "Indeed, there is no standard for a jury verdict. Nothing could be more of a guess and a gamble than what a jury's verdict will be in a closely contested case. There is no inherent virtue in that gamble." Judge Peck made clear at a later point in his report that "if the argument against jury trials rested only upon a time-saving base, I would not be so confident of my ground in advocating change. If the equality of justice can be assumed to be the same, however, the time element is a sufficient reason to change to a system of trial by judge without a jury. And we can be fairly well assured that there would be no sacrifice of justice in any way by the fact that the most traditional country in the world, England, the cradle of the jury system and the common law, quite some time ago abandoned the jury system in most civil cases without regrets."

Not only has the question been raised in the legal profession, but by lay critics as well. In January, 1957, an article "Damage Suits—A Primrose Path to Immorality" by Morton M. Hunt in *Harper's Magazine* developed the theme that the law suit for personal injuries has become a national pastime. It asserted that the avariciousness of the plaintiff and his lawyer is degenerating the moral fiber of American life, and raising insurance costs. Hunt illustrated his point with this example:

Consider the ethical virtue of the "sock the city" verdict, as it might be called. Six years ago a thirty-nine-year-old barge worker toppled, dead drunk, onto the tracks of a New York subway station. An incoming train screeched to a halt, but failed to stop short of him, and killed him. His widow sued and won on the grounds that the city was at fault; it should have maintained such operating conditions that no train could run over a drunk who fell on the tracks. It was no contest : she was a real, tearful woman, and the city was a vast, cold abstraction. She collected $101,649.86.

It is evident from this that the problem of soaring verdicts is causing a commotion in many quarters. Yet it should be made clear that this comprises only half of the criticism about jury verdicts in this area. The other half is the great number of complaints leveled where no verdicts are obtained; where the defendant is so poor that it is not worth while to file legal action against him, no matter how negligent he may have been. This is made clear in the pointed comments of Robert S. Marx in the *Ohio State Bar Journal* :

The morality of a system which attempts to put a price tag on such an item [as the agony of pain] is open to very severe questioning indeed, and if we do presume to put a value on it, we get exactly what we deserve : the widest possible variation in the verdicts of juries as to what one man's pain and suffering is worth as against another's, due partly to the awesome ability of some skilled lawyers to recreate a gruesome spectacle of violent agony in every tiny detail to the point where the jury cannot abide it; this is known as "demonstrative evidence."

What has all this got to do with ability to pay? It has everything to do with it. A rich defendant makes it well worth the plaintiff's time to attempt to trail every bit of blood possible across the floor of the court room. If that rich defendant is an insurance company, the jury will know it, in spite of all the efforts of the defendant to keep that fact away from the jury's knowledge. At present, juries assume the existence of insurance, especially in automobile accident cases, and this assumption is generally a correct one. It is correct, not because all automobiles are insured, but rather because most men of any substance are insured. This brings us to look at the other side of the coin : the ability to pay is the greatest single factor in determining which law suits are never filed. There is no point in litigation with an insolvent defendant, no matter how much of a liability case is present. When a law suit is filed, it is filed because there is some expectation of recovery and where the defendant has no insurance and no assets the matter is usually forgotten. In this case, the victim's agony, worth perhaps $50,000 under other circumstances, will never be described to any jury. Discussion of amounts of damages in negligence cases involves us in an assumption which is all too casual : there is often no point in determining an amount, because there is no ability to pay.

As we turn our attention to sky-rocketing verdicts then, let us remember that they represent only one view of what is wrong; the law suit which is never filed because of lack of ability to pay is certainly just as serious.

The casually summoned modern personal-injury jurors are indeed placed in an unreasonable position. Taken from the security of home or shop, they are tossed into the middle of this major problem, pushed and pulled from all sides, and ordered to return a semblance of justice. An incident I observed may illustrate one result of such a system. Two very capable attorneys opposed each other in the case of a fifty-seven-year-old secretary who had suffered a broken arm. Her house, on a higher level than its neighbor, had a two-foot retaining wall. One night, the secretary tripped over that wall and fell, suffering a multiple fracture of her right wrist. When this fracture healed, it did so at an awkward angle. It was clear she could no longer type so well as formerly and she lost her job as a secretary. She subsequently lost several other jobs because she could not use her arm very well. The defendant offered her $3,500 to settle and was refused. The case finally came to trial and, to the surprise of all participants, the jury brought in a verdict for $2,200—some $1,300 less than she had originally been offered.

The trial judge was astonished. He granted a new trial. It was a year and a half before the case came to trial again, this time before a different judge. More important, it also had an altogether different jury. Facts were still exactly the same and the injuries had not changed during the time. Each side presented the same witnesses. The case, in other words, had not changed in any material way. Yet when the second jury returned, its verdict was for $22,000, exactly ten times as much as the earlier jury had found on the same facts. The case was later settled for less, but it serves to show by its contrast the uncertainty of such trials.

Experts in this field of law reveal that payments are being made by way of settlements in lawyers' office to avoid court procedures and men do not turn to the jury with assurance that justice will be fair or that right will prevail. A study of cases which appear to have resulted in either inadequate or excessive damage verdicts by juries, however, will show that the courts are in almost all instances very slow to use their power to interfere with the jury in such matters. Decisions by reviewing courts seem to indicate that their only method of measuring a verdict is to determine whether or not it was influenced by passion or prejudice. This is done by comparing the verdict with the evidence in the specific case rather than with amounts involved in other cases where injuries were more or less practically the same. In essence, one expert concluded, the courts are evidently convinced that previously adjudicated cases—the basis of all other law—are rarely put into use in this area, which is so important to the general public.

Random samplings of what various state courts across the country have felt to be the tests of "excessive" verdicts should be enlightening. Here is what the appellate, or reviewing, courts have said :

OHIO : A verdict should not be set aside unless the damages awarded are so excessive as to appear to have been awarded as a result of passion or prejudice, or unless it is so manifestly against the weight of the evidence as to show a misconception by the jury of its duties (Toledo, C & O Railroad Co., v. Miller). Damages awarded by a jury must be flagrantly excessive and extravagant, or the court hearing an appeal will not disturb the verdict (Immel v. Richards).

ALABAMA : There is no limitation on the amount of an award of damages for personal injury so long as the principle of compensation is not violated (Castleberry v. Morgan). In determining adequacy of damages assessed by a jury, the court need not inquire and declare what wrongful influence or failure of duty in the consideration of the case has wrought a miscarriage of justice, but the internal evidence, the verdict itself, in the light of the facts clearly disclosed by the evidence, usually furnishes the determining data (Alabama Gas Co. v. Jones).

ARKANSAS : In determining whether the jury's verdict awarding damages for personal injuries is excessive, each case must rest on its own peculiar facts (Chicago, R. I. & P. Railroad Co. v. Houston).

MISSOURI : In determining reasonableness, consideration should be given to economic conditions, current costs, the purchasing power of the dollar at the time the verdict is rendered, and the failure of the trial court to set aside the verdict as excessive, and in days of inflation, a higher level of maximum damages is warranted (Arl v. St. Louis Public Service Co.).

CALIFORNIA : A verdict cannot be held excessive as a matter of law simply because the amount may be larger than is allowed ordinarily in such cases (Power v. California Steel Cable R. Co.).

TEXAS : An excessive verdict does not necessarily indicate that the trial was unfair or that the verdict was influenced by passion or prejudice, but if the verdict is grossly excessive, that fact may be regarded to some extent as reflecting the jury's mind in arriving at the verdict (Texas & N.O.R. CO. v. Haney).

NEW YORK : The court should not substitute its opinion for that of the triers of the facts respecting the amount of damages unless the verdict lacks proper support in the evidence or is so large that its excessiveness is clearly apparent (Kazdin v. Cooley).

In view of the increasing difficulties of lay juries in handling the highly technical personal injury trials, and with an eye to the reluctance of reviewing courts to upset jury verdicts as just shown, many people are becoming increasingly concerned with the situation. In a speech before the Nebraska State Bar Association, George L. DeLacy, attorney, said :[2]

I am of the opinion that every member of the Bar will admit that the handling of personal injury cases, where a jury trial is involved, is uncertain, is not efficient. I believe all will agree that many injustices result. I believe all will agree that litigants involved in personal injury cases are apprehensive, are fearful of the results and that many defendants prefer to pay more than they should to avoid such an ordeal. This is the year 1955; men in other walks of life, I think, wonder at the inefficient handling of such litigation by our profession and wonder why we do not improve on our proceedings.

[2] Volume 35, *Nebraska Law Review*, p. 389.

In another part of his speech, DeLacy emphasized:

Personal injury litigation in recent years has become big
business on both sides, and it should be handled with businesslike
efficiency across a desk with the opposing counsel seeking a solution and not in trial courts unless trial is absolutely unavoidable.
There is danger that if trial courts and trial lawyers do nothing
to improve the situation, disaster will result. The public will stand
just so much. Unless the present situation is corrected, we will
lose the bulk of personal injury litigation to either arbitration or
some form of compensation.

THE SASKATCHEWAN PLAN

Various plans have been proposed as a way out of this
dilemma of unpredictability of juries, uncertainty of amount
recovered, loss of any recovery where the defendant is penniless, and all the other problems of the personal injury jury
"business" just described. One such plan has been in operation
since 1946 and has captured many an eye seeking a solution
to the problem. It is the Automobile Accident Insurance
Act passed by the legislature of the Canadian province of
Saskatchewan. In brief, it provides minimum payments to all
parties injured in traffic, regardless of fault. Thus, any victim
of an accident is assured some amount of payment regardless
of the financial condition of the other party without even
having to go to court to face a jury. At the same time, it does
not prevent the injured party from bringing suit if he thinks
he deserves more. However, the amount the victim receives
from the fund is deducted from whatever he may recover from
the insured.

According to E. C. Leslie, former president of the Canadian
Bar Association, in a report in the *Journal of the American
Judicature Society,* the general principle of the act is that an

insurance fund is set up out of which the benefits prescribed by the act are paid. The fund is raised by means of compulsory insurance. Every applicant for a motor vehicle license in the Province of Saskatchewan must pay an insurance premium at the time he takes out and pays for his driver's license. The rates of premiums are fixed by regulations made by the lieutenant governor in council and have varied throughout the years.

The rates charged for this compulsory insurance depend on a number of different factors. The ordinary basic premium rate for an operator's license is $3.00. The premium rate for a private passenger car varies from a minimum of $5.00 to a maximum of $67. Cars of early vintage and those of smaller wheel base get a lower rate. The premium rates increase for passenger public-service vehicles, taxis, and public-service vehicle trucks depending upon the number of passengers carried and other factors up to a maximum of $411. Where there has been a conviction of an owner or operator for a violation of the provisions of the Saskatchewan Vehicles Act or the Criminal Code of Canada with respect to motor vehicle offenses, the adjudicating court may cancel the operator's license. In this way a "white" license may be reduced first to a "blue" license and finally to a "red" license. The fees for the holders of a blue or red license are higher than those charged to a person who holds a white license.

The second part of the plan provides for insurance for personal injuries and death. Here the "insured" means a person in respect of whom, or of whose dependents, benefits are payable if bodily injuries are sustained as a result of one of the perils included in the act, whether such person is named in an owner's or operator's certificate or not. For example, a pedestrian crossing a street in Saskatchewan and sustaining injuries by being struck by a moving motor vehicle is insured. However, such a person — that is, one who had not taken out an owner's or operator's certificate — would not be insured if his accident occurred outside the Province of Saskatchewan, but within Canada or the Continental United States of America, unless he were a passenger in a Saskatchewan-licensed vehicle; whereas the owner of an owner's or driver's certificate could be compensated if he were injured in an automobile accident outside the province.

The amount of benefits provided under this act are: In death, $5,000 to the primary dependent, $1,000 to each secondary dependent, $2,000 for housewife's death, $10,000 maximum payable to any one death, and $300 payment in lieu of funeral expenses. In dismemberment benefits—loss of limb, for example—maximum amounts payable range from $500 to $4,000. Weekly indemnity during period of incapacity from injuries where the insured person is (or, during any six out of the preceding 12 months, has been) actively engaged in any occupation or employment for profit, as well as for housewives is $25, subject to a maximum total of $2,600.

Under the public liability provision of the act, $35,000 is allowed for personal injury or death or damage to property or both in one accident. By amendments made to the act in 1957 and 1959, relief is extended to the amount of $35,000 to those who suffer personal injuries or death as a result of the negligence of a hit-and-run driver or the driver of a stolen vehicle.

By further amendments in 1964, relief is extended also to the amount of $35,000 for claims arising out of one accident on account of bodily injury, death or damage to property caused by the negligence of an uninsured motorist. Although it is thought that the number of resident uninsured motorists is negligible, the 1964 amendments provide more adequate relief than was theretofore available where an accident was caused in the province by the fault of a non-resident uninsured motorist.

It will be seen that these coverages are not large, but the

intention of the act is to provide a basic minimum coverage and to provide as broad a protective umbrella as possible. Consequently, there is nothing to prevent a person who has suffered injury, loss, or damage as a result of negligence of the operator of a motor vehicle from suing the operator and owner of that vehicle. Under the provisions of the act, the amount of judgment recovered against any such defendant who holds an owner's or operator's certificate under the act is reduced by any amounts that have been paid to the plaintiff in such action by the Saskatchewan Government Insurance Office pursuant to the terms of the act.

For example : if A is killed in Saskatchewan as a result of a motor vehicle accident and his widow sues the owner of a motor vehicle involved in it alleging negligence, and if she succeeds, she would recover a judgment, let us say, of $50,000. Under the act, she has already been paid on behalf of herself and her children the sum of $10,300. She recovers a judgment of $50,000, but from there must be deducted the sum of $10,300, provided that the defendant negligent owner or operator holds a cerificate issued under the act. However, if the death of A was caused by the fault of a person who at the time of the accident was not qualified and authorized by law to drive, or was under the influence of liquor or drugs, the operator will not be entitled to the benefit of the provision and there will not be deducted from a judgment against him the payments made to the widow under the act. Of course, the act provides minimum coverage, but this minimum coverage is compulsory, and benefits are paid even to persons who are at fault and while all applications for operators and owner's licenses in Saskatchewan are compelled to take out the insurance provided by the act, they are not the only persons insured under it.

The Automobile Accident Insurance Fund created by the premiums received pays the claims benefits to motorists and others who are victims of automobile accidents as well as paying administrative costs. If a surplus remains over outgo in any one year, it is government policy to hold such excess in the fund for the benefit of the potential auto victims. No surplus is transferred to the general operation of the office nor is the surplus credited to the consolidated revenue of the province.

Statistics show that the plan drew in $1,300,515 in premiums the first year, paid out $298,977 in losses, another $147,569 in expenses, and showed a surplus of $767,287. By the end of 1958, premiums earned were up to $5,442,686, losses were at $4,379,581, and the cumulative surplus had reached $3,900,255. By the end of 1965 premiums earned for the year were $13,758,924, claims incurred were $12,920,982 and the accumulated surplus had been reduced to $1,201,080. Any accumulated surplus above that required for reserve is returned to the people in the form of either broadened coverage or lower rates, or both. All interest earned on the investment of the money is paid into the fund.

Important though jurors are in ruling on the facts in personal injury cases — in determining who is right and who is wrong — that is only half the function of a jury. Once the liability is determined, or the blame assessed, the jury turns to a new job; it tries to evaluate the dollar value of the damages suffered. Here it finds itself in an altogether new wilderness, an area of difficulty which even experts fear. Yet jurors have no way out. The law requires them to come back with a written figure.

5

Placing the Price Tag

IT SHOULD BY NOW BE EVIDENT THAT ACTIVITIES OF JURORS in personal injury trials in state courts have become the subject of controversy. Strangely enough, however, it is in the area of personal pain that juries have their biggest job. Their work load in this area goes far beyond what they may be called upon to handle in criminal matters, contracts, will contest cases, or the other multitude of problems in the law.

With the country's rapid expansion in population, coupled with the constantly growing number of automobiles, more highways, and greater mobility of the general public, it can be seen that the number of personal injury cases has no place to go but up. And with the worsening of the problem in the sheer number of cases flowing into civil courts and clogging even more the already heavily laden dockets comes another problem: the more complicated aspects of the individual cases. Increased horsepower in automobile engines perforce results in more serious accidents and larger amounts sought to repay injuries. At the same time, attorneys in this highly specialized field are becoming more expert. As their stakes go up, they spend more time in preparing their cases. Greater attention is given to medical experts and their techniques. In response to this, insurance companies and defense attorneys must also delve into their cases with greater intensity, summoning more highly qualified experts. The problem compounds itself. The focal point for this tremendous burden of conflicting expert testimony and lengthening complicated law is—our innocent citizen juror.

DATA KEPT FROM JURORS

The law itself makes the problem of the juror seeking the nebulous figure in dollars to award the injured party a difficult one indeed. This is done by rules which force courts actually to keep from the jury information that is necessary in determining a fair price. For example : the jury is not told that the lawyer's fees should not be part of the damage figure, or that interest is not to be examined from the time of the injury and, highly important, they are not told—and rarely are aware—that the award they give is *not* subject to federal income taxes. Failure to give this information to jurors obviously creates misunderstanding, which is reflected in the damage verdict. But no one ever knows to what extent since, of course, the jury's deliberations and reasons for their conclusions are completely secret and protected.

It should be clear from the outset that juries face tough tasks : they must reach important decisions on the basis of incomplete information and conflicting evidence; they are asked to look into the future; they must consider how long a plaintiff will live and how long he will require medical care; they must guess how long his present pain will last; and they must estimate one of the hardest of questions—how much will the dollar they award today be worth in years to come?

Obviously, these questions could easily bewilder a panel of learned experts in each of these fields. Their effects on the amateurs who have been called in hastily, and without preparation, is not hard to imagine.

Question has been raised as to why the future cannot be left to the wisdom of the courts with payments to be adjusted as new problems arise. This could be done in a manner similar to that used in alimony. But that it not the situation now: the jury is asked to make a final decision for all times, and to do it quickly and under handicaps. As a result, it is not unusual for juries to reach conclusions that are in direct conflict with the law which they are given. For example, there is the problem of wrongful death. Here the law calls for payment to survivors for the loss they have suffered, so it would logically appear that a young man with high earnings and a large family depending upon his income should be worth more than an elderly man who is retired and has no dependents. However, juries have been known to ignore this basic question completely and to decide on the purely emotional question of "what is a human life worth?" Thus, the elderly's person's estate becomes the recipient of an award practically equal to that which is needed to support the dependents of the younger man.

At other times, juries have been known to put a peculiar reasoning into their decisions. For example, in one case it was reported that the victim left behind an attractive young widow and children. This would seem on the face a perfect case for a plaintiff's lawyer to get a large verdict to replace the husband's earning power. With another jury it could easily have turned out that way. But again logic and presupposition were defied. The jury which heard the case brought in a modest award. The reason, strange though it may seem, was that a widow who was that attractive would have no trouble in remarrying and having someone else support her. And, they added, if she failed to remarry it would probably be her own fault and she did not deserve the large amount from the defendant!

PROBLEM OF PAIN AND SUFFERING

Lay persons often ask how lawyers can seek unusually high amounts of money from injury cases in which the expenditures were not particularly heavy. The question arises, for example, when a jury gives, say, $50,000 to a person who has been able to show actual costs of medical care and time lost from work totaling about $10,000. The answer lies in that twilight area known as pain and suffering. It is the area at which ambitious trial lawyers aim their heaviest artillery when they seek great achievement in their profession. The target is an emotional, and often gullible, personal injury jury.

This question of "pain and suffering" has many aspects. It covers the physical pain suffered at the time of the accident, the degree of which only the victim can adequately describe. It can include suffering brought about by the medical care subsequently required to correct the original injuries. Usually the only requirement for this physical pain is that the victim be conscious at least part of the time in order that he be aware of that pain and discomfort.

In one Minnesota railroad case, the victim lived 41 hours after the accident and his own physician later testified that he was unconscious during all that time. A lay witness and a nurse, however, testified that he was conscious at intervals, that he moaned considerably and even uttered a few words. The jury granted an award for pain and suffering before death. The reviewing court upheld the verdict with the observation that all that was required to justify a recovery was that an appreciable length of time elapse between the injury and death — and that the decedent suffered conscious pain.

The area of payment for pain is obviously one in which

juries have the greatest latitude—and the least knowledge. It is territory hard to challenge. There are practically no rules to guide the fact finders or to determine if they have acted through error. As Marcus L. Plant, professor of law at the University of Michigan, has noted (in the *Ohio State Bar Journal,* Spring, 1958) no particular amount of pain, suffering, or its term or duration is required as a basis for recovery. Since it is only necessary that the sufferer be conscious, recovery is not usually permitted in cases involving instantaneous death. Aside from this, however, no quantitative or time limitations are imposed. In one California case, the evidence showed 20 minutes of pain and a jury awarded a judgment of $20,000. This was held not to be excessive.

Other instances of recovery show awards of $10,000 for pain and suffering extending over a period of two hours; $6,000 for three and one-half hours, and $10,000 for four hours. Or the period may be a protracted one which looks far into the future. For example, an award of some $125,000 was allowed to an eight-year-old boy in a Florida case who lost his left leg in a railroad accident. His life expectancy was estimated at fifty-six years.

While pain is usually regarded as part of the *original* injury, it may be transferred over effectively to cover *later* pain that stems from the original incident. In one case which I observed, the victim was unconscious immediately after her accident. She had received plastic surgery, however, to help remove severe scars from her face. When her attorney stressed the humiliation of such scars, the defense lawyer called to the stand an eminent plastic surgeon. The doctor testified such mutilations could practically be eliminated in a type of operation wherein the skin was stitched, then folded over and stitched again. Apparently the plaintiff lawyer's bid for sympathy from the jury over the scars had been foiled. But he was not defeated for long. When he gave his final summation to the panel, he stressed "the excruciating pain this woman will have to endure when her scars are cut and sewn and then sewn again, stitch . . . after stitch . . . after stitch into her living flesh." The jury was obviously impressed. It returned a large verdict for her.

This same plaintiff attorney has a great fondness for conveying to the jury the pain that comes from embarrassment. His favorite closing comment with many juries has long been: "Ladies and gentlemen, you can go home tonight and forget this poor man. That is perfectly alright. But remember when you go into your deliberations that this man can never forget. Every morning when he looks into his mirror those scars will be there to remind him; and he will carry them with him to the very last day of the long life we all hope he still has. Remember that when you go up to decide what this is worth. Ask yourselves what it would be worth to you."

What can a defense attorney say to overcome this broad expanse of money that his opposition has thrown open before the jury, particularly if the defendant happens to be a large corporation?

Thus it can be seen that the concept of pain and suffering can also include mental distress resulting from injury. This was pointed out, too, by Professor Plant. He noted that it was hard to distinguish mental distress from physical pain in every case, but certain types of disturbances which were perhaps more emotional than physical were commonly allowed to be taken into account in the recovery for pain and suffering. Among these are humiliation or embarrassment connected with scars or disfigurements incurred as a result of the injuries, inconvenience of bi-weekly visits over a long period of time for the purpose of adjustment of the victim's prosthetic equipment; "extremely nervous" fright experience at the time of injury, and the fear of death. While these forms of distress are not exactly the same as physical pain and suffering, they are generally regarded as sufficiently connected with it to be the subject of recovery by the plaintiff.

It is evident that courts have placed few restrictions on the plaintiff in his display to the jury of the pain through which he has gone. The usual is to let the plaintiff testify himself. If he appears in great pain at the moment, or if he has obviously disfiguring scars, so much the better for his lawyer, who can dramatize it to the gaping jury. Others who can testify include lay witnesses who were able to see him and his condition and can speak convincingly of his moans and groans, or who can describe vividly the way he winces with pain. The attending physician may also speak of his observations. In other words, the jury may get practically every kind of evidence which indicates the existence of pain and suffering and it is up to them to distinguish which is real and which is put on as a show to elicit their sympathy and with it the awarding of a large verdict.

There are times when proof of the basis for the jury's prediction of future pain and suffering must rest upon the plaintiff's own testimony, unsupported by anyone else. Professor Plant has done considerable research on this and concluded that the answer of the courts seems to be in the affirmative. Here are a few examples he has unearthed:

In *Orme v. Watkins,* a six-year-old school boy was struck by an automobile but was discharged from the hospital the very same day. The child complained "occasionally" that his knee bothered him and that he had headaches, but there were no objective symptoms of pain, injury, or dizziness. His mother and father testified that he was restless in his sleep, wetting his bed, and was sleepy at school. A judgment for $5,000 was upheld. In *Brown v. Campbell,* the plaintiff, who had been assaulted, testified to having headaches. His testimony impressed the court as rather weak. No corroborating evidence was adduced. Nevertheless, a judgment for future pain and suffering was upheld. In *Sarik v. Pennsylvania R. R. Co.*, plaintiff was hurt in what the court referred to as a trifling accident : a handle of an overturning two-wheel truck grazed her scapula. There was no physical sign of injury and X-rays revealed no damage to the bony structure. The court indicated that there was some basis for doubting her veracity; all plaintiff's physicians ascribed her suffering to a neurosis. Nevertheless, the court upheld a judgment for $3,000. Similar results have been reached in a case involving a throat ailment with alleged difficulty in swallowing, and one involving alleged headaches and dizzy spells. Perhaps the most extreme illustration of this type of situation concerned an injury alleged to have arisen out of the wrongful insertion of a hearing aid in the plaintiff's ear. The plaintiff's testimony on the witnesses stand commenced in a flow of tears as he recalled the pain. The court said, "the physical act of crying is painful and . . . it is reasonably certain to occur again in the future." Damages of $3,000 were awarded.

Professor Plant concluded that it seemed clear to him from those and other cases — and it was borne out by the experience of personal injury lawyers on both sides of the table — that the existence of pain and suffering is one of the easiest elements to establish in the plaintiff's case in a personal injury action. Despite the requirement that the jury must be instructed that in order to make any award for future pain and suffering they must find that such pain and suffering is reasonably certain to occur, the foundation for such a finding is fairly easily proved.

NO GUIDES FOR JURORS

Standing alone, the foregoing aspect of a personal injury case would not be too disturbing. Its significance becomes evident, however, when one considers it in relation to another element: the absence of anything like a fixed standard for measuring damages attributable to pain and suffering. The complete lack of any such standard has been freely admitted by scholars and the courts for many years. As far back as 1912 it was noted, said Professor Plant, that "for pain and suffering there can be no measure of compensation save the arbitrary judgment of a jury."[1] Other experts since then have concluded that translating pain and anguish into dollars can, at best, be only an arbitrary allowance, and not a process of measurement, and consequently the judge can, in his instructions, give the jury no standard to go by. The courts have consistently ackknowledged the validity of this view putting it in many different ways:

The rule for measuring damages for pain and suffering, past, present and future, is that there is no standard by which to measure it except the enlightened conscience of impartial juries . . . the award of damages for pain, suffering, shock, etc., for personal injury of necessity is somewhat arbitrary and depends upon the facts and circumstances of each case . . . such damages rest in the sound judgment of the trier of the facts . . . each case necessarily sets its own standard . . . the amount of the award must rest in the discretion of the jury guided by common sense . . . such damages cannot be measured by a mathematical rule.

Professor Plant commented that "the uncertainty in the award of such damages is compounded when one takes account of the fact that pain and suffering vary greatly from one individual to another.

"Not to be overlooked in any catalogue of uncertainties in this field is the great likelihood of variation among judges in their decisions to permit a damage award to stand or to over-turn it as 'monstrous,' 'shocking to the judicial conscience,'

---

[1] Plant, Marcus L., *Ohio State Law Journal,* Spring, 1958; Vol. 19, No. 2, p. 205.

'indicative of bias or improper motives,' or in violation of whatever other verbal standard is used to measure the validity of a jury verdict."

The professor concluded that the ultimate practical consequence of the absence of any certain method of evaluating pain and suffering is that in appraising the potential recovery in any personal injury case there exists a vast imponderable : no one, not even the experienced claims adjustor, can say with any reasonable degree of certainty what a jury is likely to do in awarding damages for pain and suffering. Many cases show that it is very easily possible for a jury to exceed the bounds of reason.

Harley J. McNeal, an attorney friend of mine who represents insurance companies on the defense side of trials, put it much more bluntly when he said that too often jurors feel exceedingly generous in distributing large sums of money that belong to someone else. One of the troubles with juries, he said, is that they are not spending their own money. If they had to do that, or if they were aware that their benefactions help to raise their own insurance rates as well as that of others, it might put a damper on their generosity and bring a greater measure of reason to their verdicts. It must be realized, of course, that Mr. McNeal speaks with his own interest in mind, but his point is well worth the consideration.

THE INCOME TAX ASPECT

One important area in which juries overpay a plaintiff at the expense of a defendant comes about simply because an important item of information is deliberately kept away from them. The area is that involving income taxes and the fact carefully hidden from jurors is that all recoveries from court suits are completely free of such taxes. How many times jurors have raised the amount of their verdict because they erroneously believed part of it would go for such taxes is unknown. But it is known that efforts by defense attorneys to get such information before juries, either by way of evidence during the trial or through argument to the jury at the close of the case, have been consistently rejected by the courts.

At the same time, however, courts regularly allow into evidence the gross earnings of the plaintiff. The reason for this is that it is necessary to show what loss he has suffered by not being able to work because of his injury. This loss is properly part of the damages he has incurred due to the accident. Since it is the gross figure that is introduced, the jury has no way of knowing actual earnings after such taxes have been paid. In other words, this rule makes possible a double overcompensation: first by awarding dollars he would never have received anyhow because they would have been deducted in taxes; second by adding on taxes to the award which will never have to be paid.

Reasons for the court attitudes on income taxes are most interesting. They have been gathered by Robert J. Nordstrom, associate dean and professor of law at Ohio State University. In the *Ohio State Law Journal* he summed up what is most often in the court's mind when it refuses to admit such evidence:

1) The impact of federal taxes is a matter between the plaintiff and the taxing authorities. The defendant has no interest in whether or not a tax is levied.

2) To allow the introduction of such evidence would upset a well-established precedent.

3) The amount of federal income tax is too conjectural to be considered by the jury.

Courts have argued that it would be too difficult to give juries an accurate tax picture of the plaintiff which would have to include information on such outside income as returns on investment, the number of his dependants, the income-tax bracket in which he falls. Yet Professor Nordstrom points out that all this is not necessary, since the entire problem can be pointed out by a judge in a simple statement to the jury at the close of the case. For example, the judge could say: "You are instructed that any award made to plaintiff as damages in this case, if any award is made, is not subject to federal or state income taxes, and you should not consider such taxes in fixing the amount of any award made plaintiff, if any you make." The professor commented:

This instruction does not require any speculation as to the future tax structure of this country; it merely tells the jury that there will be no income tax levied on any award that is made to the plaintiff. This instruction, therefore, does not call into question the plaintiff's future marital status, the number of his exemptions, the size of his deductions, the amount of his outside income, or the future tax rates of the country. There can be no parade of tax experts across the stand, thus prolonging even longer the trial of negligence cases. It involves merely a simple statement of no longer than two or three sentences to the jury at the close of the trial.

Why then have most courts refused to give this instruction? If we answer this question on the basis of the words they have used in their opinions, that question must be answered thus: many courts have refused to give this instruction because they have confused the problem of the instruction with the problem of whether the evidence of the incidence of taxation should be admitted during the trial. Once these are confused, the court can then point out how "confused" the jury would be with this added bit of information.

This idea is discarded by Professor Nordstrom with the thought that, when analyzed, the instruction to the jury cannot properly be refused because the jury will be "confused"—the instruction is not that complicated. In fact, it appears rather simple when compared with a charge on measuring the decrease in the plaintiff's future earning capacity. In addition, refusal cannot be based upon a presumption that juries follow instructions.

TRENDS IN AWARDS

Keeping in mind the problems facing the average citizen jury, summoned for brief service in a state civil court, only a few of which have thus far been touched upon here, it is time now to turn to the actual amounts of money being awarded for specific injuries. The trend in these has been consistently upward. A wide variety of reasons can be given. Some point to the economic chart to prove that the price of everything is going up and that the ever-higher verdicts merely reflect the declining value of the dollar. In this theory, amounts awarded have their hills and valleys in somewhat of a direct ratio to periods of prosperity and recession; but the general trend is upward in compliance with the rest of the economy.

Others contend that the climb is the result of pressure, that it comes from organized plaintiff lawyers passing among themselves new techniques for impressing juries. This includes the so-called demonstrative evidence, or better known as "dragging the blood across the floor in front of the jury," as well as efforts to publicize widely the higher verdicts in an effort to condition future juries.

Conversely, efforts are made to hide the valleys. This type of pressure confronted me recently when I published newspaper articles revealing that for a period plaintiffs had found difficulty in winning any verdicts and that those which came were comparatively low. The response was immediate. A member of NACCA, (now the American Trial Lawyer's

Association) the plaintiff lawyers association, contacted me to say such articles were not in the best interest of justice and should be discontinued. Other plaintiff lawyers, my personal friends, argued with me that such disclosures were detrimental to their business since they discouraged potential clients. Defense attorneys were, of course, quite happy and praised me on my "accuracy and good taste in the publications." Take each of these comments for what they may be worth.

Still other reasons given for the uptrend include the fact that accidents are becoming more serious; that time lost from work is worth more due to higher salaries; that the country is becoming increasingly more urbanized with jurors thus becoming more sophisticated in dealing with large sums of money.

The reasons are many, changing with the opinions of those interviewed or the circumstance of the moment. Whatever the view, however, it is clear that jury verdicts mount constantly — and sometimes mysteriously and unpredictably so.

It should be remembered that this upward trend, flowing from secret jury sessions, has a far-reaching effect. It is felt in private negotiating meetings in law offices and with insurance claims adjustors. These negotiations are based on figures that come from the jury room. If, say, a new high figure is announced for a head injury by a jury, the next lawyer with a head-injury case will quote it to the defense attorney. It is somewhat of a club bearing the figurative thought of "either you settle with us around this figure or we will take it to court and have a jury give it to us after a lengthy and expensive trial which neither of us really wants to have to go through."

Many times, however, going to court is a necessity despite the cost and discomfort it brings in an effort to set a new jury guidepost for ensuing settlement negotiations. This is due, in part, to the fact that jury verdicts can vary to such an extent as to leave a particular area in complete confusion. In view of this, editors of the *Cleveland-Marshall Law Review* made a survey of personal injury damage award trends and came up with some interesting, and contrasting, results on specific injuries. For example, in multiple head injuries with permanent brain damage, it was found that verdicts ranged from $260,000 for pre-natal injuries to an infant in South Carolina all the way down to $8,000 for a sixteen-year-old Arkansas girl who suffered cuts on her forehead and across the nose, over an eye and on either side of the jaw and tongue which brought a resultant nervousness and evidence of loss of intelligence due to organic deterioration of the brain.

In that same sampling, a man of seventy received $38,000 for deep contusions of the skull, contusion in the frontal portion of the head, subdural hematoma detected and removed several months after the accident and rendered mentally incompetent and physically helpless (Illinois). And a man of twenty-four received $30,000 for a fractured skull and cerebral concussion which brought total and permanent loss of smell and sense of aromatic taste, total hearing loss in left ear, partial right ear loss, frequent headaches and dizziness (Missouri).

For the same type of injury, a family man of thirty-three received $100,000, plus an additional $65,000 — for past and future loss of earnings — for severe brain damage, permanent disability, and severe mental condition (New York). A graduate surgical nurse, thirty-nine, was awarded $72,380 for a skull fracture, intercranial hemorrhage, bruises, lacerations, permanent disfigurement, permanent impairment of memory and thinking inhibition (New York). A man, twenty-eight, received $55,000, plus an additional $123,500 for past loss of earnings and future diminished work capacity for severe brain damage, speech impairment, and permanent inability to coordinate on the right side of his body (Texas).

In marked contrast, to illustrate the unpredictability of juries, a housewife with a permanent brain injury, future nausea, and headaches, who claimed she was incapable of performing usual household tasks was awarded only $3,000 in Mississippi. The case was sent back for new trial on question of damages because a reviewing court found the award grossly inadequate.

For the same type of injuries, awards ranged from $85,000 for a sixteen-year-old Mississippi schoolboy whose mentality was reduced to that of a five-year-old by brain and internal injuries, all the way down to $500 for a teen-age girl with serious permanent brain damage and injury to her nervous system. This award was held grossly inadequate since medical expenses alone were over $1,000 (Alabama). Other sample awards included $70,000 to a thirty-eight-year-old carpenter with brain damage and substantial memory loss as well as severe headaches (Texas). A forty-year-old service station attendant won $45,000 for serious and permanent brain injury with his earning capacity substantially destroyed (Arkansas).

In the area of injuries to the eye, the survey found a similarly wide range of awards for comparatively equal damages. For example, a seven-year-old girl was awarded $28,000 for loss of sight of one eye after being struck by the defendant's car (New York), while an eleven-year-old boy, who lost one eye due to the explosion of a soft-drink bottle was given $200,000 (New York). While both of these cases were in the state of New York, it is interesting to note the first was in Poughkeepsie and the second in New York City.

An inmate of the New York State Reformatory who was injured on state property and lost one eye was awarded $9,785, while, in Michigan, a plaintiff was awarded $225,000, which was later reduced to $175,000, when he claimed that after loss of his right eye he was permanently and totally unemployable industrially, but could get about by himself and was able to do some reading with the aid of glasses. A twelve-year-old boy received $30,000 for loss of one eye after the explosion of a .30 caliber live blank cartridge left on government property after Marine maneuvers. A thirteen-year-old girl who lost one eye and suffered facial scars was given $25,000 in Michigan, while an illiterate laborer was given $6,500 for the loss of one eye by a New Jersey court.

In Louisiana, an award of $76,000 was given to an Air Force pilot who was hospitalized one day and reported trouble with the pupil of his eye and headaches from a whiplash injury. On a $1,500 medical bill and $500 loss of earnings, a thirty-six-year-old partner in a masonry contracting business was given $65,000 when an intern in a hospital treated his eye with 75 per cent silver nitrate solution which burned his eyeballs and caused him to spend twenty-five days in the hospital. There is 87 per cent vision remaining in his left eye and prospect of a corneal transplant and restoration of 100 per cent vision (Ohio).

Injuries to the back have long been a major trouble with juries. One reason for this may be that they have long troubled doctors as an unanswerable problem. The familiar aching back often has no proof in X-ray pictures, yet it is complained of as a continuing and disabling pain. Often, with proper medical treatment, the pain is only temporary. At other times it can be a long-term inconvenience complete with uncomfortable back braces and repeated visits to the doctor's office. But whatever the type, it is a challenge to the opposing attorneys and a great problem to juries who are called upon to render verdicts that even physicians would be hard put to reach. An example can be seen in such verdicts as $5,500 in New Jersey, despite medical costs of more than $8,000, to a woman whose back was sprained. She claimed continuing disability which the jury found might have been simulated or grossly exaggerated. In Missouri, medical expenses of $125 and loss of wages of $1,325 brought a verdict for $3,950 even though the X-ray indicated no bone fractures. And then there was the pregnant woman in Louisiana who was given $650 for minor injury to the muscles of the back and hip. This award contained $500 for worry and fear as to possible injury to an unborn child. In New York, an unemployed mason sustained injuries consisting of a back and neck sprain, and a laceration of the leg. For $40 in medical expense he received a return from the jury of $1,000.

In New Jersey, subjective claims were made of back and head pains, with loss of hearing. It wrung from the jury an award of $15,000 which was later reduced to $8,500, and finally down to $6,000 on review. In Louisiana a storekeeper's low back sprain, still causing trouble at the time of trial, got $15,000 from the jury and was later reduced to $10,000. In Missouri, a soft-tissue injury to the neck and lower back area of a thirty-year-old man, plus contusions of the knee, brought an award of $30,000 which was later cut to $20,000.

A married woman in Washington suffered pain and disability for two years, she said, as the result of a severe lumbosacral strain. She was hospitalized and in traction for all of five days and had medical expenses of $307 for which the jury gave her $10,307. The purpose, obviously, was to pay her costs, but with practically all the money going to that previously described elusive area of pain and suffering. In Kentucky, a jury awarded $5,000 for a subjective claim of back injury with continuing pain, but the reviewing court noted that the victim had not made any attempt to have medical attention and that normal activities were not limited, returned the case to the lower court for a new trial on damages only. In Louisiana, complete recovery was shown from back injury in two weeks; there were also lacerations of shins and face and shoulder sprain. The victim was hospitalized for twelve days and his medical expenses added up to $115, but the jury awarded him $865.

Why? Ask the jury.

Of all cases pouring into state civil courts on personal injuries, one of the most common is that for the so-called whip-

lash. This comes about when the body has been jerked and
the freely movable head has been snapped. Its most common
cause is the rear-end collision where the plaintiff's car has been
standing at a stoplight and has been struck by the car following.
Here, quite often, as in back injuries, it is hard to show positive
proof of injury on X-ray pictures. It often comes down to how
the plaintiff says he feels and how others describe his actions.
Here, too, the jury is completely on its own in a wide open
field of money, free to bring back almost anything.

What juries can do here is seen in the New York case where
the jury gave a verdict of $21,000 to a woman, although
evidence showed no traction was needed, no hospitalization was
involved, and that the woman continued working for several
months after the accident. A Thomas collar was not used
until some time later on the advice of a doctor. Here, however,
an appellate court showed an unusual degree of courage and
lowered the award to $10,000. In New Jersey, a jury awarded
$20,000 to another woman despite the fact that much medical
dispute centered on the extent of injuries. She stated loss of
balance and buckling of the right knee. Her doctor testified
that she would have a 15 per cent disability not in respect to
bodily function, but insofar as her daily activities were concerned. This was sent back for a new trial later on the basis
that the award was excessive. In another case, in Illinois, a
woman who spent five days in a hospital and slept with a
cervical collar for about six weeks after leaving the hospital,
was awarded $750 by the jury after proof that her medical
expenses alone were $429.61, not counting time lost from work.

A significant factor in all the reports on injury verdicts was
a sentence which ran through each report with only minor
variations. It said: "In viewing more than 100 recent appellate
cases . . . one is struck by the lack of any definite standard or
pattern of awards; and in reviewing these cases in order to de-

termine a trend, the conclusion is that if there is a trend it is not discernable . . ."; and again "no clear trend may be noted from the cases reported."

Repeatedly, surveys underscored what practicing lawyers had long said : that juries are unpredictable and do not set a clear pattern in their decisions — even on similar injuries — which claimants and insurance adjustors can use in the future to reach agreement in negotiations. They are, in effect, pushing the cases into the grab bag of the courts and adding to the congestions that keep other cases waiting for years to get their turn.

While most lawyers will argue that jurors acting on money verdicts are doing so completely without an earlier precedent to guide them, they will concede that there is, in fact, a sort of crude system of precedents that does influence them somewhat. I would describe it in this way : The jury does have an informal sort of precedent. It comes from jurors with prior experience, from cases reported in the newspapers, and from general gossip in the jury pool. The lifting of the award "ceiling" in a given locale, which has been a major target of NACCA, is one aspect of this. The impact of the "precedent" of one well-publicized high award appears to be considerable. Others describe it more bluntly by saying prospective jurors are conditioned by page-one stories which tell of high awards and, conversely, by the fact that cases involving small awards — or no awards at all — rarely get prominent space in the press because they are not ordinarily regarded as big news.

A LOOK TOWARD A SOLUTION

A highly capable defense attorney I know, after many years in the courts, has a plan which he thinks would bring a little more stability and justice to the problem of money verdicts. His answer is deceptively simple. He would divide between judge and jury the responsibility now given only to the jury.

He would allow only the task of deciding on the facts to remain with the jurors. Thus, they would continue to hear the story of how the accident happened and would have the responsibility of deciding whether the defendant was negligent and should be required to pay. In effect, they would be ruling only on the question of "guilt or innocence" and would have no hand in imposing the "sentence" of the civil court : the setting of the amount of money damages. This latter task would be the province of the judge alone. He, in full knowledge of the facts, and thoroughly familiar with what the trend for this type of injuries has been in preceding cases, would be in a much better position to decide how many dollars would, in all justice, be required to compensate the plaintiff who brought the suit.

This could be a partial solution. It would retain the jury for those who find a sentimental attachment to it, yet take out of its hands the power to do the great financial harm of which it has been accused. It would, however, be an incomplete solution, since it would still leave great power to the jurors.

Others would prefer a more complete solution such as the compensation insurance plan discussed previously and now operating in Saskatchewan, Canada. This would take the entire question away from juries and place it in control of a board financed by insurance on every car driven in the state. The amount paid by way of compensation to the injured would be set by schedules.

It goes without question that most lawyers would raise loud objections to this. It would take much of their practice from them, converting it into a routine matter that would not require the services of a specialist. Any neophyte lawyer could prepare the proper forms and present his facts to the board of commissioners.

Therefore, the very lawyers who would raise the noisiest opposition must look to themselves for such a change. Had they the courage to waive juries and present their causes to the judge alone for more prompt and equitable disposition of the matters, the present situation in all probability would never have arisen. Or had they stopped short of making a personal injury trial into an emotional drama calculated to sway naïve jurors into higher — or lower — verdicts, the injustices would not have been such as to cry out for change. Or had all motorists been forced to provide some sort of insurance, so that their victims might have some guarantee of recompense for their injuries, the situation would have been more equitable. None of these solutions, obvious though they are, has taken place and it is apparent that the time for needed adjustment is approaching.

But what about the handling of negligence cases other than automobile accidents? While damages can be assessed against specific drivers in highway accidents, other injuries, such as those occurring in the home or place of business, cannot be determined so easily. Here is another jury problem.

It should be clear from the wide variety of views presented that dissatisfaction is strong in the present method of handling the law's great burden : the question of personal injuries. It requires deep consideration not only from the courts, but from the general public — those hurt in the accidents, those sued for large payments, the jurors who must make these important decisions.

6

Blood Across the Floor

COMPLICATING THE EFFORTS OF SINCERE JURORS IN BOTH
laying blame and assessing value in today's accidents are complex rules of evidence, irresistible dramatics by lawyers, and the
involved routine of normal court procedures. For example, in
an incident I observed, a middle-aged nurse in a starched white
uniform slowly wheeled a little boy, awkwardly slumped in his
wheel chair, down the length of a courtroom one sunny afternoon. Eyes of the twelve jurors were fastened unwaveringly
on the crumpled figure as it was hesitantly brought toward the
judge's bench. Out of the shocked silence, the defense lawyer's
voice sounded suddenly loud as he raised an objection. The
nurse hesitated and then, at an order from the judge, slowly
turned and gently wheeled the little boy out again. Two
lawyers, Craig Spangenberg for the little boy and S. Burns
Weston for the defendant, whispered urgently with Judge
Arthur H. Day. Then the judge announced that the objection
was overruled and that the youngster could, in effect, be used

as a part of the evidence in his own case. Again, the nurse, called from the outer corridor, began her long walk, pushing the boy slowly toward the front of the room. And again every eye was riveted to the pitiful figure as the silent rubber wheels seemed to float him toward the judge. At last the boy sat before the bench.

His lawyer, softly dramatic, asked the boy his name. Every ear strained to hear. The boy sat in silence as though trying to comprehend the meaning of the question. Then, in a sentence broken with long pauses, as though it were an effort to form the words, the twisted little figure, its head leaning to one side almost on its shoulder, gave the answer. He was slowly wheeled out again.

The spell remained with the jurors. A few days later they returned with a verdict of $300,000 for this youngster, who had been hit by a car near his home as he alighted from a school bus. Brain damage was claimed. The case was heavy with drama.

This pitiful little boy was only one small example of the drama that is being created every day in courts across the country in the constant battle for the emotions of the jurors. The aim is to transfer this natural sympathy into high dollar verdicts, hoping each time to set a new record that must be surpassed with the next case. The clank of leg braces are normal sounds in courtrooms and skilled lawyers add their own personal dramatics, the whispered question and the thundered argument, to push the verdict up another notch. Angry defense attorneys, who fight with equal dexterity to minimize the injury and with it the ultimate verdict, denounce this absurd practice as "dragging the blood across the court-room floor."

Some attorneys are more inhibited than others; they present their cases in a more academic way, having the facts recited by a physician from the witness stand and keeping the "blood" to a minimum. They too often pay the penalty in lower verdicts. There is nothing like actually seeing the poor victim stagger panting to the witness stand—and if he is forced to crawl there on his knees, so much the better for the jury—to tie the jury's emotions into a neat little package for the plaintiff's lawyer.

Sometimes the "blood" is a little more subtle, particularly if the attorney is a veteran at such things. In one case I covered, a young man seeking money recovery claimed he was paralyzed from the waist down. Every morning he was pushed into the courtroom on a wheeled stretcher and then, with a great to-do involving attendants clad in white, he was carried from the stretcher to the chair at the trial table while defense attorneys stood in silent agony, unable to stop this great and constant appeal for sympathy from the jury.

They finally raised objection, however, that the empty stretcher, stark and white, stood prominently in the middle of the courtroom during trial sessions, distracting the attention of the jurors during testimony. The judge agreed it was unreasonable and the plaintiff's attorneys, appearing suddenly awakened to their misdeeds, apologized profusely in the presence of the jury and personally wheeled it out of the courtroom—and just happened to place it right outside the only door to the corridor. There, of course, the jury had to walk around this mute, crisp reminder of helplessness when it went out for recess in the middle of the morning, for lunch at noon, for recess in the middle of the afternoon, and at the close of day. No one said a word about it in the courtroom. It was never entered as evidence. Yet as jurors brushed against its white sheets it struck their emotional nerve centers as nothing else could—and the defense attorneys had nothing to which they could object.

Interestingly enough, such things appear to happen only when there is a jury present to view it. In preliminary hearings which involve the injured, but which are handled by the judge alone, evidence is presented with dispatch. No time is wasted by wheeling the victim about. If he is pushed in, it is by a relative in street clothes; there is no dramatic white uniform. There is usually an absence of shouting, with the plaintiff figuratively held aloft as a sparkling bit of evidence. His injuries are recounted calmly and the negligence of the defendant given. The case proceeds in dignity.

It is this need for demonstrations before juries that often makes many claimants and their more modest attorneys seek settlements. They simply do not possess the dramatic nature required for such a trial. Defense attorneys and their insurance-company clients are aware of this and often keep their offer far below what would be required in a trial. In this way they, too, are contributing to the pressure for dramatic trials by those able to make of them a sort of retribution.

Thus it can be seen that juries are, in effect, captive audiences for a real-life form of dramatics in which they are pushed and pulled from both sides. Conditioned as they are by soap operas and movies, they react to such things much more than would the scientific mind of the trained analyst.

For example, there was an instance I observed where a public utility company supplying electricity was being sued in a wrongful-death action. A man, the father of several children, had been in his car during a heavy snowstorm. A live wire broke under the weight of the soggy snow and fell on his roof. Despite warnings from bystanders, he stepped out of his car and was immediately eloctrocuted. The evidence brought out that he had been jailed several times for failing to support his wife and large family, that they had been on poor relief, and that a half-empty bottle of wine was in his car with him. The case of his widow seemed to be diminishing rapidly.

Her attorney was quick on his feet, however. He brought to

the witness stand each of the dead man's many children to "show how much they had relied on their departed father for friendship and guidance." The fourth child to be called had been the victim of a fire accident a few months before her father's death. The two incidents had nothing to do with each other. But as she ascended to the witness stand, her legs swathed in heavy bandages, raw red flesh pulled taut between her chin and her chest, sympathy could be seen written across every face in the jury box. The defendant, sensing impending disaster, was quick to offer settlement — partly on the basis of this surprise witness who, in reality, had nothing to do with the accident being considered in the trial.

How much of this will arouse the "passion and prejudice" of a jury to the point where it would be reversed by a reviewing court? Practically none. The typed transcript of the trial cannot show the scars of a little girl or the sympathy of the jury, the friendly and seductive smile to jurors by a lawyer, or an "accidental" coughing spell at a dramatic point in an opponent's evidence. Judges are well aware of these little things and know their purposes. Not so the innocent juries.

IMPORTANT EVIDENCE KEPT OUT

In addition to promoting the skill needed for bringing in such damaging and often unrelated subtle evidence to influence the jurors, the growth of the jury system has also brought about rules to keep out other important evidence. The effect of this is to block the road to a better finding of facts. The reason for these rules has been the growing realization that jurors are highly incapable of separating important information relating to the issue at hand from meaningless data. Jurors have been found unable to give proper perspective to what is told them, and so major data is kept from them deliberately. These restrictive rules grew in proportion to the power and independence of juries in an effort to keep their attention focused on the matters at hand.

This situation has often raised question of the hindrance brought by juries to a search for the facts. Its growth is described by Lewis Mayers in *The American Legal System* in this way :[1]

Historically, the development of many of our rules of evidence is closely bound up with the development of trial by jury. The English judges of the fifteenth and sixteenth centuries were attacking a novel problem—that of obtaining reasoned decisions from a group of laymen, often illiterate, brought together only for the particular case in hand, having no organization, tradition, or experience.

They early sensed the need for assisting this lay tribunal to keep clear the issue before it by thwarting attempts to introduce before it irrelevant testimony—that is, testimony as to occurrences which, while perhaps related to the subject of the action, could have no bearing on the legal right or liabilities of the parties. Equally clear was the need of checking the invariable tendency of witnesses to relate not merely the occurrences that they themselves had seen or heard, but what someone else had told them about the events in question. The receipt in evidence of alleged dying declarations was also surrounded with safeguards. Rules as to the admissibility of secondary writings and records also arose.

As the use of the jury and its independence and power grew, the body of restrictions on admissible testimony took shape as an extensive and increasingly technical body of doctrine. United with it was a similarly developed set of rules excluding or limiting the testimony of a particular class of persons, especially the parties, their spouses, etc. It is this body of doctrine, supplemented by a considerable body of statute law, that the judges must apply in determining whether the proposed testimony or the proffered document or exhibit is admissible.

[1] Pp. 103–104.

In theory, it is just as incumbent upon a judge sitting without a jury to exclude evidence or offers of proof which are repugnant to the rules of evidence as if a jury were present. In practice, however, there is often a disposition on the part of both counsel and the court not to insist too strictly upon the application of technical rules of evidence. As one learned in the law, the judge, it is supposed, will not, as might a jury, accord to incompetent or irrelevant evidence a weight to which, in the eye of the law, it ought not to have.

Operation of these rules which keep out certain evidence might be made clearer by a few simple examples. It is quite common in a trial before a jury to have a witness begin to say, for example: "When I saw the accident, my sister-in-law turned to me and said she thought the driver had been drinking from the way he . . . ." Suddenly a heavy objection is heard from a lawyer and sustained by the judge. The reason for this is the hearsay rule. A witness cannot tell what someone else saw or said, with certain minor exceptions, even though it might be highly important to the case at hand.

When exactly the same incident takes place in a trial before a judge alone, the same objection is raised at the same point. But the judge here will probably say: "The evidence will be received for whatever value it may have. The witness may proceed." In other words, it is felt the judge is more capable of separating the legally important from that which is not admissible, and assigning it proper value; so the trial by judge opens the door for presentation of a great deal more evidence.

Another example is the "leading your own witness" rule. This simply means a lawyer is barred from asking his witness a question in words that indicate what the answer should be. For example: "You did not stop for a drink at a bar before the accident, did you?" as compared with: "What, if anything, did you do before the accident?" Before a jury, such methods are highly objectionable. But before a judge, who clearly sees exactly what is being done, such questions often are allowed with the idea of speeding matters along.

Experts have long held that our complicated and cumbersome rules of evidence could be simplified greatly if we could do away with the jury system. In just these two simple illustrations here it can be seen technical blockades are in use because of the mistrust of the jury's competence to weigh such evidence properly.

"DISREGARD THIS": LEGAL FICTION

One of the neatest little tricks in a jury trial revolves around a judge's order to "strike this evidence from the record and the jury will disregard it." Although all too obviously a legalistic fiction, it is nevertheless indulged in regularly by the courts. Of course, the jury cannot pretend that it has not heard something which it has. Neither can anyone present in the courtroom imagine the jurors have put it aside in their mind. Yet on the trial record it is a continuing pretense and once the judge has uttered those magical words the record is believed to be cleansed. The reviewing courts will not touch it no matter what the protests of the opposing lawyer who lost his case.

Lawyers many times have been known deliberately to ask a question that they are fully aware is not allowable under rules of evidence. They know their opponent will leap to his feet with objections and the judge will order it stricken. They also know, however, that it will be pressed into the jury mind as indelibly as if it had been branded and will be brought up at their secret deliberations as strongly as proper evidence. It will have as much influence — or more — as will proper evidence, correctly admitted.

Tests have been made with jurors on this point and the result has been interesting. In one mock trial, the judge ordered this testimony stricken from the record and disregarded by the jury: "Sammie had alcohol on his breath when he asked me to 'step out in the back alley' with him. Of course he had the intention of fighting with me." Later the jurors were asked what influence this testimony had on their decision. Some thought it was important, and others did not. But only one, who had served on juries before, remembered that the jurors were supposed to disregard it.

In another such test case, this time involving rape, the attorney for the defendant, in his cross-examination of the girl, asked if she had informed the defendant that she was a virgin. When she answered that she had not, the lawyer remarked with obvious sarcasm that it was unfortunate she had failed to use the most effective weapon at her disposal. Quite naturally, opposing lawyers objected to this little byplay that had no relation to the trial and the judge ordered it stricken from the record. He carefully informed the jury not to consider it. Yet all the jurors later questioned wholly ignored the instruction of the judge, and in fact all gave it considerable attention. One juror stated the jury should not consider this statement in favor of the defendant because "a man intent on rape hardly would stop because the girl told him she was a virgin. In fact, it would probably heighten his desire." Another felt the jury should consider it, for "she should have explained that she was a virgin and wanted to keep her maidenhood." Another said: "I don't think under the circumstances he would have listened." Still another said: "No, because if she was objecting, she wouldn't have had much time to think of anything. I know, for myself, if I were in her position, I'd fight."

It was clear that this attorney, with an off-hand comment that was not really part of the case, had rammed home the point with the jury despite the judge's caution that it was not even to be considered. Here is an obvious weakness of the jury system which can be, and quite often is, deliberately taken advantage of by lawyers.

THE LAWYER'S RIGHT TO DRAMATICS

Many times during a particularly dramatic trial the lawyer is himself apparently carried away by his own imagined talents as an actor. Or it may be that he feels his case is weak in the dramatic attributes necessary to influence a jury and that he must make up for it with his own performance. In any event, it is not rare to have a lawyer's voice break with choked sobs in his final summation to the jury and it is quite normal to see him pound the jury rail as he drives home a point.

The more subtle attorneys may prefer to underplay their part. They make their performance by the whispered voice, the lengthy pause after a telling point. Sometimes they use evidence as props and shake leg braces or an artificial limb over the jury box as they give their arguments.

In one case I observed, a young attorney shook a blond woman's wig at a box filled with male jurors to prove the humiliation his client had been forced to endure. His case was that the woman's hair had been singed close to the scalp by chemicals in a hair-curling package. Unfortunately for him, her hair had all grown out again to its former luxuriance by the time of the trial and so he had nothing to show but the wig she had once worn to cover up her embarrassment. He used it to the fullest—and evidently quite capably, judging from the hefty verdict he won. It surprised even the trial judge who just shrugged his shoulders and said : "Who can predict how men jurors will react to a woman's hair?"

This drive for dramatics is not simple happenstance. In 1946, the association of plaintiff's lawyers was formed : the National Association of Claimant's Compensation Attorneys (the NACCA), and as part of its functions, it advised and taught the use of demonstrative evidence. Surgical instruments were produced, colored photographs were encouraged to show wounds and blood in their most realistic manner. Plaintiff lawyers were cautioned not to rely on the doctor who actually treated the claimant but were advised, rather, to employ special doctors. The natural sympathy which all jurymen have is being deliberately inflamed. In this way, evidence ceases to truly assist, as one critic has said, and begins to create impulsive verdicts in a contest among plaintiff lawyers to somehow get a larger verdict than has been returned before.

Thus far, apart from a few rules such as those preventing the admission of extremely prejudicial evidence, the courts have done little to restrain lawyers from stirring the prejudices and awakening the passions of jurors. For example, in Tennessee, a lawyer's right to weep before the jury has been placed above the Constitution as "one of . . . [those] natural rights . . . which no court or constitution [can] take away." (*Ferguson v. Moore,* 98 Tenn. 342.)

It is evident from the stories told in courthouse corridors that the attorney who can successfully arouse jury passions, becloud the issues, and appeal to prejudice is hailed as an ingenious hero rather than looked down upon by fellow lawyers.

An old trick which I have seen used on jurors goes like this: The doctor, a kindly looking man who is a veteran at this play, testifies from the stand about the victim's injuries. He is cross-examined in normal manner by the defense attorney. Finally he is excused and walks to the courtroom door with great dignity. But, just as he puts his hand on the door, the plaintiff's lawyer calls out: "Just one more question, Doctor. Do you think this man will ever recover?" The doctor looks down, sadly shakes his head, and says: "No, he will never walk again." Then he steps out the door.

The impact on the jury is evident. But on the defense attor-

ney it is even more so. He has no chance to cross-examine the
doctor on the last statement to see on what it is based. The
doctor's words hang clear in the courtroom while the lawyer
sputters objections at their unorthodox use. Whether or not the
judge sustains the objections becomes meaningless. The words
have hit their target, the jury, and little else matters at this
point.

Thus it is that juries have developed in some lawyers a
whole new skill: the dramatic and emotional method of
presentation of evidence that is never dreamed of before a
judge alone. It is often both unfair and time-consuming in the
conduct of a trial. But attempts to cut through it ordinarily
run into vigorous objection from those who benefit from it
the most.

One example of this is the attempt to make more widespread
the use of the independent medical panel. This plan, which
has been used with some success in eastern states, calls for the
setting up of a voluntary group of doctors, experts in various
fields. When a contested injury case comes to court, it would
be turned over to a three-man panel of doctors who specialize
in that field. They would not represent either of the litigants,
but would be the eyes of the court. Their information would
be presented at early settlement negotiations and, failing that,
could be summoned to the witness stand by either party if
they so desired.

Defense attorneys in Ohio have hailed the idea. Not so the
plaintiff lawyers. They protest that it takes from them their
freedom and right to hire any doctor they wish in their case.
"Keep this up and you won't even need two lawyers; one
lawyer could present both sides of the question and have done
with it," one plaintiff attorney said sarcastically. It is obvious
they do not want to give up any part of their dramatic
presentation of evidence in order to impress jurors, such as that
doctor with his hand on the door.

It goes without question that the presence of jurors makes for a more exciting trial as a form of human drama. Their form of democracy-in-action turns itself into a participation show where the audience sits, in effect, as a sort of super critic on the actors performing before them. Far too many times that is all the jury is. The party putting on the better show is the one with the best chance of emerging victorious.

7

The Grand Jury:
An Outmoded Ritual

LET US TURN NOW TO THE CRIMINAL ASPECT OF THE LAW, AND
examine another problem in American courts: the grand jury,
a curious animal with a most impressive name. It has been
described many times as "neither doing an effective enough
job to arouse much praise nor is it visibly doing a poor enough
job to receive violent criticism." While that is largely true, it
is still lively enough to create major front-page headlines while,
at the same time, leaving the observer feeling more than just
a little confused.

JUST WHAT IS A GRAND JURY?

Where it still exists, it is usually a group of citizens named to
serve for a full term of court. Their function is two-fold: to
return indictments against individuals accused of crime, and to

120

give formal reports of evil doings in the community whether they be political, social, or economic.

A large part of its function appears to be that of garnering publicity for the courts. It starts when a presiding judge in criminal court appoints the new foreman for an incoming grand jury at the beginning of the term. That person is usually someone well known in the community and the appointment is a fine occasion for a page-one picture in the newspaper of the foreman and the judge. (The latter probably will soon be running for re-election, and is, of course, most appreciative of any favorable publicity he may get.)

The publicity continues in varying degrees for the following four months of the court term as various indictments are made public. It reaches a climax at the end of the term with the jury's report which, again, is front-page news. Then the jury is dismissed and the entire cycle is repeated with a different cast doing the same thing.

Other than this ready-made vehicle for publicity, it is sometimes difficult to see the purpose of this long outmoded ritual; all its tasks could be performed much more efficiently if this cumbersome procedure were not in the way.

THE JOB OF ACCUSATION

Take first its more routine task of returning indictments. This is nothing more than returning an accusation against an individual of having broken a criminal law. It is done, generally, on a three-quarters vote and means nothing more than that the accused must stand trial before a regular court.

With rare exceptions, the grand jury hears only the evidence of the state and is not even made aware of the defendant's side of the picture. It is deliberately one-sided so that the jurors can determine if there is enough evidence for the trial. The evidence is usually presented by the prosecutor or one of his assistants who could, of course, examine the same evidence himself and determine whether he had enough to prove his case. Once having been convinced that he had enough material, the prosecutor could easily present an indictment and proceed with the case without having to go through the citizen jurors and having them act in his behalf. It is very seldom that a grand jury refuses to return an indictment if the prosecutor is convinced he has a proper case, and even rarer when it will push a case which he feels has no merit. Thus, it usually is a rubber stamp for the prosecutor and is an extra, costly procedure with which he could dispense quite conveniently.

The grand jury indictment as it is known today began in 1166 when Henry II of England gave instructions that in the future no man was to be brought to trial unless first found guilty by "twelve knights, good and true." The knights have long since disappeared from the scene, but the grand juries still persist in many areas of the United States. It is interesting to note that they have long since gone out of existence in England, their birthplace.

Question may be raised even of the grand jury's effectiveness in relation to justice in its simplest job, that of returning official accusations. A good example of this that received wide notoriety was a 1959 case which took place in Mississippi. According to a report published in *The New York Times,* the United States attorney general (at that time, William P. Rogers) branded the handling of the Mississippi lynching case as a "travesty on justice." It was reported he was so disturbed that he told a news conference he was considering a new criminal statute to let the federal government move in more strongly when states refused to act in racial crimes.

The case in question concerned Mack Charles Parker, a twenty-three-year-old Negro charged with having raped a white woman. On April 24, 1959, he was dragged from a jail in Poplarville, Miss., and nine days later his body was found in the Pearl River by agents of the Federal Bureau of Investigation. Parker had been shot twice. Mr. Rogers told his news conference that the F.B.I. had spent $80,000 investigating the lynching and had performed "one of the most complete investigations I've ever seen conducted." The Justice Department then turned over to Mississippi officials its report. Mr. Rogers claimed murder was a crime "more appropriate for a state to handle under our Federal system." A band of men had been arrested, accused of being the masked group that had stolen Parker from his jail cell.

Early in November of 1959, a Mississippi grand jury considered the case. According to news reports, Mr. Rogers said the Justice Department had written to the grand jury and local officials with the offer to produce F.B.I. agents to testify and to bring evidence, including fingerprints. Yet not one F.B.I. witness was called and the grand jury adjourned without ruling on the Parker case. In pointing to the failure of the grand jury to call any witnesses, Mr. Rogers said : "It was as flagrant and calculated a miscarriage of justice as I know of. This man was taken from the county jail and brutally lynched. When the evidence is eventually adduced, I think the nation will be shocked."

This was obviously an incident wherein a grand jury reflected the attitude of the community from which it was drawn to the point of shocking even a veteran of law enforcement. This was not justice, but a layman's concept of what he would make justice to be. It was surely not equal for all persons but was twisted to fit a specific incident. It shows how far such a group can go with impunity from its original ideal of protecting the innocent against unjust accusations.

STAR CHAMBER PROCEEDINGS

While such happenings as shown above are possible, they

are not the general rule. Indeed, the opposite is more the usual. For in what is in reality a secretive, locked-door, star-chamber proceeding, it is the innocent who have no chance to protect themselves from their accusers no matter how false the evidence may be. In the grand jury accusatory proceedings, which I have covered as a newspaper reporter, no outsider is permitted near the chamber. No one can ever know if the jury's action is the result of cool deliberation on facts or is based upon prejudice or enflamed passions of an aroused community bent upon revenge at any cost. The persons most *non grata* at such secret hearings are the defendant and his lawyers. They are not even given the slightest opportunity to present their story or an explanation of the happenings. The indictment is returned solely upon information given by the prosecuting attorney.

It turns out, therefore, that the grand jury ordinarily is nothing more than an arm of the prosecutor which serves to take the pressure of public distaste off him should the action prove unpopular. It is the action of a group of untrained citizens responsible to no one at election time.

As far back as 1850 discussion was under way in America to abolish the grand jury system. According to the *United States Monthly Law Magazine* in February of that year, claims that complete reliance upon public prosecutors would be "a dangerous innovation" were countered with arguments that no district attorney could possibly be more arbitrary or dangerous than a secret *ex parte* (one-sided) body which held its sessions like the inquisition of the star chamber. It was pointed out that the average juror had complete ignorance of the law and it was noted that there was a great expense in maintaining such a useless institution. Some at that time hailed the grand jury as an essential bulwark of liberty, while others denounced it as a "remnant of the barbaric past," according to an article in the *1955 Journal of Criminal Law, Criminology & Police Science* by Richard D. Younger.

That the criticism of grand juries did not fade away with time can be seen in an editorial in the *Winston-Salem* (North Carolina) *Sentinal* of March 14, 1959, which said: "It is the unanimous feeling of the members of this grand jury that there has occurred an unnecessary waste of time and a consequent waste of the taxpayers' money in the performance of a function of questionable value or usefulness."

This is what has descended from the old argument (before our public prosecutors of today) that the main reason for retaining the grand jury was to protect defendants from unjustifiable prosecutions at the hands of overzealous prosecutors.

THE GRAND JURY'S REPORT

The other major function of the grand jury is described as "investigatory, or inquisitorial." In his article, "Grand Jury: Sleeping Watchdog or Expensive Antique?", Lewis Poindexter Watts outlines this area succinctly:[1]

In the beginning the jurors inquired among themselves for knowledge of crimes committed within the county. Later they sat as an inquest and heard witnesses in this regard. Also the grand jury served as a kind of supervisor of the local government machinery apparently with the power to make the necessary investigations.

With the professionalization of law enforcement and the rise of the modern police force, there has been a steady decrease in the need for the grand jury as an investigator of private crimes, and the investigatory function of the grand jury is today thought of mainly as a check on the efficiency and the honesty of public officials. As investigators, they can go from such routine activities

---

[1] *North Carolina Law Review,* Vol. 37, p. 290.

as inspecting the courthouse to the presenting of public officials for malfeasance in office. Exact limits on powers are not clear since they vary among states.

It is in this area, too, that the grand jury can become the most foolish or the most vicious. The viciousness comes when the jurors, in their reports, make accusations against persons who have had no chance to defend themselves or to show reasons, of whatever value they may be, for the activities of which they are being accused. It has often been pointed out that which public official is accused of wrongdoing as a result of these secret investigations depends upon the political party to which he may happen to belong. Reason for the accusation sometimes becomes clear if he belongs to the one opposite that to which the grand jury foreman happens to belong. Thus, it is a good opportunity to throw a little political mud at the opposing party without having to give the other a chance to answer.

The grand jury, however, begins to look foolish when, after a lengthy "investigation" it comes out with the profound report that, for example, illegal gambling is wrong. Obviously, it is hard to quarrel with that. This is especially true when local newspapers have been drumming at that situation—in all probability for months—and have even gone to the point of reporting exactly where these gambling activities have been going on, and who is running them.

An example of the vigor and originality of a usual grand jury report can be seen in one made in Cleveland where improved street lighting as a deterrent to crime was recommended. The jurors found "70 per cent to 80 per cent of crimes occur in the dark hours and that this has been cut in half where streets are well lighted." The newspaper account of this report added : "The report's recommendation followed articles in the Cleveland *News* pointing out the dark spots on

Cleveland's streets and their relation to street crimes and hoodlumism."

In other words, this grand jury came up with facts that were already well known not only to the police and the courts, but to the newspapers and the reading public as well. If anything were going to be done about it, it would already have been under way long before the group of jurors reached their conclusion. The report, in effect, was worthless and repetitive.

It is obvious that professional police are well aware of these problems to a much greater extent than a four-month-old jury. The police deal with these matters daily and have done so for a great many years. In areas where they may become lax in their enforcement, alert newspaper reporters are only too eager to jog them awake with blazing stories that may win a Pulitzer Prize. Newspaper pressure can be a much more telling prod to elected prosecutors and legislators sensitive to public reaction than a single-shot jury report.

An interesting point about a jury report is that its foolishness, in whatever degree it may be, usually does not last long. It makes a newspaper story for a day and then is usually filed away to be soon forgotten. A casual glance through the files of any newspaper will disclose such reports which have long faded from memory. It is rare when they have been found to bestir official action even when they are fresh. Indeed, the more modern approach appears to be not even to release them to public appraisal. As far back as 1953 in "Application of United Electrical Workers" (III Federal Supplement, p. 858) a federal judge ordered a report expunged from the records of the court and stated that "the great weight of authority is that such reports exceed the power of the grand jury and may be expunged." This conclusion appears to have found support from other quarters of the law.

More recent was the case of a Schenectady County grand jury, which investigated claims against the county highway department. It developed that the jurors failed to find any evidence upon which to base a criminal indictment. It therefore turned to its traditional function, and filed a report of its findings which criticized the department's practices as contrary to the public interest.

One can imagine the jury's surprise, however, when the presiding judge who had impaneled the members refused to disclose the contents of their report. He accepted the report for filing and, except for a minor portion, he ordered the contents sealed. The grand jury, of course, could not release the report to the public because, as a result of its oath, its proceedings are completely secret.

The foreman of this grand jury tried to force publication of his report, but his petition was dismissed by the court of appeals. The reviewing court said no such power was conferred upon the grand jury by its constitutional provision or statute. It concluded that there was no authority for the grand jury to make a report censuring public officials for noncriminal misconduct. The foreman should not have been disheartened, however, since he should have known that professional government watchers—such as newspapers—would probably do a much more effective job of it anyhow.

The courts, in refusing to free the reports, were evidently cognizant of the fact that the weight of authority (by far the majority) holds that juries may not issue reports that criticize persons for inefficiency, neglect, or criminal or quasi-criminal conduct. The legality of the typical grand jury report has been in dispute since about 1900. The grand jury is a creature of statute, which means that each state sets up its own grand jury and gives it special powers. No matter what powers have been given, however, it has been common practice for grand juries to inquire into what they considered the willful and corrupt misconduct of public officials as well as into the more ordinary problems of the local jailhouse or court building.

As Richard H. Kuh, an assistant district attorney for New York County wrote in his article "The Grand Jury 'Presentment' : Foul Blow or Fair Play?" :[2]

Continued appearance of these reports might be attributable to the common belief among lay jurors, uninstructed in the law, that they are a power unto themselves and can peer into any matter that their civic conscience indicates needs investigation. Possibly, reports continue because of a disregard of legal precedents by prosecutors who guide the grand juries and by the judges who accept these reports and permit them to become matters of court record.

Kuh also noted that "allegedly, the jury's proper function is to serve as a buffer between the individual and the power of the state, to protect the citizenry from despotic prosecution. A jury report does not protect a person from an improper charge; further, opponents of reports urge, it of itself constitutes an improper charge in that the persons criticized are deprived of a judicial forum in which the truth or falsity of the attack may be determined."

Grand juries have not all been bad as the foregoing would seem to indicate. On rare occasions they have performed valuable services. For example, a probe of the city police department was begun in October, 1933, in Cleveland, Ohio, under the leadership of an energetic and fearless foreman, William Feather. Reports in the Cleveland *Plain Dealer* of that time showed that the panel spent three months in investigation and issued a report which shocked the citizens. According to the *Plain Dealer,* the grand jury denounced law enforcement officials and declared that the local criminal court "neither merits nor receives the respect or confidence of the people."

At about the same time in New York a fighting group of

[2] *Columbia Law Review,* Vol. 55, p.1103.

grand jurors shook off the hampering tactics of city officials. It rallied public opinion to launch a complete investigation of the rackets in the city. It was in March, 1935, that the grand jury continued the study of policy rackets which had been started by an earlier body. As its probe uncovered new areas, it broke with the district attorney. After racketeers had threatened jurors, an appeal was made to Governor Herbert Lehman to call an extraordinary grand jury with a special prosecutor. Thomas E. Dewey was the special racket prosecutor who was named and, in December, 1935, the jurors returned 29 indictments. Further investigations by this special unit in 1936 turned toward criminal infiltration into labor unions and trade and protective associations. It was noted, however, by Watts (*North Carolina Law Review,* Vol. 37, page 290) that "there is reason to believe, though, that the experience in New York County is somewhat different from that in the rest of the country. The successful New York grand juries are taken from 'blue ribbon' panels which are carefully screened. It seems unlikely that the New York jurors selected in another manner would have been so consistently effective."

Despite these rare splashes of light, the general picture of the grand jury has been far from bright. In 1920, at the Illinois Constitutional Convention, the American Judicature Society advised delegates that grand juries were of little value except to delay the courts. Its warning that time was of the utmost importance in criminal justice drew whole-hearted agreement from the State's Attorney's Association of Illinois which also called for abolition of grand juries. All this was to no effect, as delegates refused to act.

HISTORY OF THE GRAND JURY

As was noted here earlier, the grand jury, with its system of indictments, can be traced back to England in 1166 and the instructions of Henry II that twelve knights must first find a person guilty before he could be brought to trial. Since then the system has had a speckled career and over the years has garnered a great deal of opposition. In the previously-mentioned article, "Grand Jury Under Attack," Mr. Younger reported that by the mid-nineteenth century a strong movement developed in its English birthplace to wipe out the grand jury entirely. Curiously enough, it was described as a potential menace to the country because it assisted rather than suppressed crime. The committing magistrate of famed Old Bailey prison declared that the grand jury was the "first hope" of the criminal because it offered "a safe medium for buying off a prosecution and is often resorted to for that purpose."

It was reported that another lawyer of that time claimed that the intelligent and respected jurors were ashamed and disgusted with their functions. The cry against grand juries was echoed in America in February, 1850, when the *United States Monthly Law Magazine* described the movement in England and commented that it hoped American judges would follow the example of British judges.

Also, in 1850, state constitutional conventions in three states seriously considered erasing the grand jury. They were Michigan, Indiana, and Ohio. In Tennessee, where judicial decisions had successfully restricted inquisitorial powers, the Supreme Court in 1851 reaffirmed its policy. New York followed the broad rules adhered to in Missouri and allowed the juries freer rein in their inquiries. In the Federal courts, however, the grand juries tended to become more and more an arm of the court. In 1856, as part of an economy measure, Congress empowered Federal judges to discharge jurors when in their opinion such action would best serve the public interest.

For ten years after America's Civil War, movements to end the grand jury system grew and flourished. While it was agreed that its inquests might have been needed as safeguards against the power of royalty at one time, it was argued that there no longer was such a need. It was protested as being too inefficient for modern justice and too slow for society's increasing pace.

Debate over the need for the grand jury mounted. Opponents pointed to the smoothness of the Michigan system where the grand inquest was no longer in use. But the supporters of the system also had heated comments. In Wisconsin, the Milwaukee *News* of that time asserted that the end of the grand jury would surely be "another step toward the concentration of power." On November 7, 1870, by a referendum, Wisconsin voters went for reform, however, and the grand jury was changed to a sometime institution that came into existence only when specifically called for by a judge. Even before the change in Wisconsin, the grand jury inquest disappeared in Nebraska. This was the result of the Nebraska constitution of 1857 which gave the legislature the right to abolish, limit, change, or amend the system. By 1867 the legislators had done that. Thus the path was well marked when, in 1876, the matter was put up to the legislature of Colorado. It was erased there, too, soon after. A compromise change was evolved in California when its 1879 constitution permitted criminal prosecution simply on the information of a prosecutor, while, at the same time, set up that a grand jury should be called in each county at least once a year. The temper of the times could be seen in this quotation by Eugene Stevenson, a New Jersey police prosecutor in 1886 :

The grand jury is an arbitrary, irresponsible, and dangerous part of government which long ago should have come within the range of official responsibility. I much prefer the efficiency and decisiveness of a public prosecutor. It is difficult to see why a town meeting of laymen, utterly ignorant both of law and the rules of evidence should be an appropriate tribunal. The summoning of a new body of jurors at each term insures an unfailing supply of ignorance.

Three years later, with the admission of six omnibus states into the union, grand jury opposition stepped up its victories. The grand inquest was now ignored, except for special occasions, in Idaho, Montana, and Washington. The question was put into the hand of legislatures, which quickly tossed out the grand juries in North Dakota, South Dakota, and Wyoming. By 1931 24 states had more or less dispensed with the requirement of an indictment returned by a grand jury. As of now, 30 states have abolished this cumbersome method of indictments by turning their functions over to prosecutors.

It is interesting to note the parallel activities to dispose of the grand juries in England. They were believed to have been launched there during the time of King Edward III in the fourteenth century as the "grande inquest" of 23 men appointed by the sheriffs. Over a span of about two centuries, this single jury began to displace the earlier juries of 12 men, which had, in turn, replaced the 100-man juries.

As time passed, the "grande inquest" absorbed (as new governmental offices have a habit of doing) most of the duties of the former juries. The major exception, however, was the police function of the 100-man juries. These new grand juries copied from the precedents of their predecessors. They made inquiries into criminal cases and also supervised the whole administration of local government. Therefore, when the American revolutionaries undertook to guarantee constitutionally the existence of the grand jury, their thought of it was mainly as an institution to protect the citizen from unjust political prosecutions.

In England, the grand jury was suspended during the First World War for at least two reasons: the loss of manpower to the war effort, and the possibility of hysteria. The body was virtually abolished there in 1933 largely as a depression measure. It died completely by act of parliament effective

August 31, 1934, after it was noted that nobody missed them during their wartime suspension.

Individual states in America have been free to abolish the grand jury if they wished since a majority of the members of the United States Supreme Court has held that the Fifth Amendment to the Constitution applies only to the Federal government. In fact, some states have strongly urged the feasibility of a modified grand jury. This is the situation in Michigan where the "information," a legal document, early replaced the indictment and provisions for the calling of grand juries became dusty mementoes of a bygone age. Since a need was still felt, however, for a substitute investigatory body to check for corruption and inefficiency in local government, the legislature finally passed a one-man grand juror law in 1917, which the state's bar had sponsored.

As originally construed, this law gave any judge the right to hold secret hearings, issue indictments, grant immunity from prosecution to witnesses with important testimony, and yet retain his judicial immunity from suit and his power to punish summarily for contempt. The greatest problem, however, lay in the fact that nothing apparently was to prevent the judge from also trying the defendant he had indicted. This obviously put him at cross purposes and it took a case in the Supreme Court to begin the changes. This case questioned the constitutionality of putting such all-embracing power into one man. The legislature then changed to a three-man judge-and-juror system in 1949, but in 1951 the Michigan legislature brought back the one-man system and set up measures which divested the conflicting powers. When they assume the role of inquisitors now, the judges must give up their later judicial role in the same case.

COURAGEOUS MEN OPPOSE

Weaknesses of the grand jury system are not now of major importance simply because these faults have long been recognized. The institution has already been changed in almost every country of the world as well as in more than half of the states. This is because men have had the courage to stand up in opposition against what was once regarded as another sacred cow in the administration of justice. For example, in June, 1915, William Howard Taft appeared before the judiciary committee of the New York Constitutional Convention and used his appearance as an opportunity to voice his opposition to the system. Furthermore, the pressure of the opposition was continuous, coming from all sides. Thus, in October, 1921, a Massachusetts judge, Robert Wolcott, told members of the state bar association that abolishing the grand jury was one means of ending congestion in criminal courts. Thus it is evident that the role of the grand jury has decidedly declined in importance in the last hundred years, especially in the Western states.

By the year 1930 the American Law Institute was proposing, as part of a model code, that all offenses heretofore required to be prosecuted by indictment only, might now be prosecuted either by indictment or by information, thus paving the way for extinction of the jury's indictment procedure. In suggesting when the grand jury might be summoned, the Law Institute proposed that no jury be called to attend in any court except upon order of the judge thereof when, in his opinion, public interest would so demand, except that a grand jury shall be summoned at least once a year in each county.

Even though there are many states which still ostensibly retain the grand jury system in all its glory, some question may be raised about its popularity and effectiveness even there. I have seen many instances in which an incoming presiding judge in criminal court in Ohio, who has the duty to appoint a grand jury foreman, has been hard put to find one willing to serve who has even the minimum capabilities for handling the job. It is common to see the judge telephone friend after friend with the offer to head the grand jury—with all the fame and prestige that it carries—only to be rejected for a variety of reasons. Some offer the press of business. Others bluntly say they have no background or interest in such an appointment. One judge in desperation turned to former business executives who are retired and who presumably would welcome an opportunity to do something meaningful. The excuses for turning down the job by these men varied all the way from saying it would briefly delay a forthcoming trip to Europe to refusing to give up the pleasures of loafing even for a few months.

The grand jury is the first step in criminal law. Once it has heard the facts and returned an indictment, the case proceeds to the second step—the criminal trial jury. The accused then faces determination of his innocence or guilt, and new problems with jurors.

8

Crime and the Jury

In 1965 a 90-minute movie was made at the University of Texas' Radio-Television Department. It was a low-budget film about a real-life murder, using real-life courtroom performers (excepting defendants) rather than actors. Where it was presented before live audiences, the judgment sometimes was left to them. *Based on the same evidence, the mock jurists' verdicts have ranged from acquittal to the death penalty.* These are the same people who would be chosen for actual murder trials where a man's life hangs in the balance.

Of the many different areas in which trial juries are used, criminal cases would seem to be one in which they could function most efficiently. Here they deal with basic human problems and emotions not too often complicated with technical difficulties found in complex contractual situations or questioned personal injuries. Here their task is most often a simple decision of facts: did the facts alone prove that the accused performed the specific act of which he is charged?

Did he rob? Did he rape? Did he kill? It is as simple as all that.

In criminal matters the public has a very direct interest. A crime, after all, is an act committed against the people. It is the breaking of a law made by the people themselves to protect their peaceful society.

In criminal courts which I have covered as a newspaper reporter, a maxim often repeated by the lawyers and prisoners went to this effect: "If you are innocent, waive a jury and ask for a judge alone; but if you are guilty and want to beat the rap, always ask for a jury because you have more chance to raise a doubt in the mind of one out of twelve jurors." In a jury there is a wide range of bias, prejudice and personal problems which can deftly be turned to the accused's personal advantage.

This writer is not alone in this view of the criminal court jury. For example, Jim Bishop, well-known author and nationally syndicated newspaper columnist wrote in April, 1961, in his column:

The lawyers and judges of the land point to our jury system with pride while, in secret, they despise it. Offstage, the jokes about the "twelve good men and true" are vicious. In civil cases the juries vote exorbitant sums for minor injuries. In criminal cases, they extend mercy in cases where premeditated murder has been proved.

Mr. Bishop noted, in passing, that he could not sit on a jury in a case involving capital punishment because he is personally opposed to executions. "However," he wrote:

As long as execution is on the books, it should be voted by juries whenever a first-degree murder indictment is proved beyond a doubt, coupled with time for premeditation on the part of the defendant. The juries in the Finch case and the Peel case voted mercy.

My opinion has no standing in law. In each of the three Finch trials, it seems to me, the prosecution proved that the lovers—Dr. R. Bernard Finch and Carole Tregoff—came to the home of Mrs. Finch to kill her. The doctor had to chase his wife down a garden path to do it.

The first jury forgot its duty entirely and became embroiled in a fight about bigotry and race hate. The second one was too confused to do anything. The third convicted the doctor on a first-degree charge, the woman on second-degree, and gave them both the same sentence—life.

In the Peel case in Florida, the members of the jury said afterward that they had no doubt about guilt. It was a matter of punishment that concerned them. Almost magically, six men wanted to send Judge Peel to the electric chair. Six wanted to give him life imprisonment.

The six who wanted to extend mercy put it on the line : If you want to fight, we'll sit here and fight right through the weekend. The six who favored the chair realized that tomorrow was Good Friday and Sunday was Easter Sunday. They capitulated.

Two murderers sat on the stand and told how they drowned Judge and Mrs. Chillingworth for "Joe Peel." The murderers had no motive other than that. They did not know the Chillingworths and Peel had to point out the victims to them. State Attorney Phil O'Connell's rebuttal witnesses, Florida Sheriff's Bureau agents, listened behind a door as Peel bargained for his life with O'Connell five years after the murders.

No, the consideration in this case was exactly what the jurors said it was : They wanted to go home. They didn't want to spend Easter weekend in a room. It came down to creature comfort.

Under the current system, men get away with murder. The judge is reduced in stature to a legalistic umpire. The defense seems to fight harder for a mistrial, or reversible error, than for acquittal.

A disparaging point of view toward criminal juries this is indeed, but it appears to be the rule among persons who have had long experience with them as observers who are not emotionally involved with the outcome. To a large degree, this would exclude lawyers. The affection of a lawyer who has just won a victory can be almost embarrassing when he speaks of the kinds and capability of his jury. But ask newspaper reporters and court stenographers, and the response is likely to be very much the opposite.

THE TRIALS OF SAM SHEPPARD

What can be described as a classic in jury conflict was the case of Cleveland's Dr. Samuel H. Sheppard. On the night of July 3, 1954, he was rapidly rising young osteopathic neuro-surgeon in his family's hospital in suburban Bay Village. The next day, at the age of thirty, he stood accused as the murderer of his pretty wife, Marilyn Reese Sheppard, four months pregnant. She had been beaten to death in an upstairs bedroom of their comfortable lakeside home while, he said, he dozed downstairs and their seven-year-old son, Sam Jr., slept in the next room. This was the beginning of one of the most bizarre court-room tales on record in the world, certainly the strangest I covered as a reporter.

Before it came to an end 12 years later, reputations had been ruined, the names of dead men smeared, and the first jury told, in effect, that it had made a terrible blunder in convicting the young doctor. At the same time, there are many who to this day are convinced it was the *second* jury which erred when it brought in an acquittal at 10 : 23 the night of November 16, 1966, after eight hours and ten minutes of deliberations.

The fateful night of the murder started quietly enough with a dinner at the home of the Sheppards. Dinner guests were Don and Nancy Ahern, who lived nearby. The children ate first in the kitchen; the adults had their meal on a porch over-looking Lake Erie. Then Marilyn Sheppard put Sam Jr., better known as Chip, to bed. Ahern took his two children home and returned after they had been put to bed.

The evening passed pleasantly. The men listened to a base-ball broadcast of the Cleveland Indians playing the Chicago White Sox while the women watched a television movie entitled *Strange Holiday*. As the evening wore on, Sam Shep-pard became drowsy and fell asleep on the couch, as he was to testify later.

The Aherns decided to go home about 12:30 A.M. Mrs. Ahern said she walked with Marilyn to the door opening on Lake Erie and turned the key in it for her hostess. Then the Aherns left by the door facing the road. Sam said later he did not hear them leave, but remembered vaguely that his wife stirred him and told him she was going to bed.

This was the preamble. The main story started sometime during the night. Dr. Sam Sheppard was to testify later that he was awakened when he heard his wife "cry out or scream." He never made a guess as to how much time elapsed between the time his wife went to bed and when he said he heard the scream. He said he ran upstairs thinking she might be having a reaction similar to convulsions that she had at the beginning of her pregnancy.

He said he charged into the bedroom and "saw a form with a light garment." He testified he could hear loud moans or groaning sounds and while grappling with "this individual from in front," he was hit from behind somehow and knocked out. He could never say for sure if it was one or two people in the room.

Sheppard said when he came to his senses he looked at his wife, covered with blood, took her pulse, and felt that she was gone. Then he thought he heard a noise downstairs, ran down and "saw a form progressing rapidly somewhere between the front door and screen porch toward the lake." He said he pursued it, down the steps to the beach, where he lunged and grasped either body or leg. He again became unconscious, he said, and came to with his head toward the bank at the lake's edge.

He said he staggered back up to the house, checked his wife's pulse in her neck, and then went downstairs into his study, searching for what to do. A number came to him, he said, and he called it. It turned out to be that of J. Spencer Houk, a prosperous butcher, who was then mayor of Bay Village and who lived a few doors west of the Sheppards. Sam and Houk were friends and, in fact, partners in the ownership of an aluminum boat. The Houks drove over, surveyed the situation, and Houk called the police and Sam's brother, Dr. Richard N. Sheppard. Dr. Stephen Sheppard, Sam's other brother, also was summoned, and they took Sam to Bay View Hospital in their station wagon (avoiding a waiting ambulance). The family owned the osteopathic hospital. Fourth family member in the hospital was the father, Dr. Richard Allen Sheppard.

Houk testified at the trial he received Sam's call at 5 :45 A.M., more than five hours after the Aherns had left. Bay Village patrolman Fred Drenkham, now the city's police chief, said he received Houk's call at 5 :58 A.M. Upstairs Marilyn's body had drenched the bed with blood. Some was spattered on Sam's bed next to hers and on the walls from the severity of the repeated blows — a total of 35 wounds, most on the left side of the head, had smashed her skull.

After Sam had been hurried away to the family hospital by his brothers, a police fingerprint expert made a thorough examination of the house and found, to his surprise, not a single print anywhere, except for a partial palm print of Chip on the inside of a drop leaf of the living room desk and Sam's fingerprint on his wife's bed. He testified he saw a number

of parallel scratches which indicated to him that someone may
have rubbed the surfaces.

Two other important clues were also reported. Sam was
seen wearing a Tee shirt when he dozed off on the couch.
Later Sam was bare to the waist. His shirt was never found
despite long, intensive search, and he had no recollection of
what happened to it. And the murder weapon was never
found. Dr. Samuel R. Gerber, the county coroner, later testified he saw a blood stain on the pillow's underside that bore
the bloody outline of what he thought looked like a surgical
instrument used in removing a cast. Long search again failed
to turn up the weapon.

By 2:00 P.M. two Cleveland detectives told Bay Village
Police Chief John Eaton that they were convinced Sam Sheppard was the killer. The lack of proof that anyone else had
entered the house, the fact that Sam was not touched by the
same weapon that killed his wife, the absence of fingerprints,
the pulled-out drawers that appeared calculated to throw
suspicion off, the fact that Sam was hurried off to the family-
owned hospital before he could be questioned closely, all this
and more, they said, pointed the finger at him.

The next day, Sheppard's brother, Stephen, said X-rays
indicated Sam suffered a broken neck. At the same time, Sam
told a deputy sheriff that the man who killed his wife was
middle-aged, six-feet-three and had dark bushy hair. By July 8,
sheriff's deputies and Bay Village police said they were still in
the dark and Cleveland Detective Chief James E. McArthur
charged his men were being given the runaround and not permitted to question Sheppard.

In the meantime, pressures began to build up in newspapers.
It was reported that Sam Sheppard had refused to take a lie
detector test, that the reportedly "broken neck" was not a
serious injury after all. It was reported that Sam was running
around with other women, which he denied (it came out later

in court that he was repeatedly intimate with a young woman
who worked at the family hospital). Editorials came out
demanding that authorities "quit stalling" and arrest the murderer. They criticized Sam Sheppard's "protective shield."
They demanded the coroner hold an inquest.

On July 22, Coroner Gerber opened a public inquest in Bay
Village that grew noisy and unwieldy, largely through the
obstinate efforts of Sheppard's lawyer, the late William J.
Corrigan. The inquest finally ended July 26 with the ejection
of Corrigan.

By July 30, Sheppard was arrested and on August 17, the
Grand Jury indicted him on a first-degree murder charge. He
pleaded innocent. His trial began before Common Pleas Judge
Edward Blythin on October 18. Judge Blythin, a man of im-
peccable decorum and unimpeachable character, a man who
stood high in the community with his reputation for straight-
laced honesty, later had his name dirtied after his death by
an affidavit from the late reporter Dorothy Kilgallen, which
alleged Judge Blythin confided in her he thought "Sheppard
is guilty as hell." Anyone who knew Judge Blythin was confident it was not his way of thinking or speaking.

As the trial progressed, the smooth veneer of the Sheppard
family life began to come off revealing more difficulties than
had been realized. Nancy Ahern, who had been a dinner guest
the night of the murder, testified she had heard Sam was con-
templating a divorce from Marilyn, his high school sweetheart,
but had been dissuaded by friends. Houk, Sam's friend and
the first person the accused osteopath thought to call, testified
he (Houk) told Sam that "we all know if you did it, it was
in a fit of rage. Sam, if you did it, come out and admit it and
we'll all still be behind you." Sam replied with a warning that
Houk was himself a suspect since a psychiatrist had shown
interest in the middle-aged man's possible involvement.

As I sat in the crowded courtroom scribbling notes of the

testimony, I was increasingly aware of Sam's aloof manner. He was cool and detached, unconcerned with the public's reaction to him. This attitude was most clear when he was on the witness stand giving his answers in too-intellectual, stilted language, oblivious to the effect of his personality on the jury.

Other evidence piled up to make Sam Sheppard look more and more guilty. A policeman testified that there were no signs of forcible entry and no sign of struggle in the house. There was testimony about angry outbursts by Sam. And there was testimony that Marilyn's blood was spattered on Sam's wrist-watch and that the watch and other articles of jewelry had been thrown into underbrush in an effort to make it look as though a robber had discarded part of his loot.

A highlight of the trial was testimony of Sam Sheppard's illicit love affair as told by his mistress. Sam had vehemently denied he ever had sexual intercourse with her. She was an exceedingly pretty girl of twenty-four who took the witness stand in a black wool dress with a Peter Pan collar. She was a medical laboratory technician who often worked with Sheppard. She told of sharing a bed with Sheppard for seven nights in Los Angeles when he visited there. Under persistent questioning by Assistant County Prosecutor (now Judge) Thomas J. Parrino, she admitted having had sexual relations with Sheppard frequently when she worked at his family's Bay View hospital. She said the sexual adventures took place in automobiles and in an apartment, and she recalled that Sheppard had spoken of divorce from the murdered Marilyn. She was the last witness for the state and ended the prosecution's case dramatically. But she never even appeared at the second trial.

Finally, on December 17, 1954, the case as presented by Assistant Prosecutors John Mahon, Saul Danaceau, and Parrino went to the jury. Some 102 hours later, including nearly 40 hours of actual deliberation time in the jury room (in contrast to the second jury's eight hours and ten minutes), the jury of seven men and five women had reached a verdict: Dr. Samuel H. Sheppard, aged thirty, was guilty of murder in the second degree (meaning without premeditation). He was sentenced to life imprisonment which, in Ohio, meant he could be eligible for parole in ten years.

Most people in Cleveland were satisfied with the verdict. Some thought Sam was lucky, that he should have faced the electric chair. The community's opposition to him was obvious — and the jury came from that community.

Then began the series of appeals and motions in various courts. Judge Blythin overruled a motion for a new trial on January 3, 1955. On May 31, 1956, the Ohio Supreme Court upheld the conviction, 5 to 2, and denied a rehearing on July 5. On November 14, the United States Supreme Court refused to review the trial and conviction. It later refused to consider a request for a lie detector test. On September 5, 1958, the Ohio Supreme Court denied a writ of habeas corpus on the claim the trial had been conducted in a "circus atmosphere." As the years passed, the governor refused to let Sheppard be interviewed in prison by a hypnotist and the Ohio Supreme Court refused to order a lie detector test or hypnosis.

In the meantime, Dr. Sheppard's mother shot herself to death on January 7, 1955. Her son had been convicted and her husband had become seriously ill. On January 18, the father, Dr. Richard Allen Sheppard, died in the family hospital. In 1963, Marilyn's father, Thomas S. Reese, also committed suicide.

Still the legal battles dragged on, tedious and expensive.

In 1961, a young lawyer in Boston became interested in the Sheppard case. His name was F. Lee Bailey and he gradually took over more of the legal aspects until he emerged as the mastermind of the defense. He continued the legal appeals and more.

Suddenly we became aware new things were happening in the case.

On January 29, 1963, when Sam Sheppard was due to appear before the State Board of Pardons and Paroles, it was suddenly announced he was engaged to marry a thirty-three-year-old divorcée. She was a tall, stunning platinum blonde from Dusseldorf, Germany, a lady in sables and clothes with Paris labels.

The lady, Mrs. Ariane Tebbenjohanns, appeared on the scene quite unexpectedly, wearing long, dangling earrings, which became her trademark, and told newsmen that she had decided to become engaged to Sam after one letter from him and a four-and-a-half-hour talk with him. She said she had written to him previously, but he had not been allowed to answer. She had a nine-year-old daughter in West Germany and, it turned out, she had Nazi relatives — her half-sister was the wife of Hitler's propaganda chief, Dr. Joseph Goebbels, she said.

Hovering conveniently in the background was F. Lee Bailey. When it was noted she was here on only a four-week visitor's visa, Bailey assured everyone it could be renewed without any trouble. To say that the more prosaic population took a dim view of the whole Tebbenjohanns situation was putting it mildly. M. C. Koblentz, chief of the state's correctional institutions, issued an edict that she could neither write to or visit her convicted fiance. But the blonde from Dusseldorf was not to be stopped. With surprising enterprise for one so new to the ways of this country, she sent a letter to the Columbus *Dispatch* asking that it publish a letter to "My dearest Sam." The *Dispatch* was delighted to oblige and published a mushy letter that ended with "And you be a good boy, darling, as always — I am always at your side." It couldn't have been more touching if it had been written by an ambitious lawyer.

To many Cleveland lawyers the plan seemed sophomorically obvious. They told newsmen the purpose was to create a new image for the aloof convict. The world loves a lover, they reasoned; so what better way to create a new climate of affection for Sam Sheppard? If he came up for parole—or a new trial—the image of a rehabilitated, settled Sam Sheppard, with a lovely bride at his side, would be a decided help. The next jury would come from the community conditioned by this new image. It could be these veterans of the law were unduly cynical. In any event, the love affair was widely publicized.

The headlines now read:

DIVORCEE, EYE
ON ALTAR, WANTS
SHEPPARD FREED

As the publicity continued, keeping the matter alive in the public view, so did the legal proceedings. Finally, on July 15, 1964, the U.S. District Court in Dayton ordered Sheppard freed on a writ of habeas corpus, ruling he had not received a fair trial because of newspaper publicity.

Things started to move quickly for Sheppard. While the prosecutor's office made moves to appeal the ruling, Sam was released on July 16 and married Ariane on July 18. They nuzzled each other on television shows, and I met them strolling around Cleveland's Public Square with arms around each other, attracting a multitude of public stares. They were indefatigable in their loving appearances.

On May 6, 1965, the 6th U.S. Circuit Court of Appeals reversed the Dayton court's decision and ordered Sheppard returned to prison, to the consternation of the more sentimental

Clevelanders. But Sheppard remained free pending an appeal to the U.S. Supreme Court. On November 15, the nation's highest court agreed to review the matter.

It was on June 6, 1966, that the top court ruled Sheppard had not received a fair trial because of publicity and commotion in the courtroom. This indirect criticism of the late Judge Blythin drew bitter opposition from all who knew the highly respected jurist. Newsmen who covered the trial drew up a petition of protest. Now the stage was set for a new trial — long after the original evidence had faded and witnesses found it hard to remember exact words and voice inflections of the murder morning.

Sam Sheppard, by now forty-two years old, balding, and somewhat huskier than at the first proceedings, was ordered to stand trial on October 24 by Common Pleas Judge Francis J. Talty in the same building in which he had been convicted almost 12 years earlier. Now the prosecutor was John T. Corrigan. His assistant was Leo M. Spellacy.

This time, remembering the judicial criticism placed against his predecessor, Judge Talty was especially careful in handling the case. He placed severe limitations upon newspapermen. No photographs were allowed anywhere in the building. Few reporters were allowed in the courtroom and preference was given to local men. Any problems which arose during the trial were worked out in whispers, far from the ears of newsmen. The case was conducted with ultimate dignity. Controls were so stringent that Bailey later commented he was amazed that newspapers would accept such limitations without a whimper.

By November 2, 1966, a jury had been seated and Bailey was smiling and leaning into the jury box to give the opening statement. Gone was the claim of 12 years ago that "a bushy-haired intruder had done the killing." Now Bailey alleged it was someone familiar with the Sheppard home, someone who had had a key to that house for a long time. He claimed the weapon, which had never been found, was 12 inches long, rounded, similar to a flashlight, and "wielded by a person with physical strength compatible with that of a woman." He noted that as "the weapon was flailed time and time again, blood spatters were made on the walls and ceilings."

As the trial got underway, we soon found it to be a very pallid copy of the first. The original fervor was gone from both sides of the trial table. Memories of witnesses had weakened with time. The pretty twenty-four-year-old medical technician, the "other woman" who got top billing in 1954 and provided a dramatic windup to the state's case, was not present and her name, barely mentioned by a witness, was quickly shushed by an objection from Bailey.

It appeared to those of us who had covered the first trial that formerly important witnesses were now wearily only going through the motions. A police sergeant testified there was a trail of blood throughout the home, but the blood had long since disappeared and the jurors never saw it on their visit to the murder scene. Coroner Gerber and Bailey conducted a duel of sorts, but newspapers later described it accurately as a "kid-gloves duel." The coroner said he had concluded Sheppard was "not hurt" when he questioned him after the killing and Bailey objected mildly. Gerber also denied saying the killer was a woman.

The former neighbor, Houk, since divorced and remarried, came to the stand, now grey-haired and slower moving, to repeat his story of urging Sam to tell the truth and of being told by the Sheppards that he, too, was a suspect. Sam never went to the witness stand, as he had in the first trial, and so he could not be cross-examined. This jury never heard his story of the murder night. A witness, held in reserve for rebuttal by the prosecution, was never heard.

When the case finally went to the jurors, we speculated about what they would do. Several said they would be swayed by sympathy, by the picture of the solemn young man who had already served the minimum required ten years and should not be sent back to repeat that even if they suspected him. Others thought the community attitude had changed with Sam's new friendly image and that the jury would reflect that.

At 10:23 P.M., when Judge Talty read the jury verdict declaring Sam not guilty of the murder, Sheppard victoriously slammed his hand down on the trial table. He had been determined an innocent man, cleared of the guilt he had carried for 12 years. A woman in the back row screamed: "Thank God!" Other women screamed in the corridor. A Cleveland reporter who knew the details of Sam's second marriage leaned across to Ariane and asked "will you divorce Sam now?" This, the reporter explained later, was because of rumors that the Sheppards had been quarreling recently. An out-of-town reporter piously described this as "amazingly bad taste."

The foreman of the jury, Ralph J. Vichill, said he thought "the prosecution case was weak and that the gathering of facts also was weak." He would not comment on the number of ballots to find Sheppard innocent.

The osteopath was obviously lucky the first jury had not decreed the electric chair. After all his appeals had failed, he would have been long dead instead of now standing victorious.

The public was opposed to long appeals after the experience of Caryl Chessman in California.

F. Lee Bailey stood in the limelight. According to an article the next morning in the *New York Times*, he told reporter Sidney E. Zion:

The jury system is good only because there is no better system. In every other respect it is bad. The worst feature of the jury system is the fact that a verdict is not reviewable on the facts by an appellate court. There is a far greater likelihood of an innocent man being convicted because of a mistake by the jury than because of an error of law by the judge. For every guy who gets off who is guilty, an innocent man is convicted.

THE FINCH CASE

The trial in Los Angeles of Dr. R. Bernard Finch is the story of an ordinary American jury which was suddenly bared in the bright spotlight of national publicity. It brought into open discussion happenings that are not usually revealed in most jury trials. It made the public stop in its daily routine and, for at least a moment, reconsider its system of justice.

Dr. Finch was a handsome California surgeon who evidently had a weakness for pretty secretaries. At the time of being caught up in the web of murder, the doctor's current passion was Carole Tregoff, described by courtroom reporters as a pretty redhead. Under ordinary circumstances, the doctor's clandestine romantic interlude with his secretary would have occasioned no more than a few knowing grins from his men patients. It might have caused a little titillating gossip among the more knowing, or more suspicious, women whom he treated. It might even have enhanced his practice as a doctor of some modest extracurricular fame. The entire affair, however, suddenly sprang into public view when it erupted into murder of the doctor's socialite wife, Barbara Jean, on July 18, 1959. The defendants, the doctor and his girlfriend, were accused of plotting and murdering the wife who, only too evidently, had been somewhat in the way of things. Of course, the handsome surgeon had an answer to these accusations. He claimed the killing was an accident, although he was a little hard put in explaining how the bullets happened to be entering his wife's back. Miss Tregoff, however, had a much better defense. She claimed that she was only an innocent bystander all during the time of the killing.

The drama did not really move into high gear until the time

of the trial. Engaged to defend the couple was an attorney by the name of Grant B. Cooper. His fee, according to the newspapers, reportedly was a $25,000 retainer from Dr. Finch and $350 per trial day. Miss Tregoff's fees were estimated at about $20,000.

Finally, the matter was ready for trial. The court turned its full attention to that fundamental of justice, the procedure of selecting a jury of objective, unbiased, reasoning citizens who would be aware that they held in their hands the lives of two human beings and could, at their own disposition, reduce them eventually into corpses in California's gas chamber. With the heavy realization of the importance of this democratic citizen panel, the lawyers were most cautious in their selection. A full 19 days were devoted to the picking, examination, rejection, and final acceptance of this all-important unit of the trial. At last a panel of seven men and five women was agreed upon as the best that could be achieved for this important task.

The procedure of the trial was routine for such matters. Witnesses were given the oath and they testified; evidence was presented, argued over, and accepted, and it was presumed that the jury was fully captivated by this life-and-death struggle to the exclusion of all else. On the bench was Superior Court Judge Walter R. Evans, very properly doing what was permitted him under the California state criminal law.

To all outward appearances, the jury was fully qualified for its work; it looked and acted just like any other such body. The jurors presented a compatible and smiling appearance; all was evidently going well. Finally the trial was done. It had taken three months and that, alone, attested to its seriousness and importance. Final arguments had been made, the judge had read the jury the law in the case, and the jury retired to deliberate. The date was March 4, 1960.

As the hours passed while two lives hung in the balance, the tension grew measurably. Increasingly nervous court observers fell into the old pattern of trying to guess what was tying up the jury over the passing hours. Had they believed the story of Dr. Finch? What part could have placed a reasonable doubt in their minds? How much of Miss Tregoff's account had they accepted? Such questions and guesses are a normal part of every important trial while the jury is out.

Still the hours passed without report.

The hours became days, but still no word on a verdict. Finally, on March 12, after nearly 40 hours of actual deliberation time had been consumed, the jury at last brought out its report: it was hopelessly deadlocked. No agreement could be reached; it was a hung jury.

The scene was dramatic. As the jury was polled, the two defendants broke into tears. The prosecutor promised the newspapers a second trial soon. As is usual at such times, Judge Evans told the jury of the court's appreciation for its fine efforts. In his brief farewell talk to the members, he said: "I am extremely sincere when I tell you thanks for your help. You have been hard-working, attentive, and punctual. You deserve the utmost praise." Then he added that if anyone asked them for opinions, they should reply: "That mean old judge told me not to talk about it."

And the jury was dismissed. For all purposes, the incident was over: the citizen jurors were, as usual, beginning to fade back into the community from which they had come. Then, slowly, the leak, which is too often lacking in other trials, began. One juror, Mrs. Genevieve Lang, a stenographer, told the Associated Press that she had some doubts about the doctor's guilt. She had voted him guilty anyhow, she told a reporter. Then, as an explanation, she said: "That's why I voted for second-degree murder."

After this, despite the admonition from Judge Evans that they should not talk about it, more and more of the inside story of the jury's deliberations slipped out. The nation was treated

to a shocking full-dress picture of what had taken place at that
aspect of modern justice that the law so zealously wants to keep
hidden from public view—the secret discussions of the first
Finch murder trial jury. Here is the report from the scene as
given to the nation by the United Press International office in
Los Angeles:

Prejudice, violence, and obstinacy caused the Finch-Tregoff
murder trial jurors to become hopelessly deadlocked. The
accused lovers face a second trial.

A "gas them or free them" stand by two jurors prevented
efforts of the ten other panelists to free Carole Tregoff, twenty-
three and convict Dr. R. Bernard Finch, forty-two, of the
murder of his wife, said one of the jurors, Mrs. Lang.

Mrs. Lang said the outwardly compatible, smiling appearance
of the twelve jurors during their recesses was far from the real
state of affairs among them.

"At the height of one heated debate, a male juror threatened
to throw a woman juror out a window and turned over a jury
table—he used to be a boxer—before she ran to the door," said
Mrs. Lang. "She was hysterical and pounded on the door for
the bailiff."

The threatened woman was reported to have said she would
seek protection from the district attorney because she was afraid
of the male juror.

Another juror said one of the male panelists passed at least
three propositioning notes to women on the panel. She said an
extra bailiff was brought to the hotel where the jury stayed to
guard a woman's hotel door after she had received the notes.

"We could have voted Carole free at any time," said Mrs.
Lang. "But we were trying to get these other two—they refused
to listen to the law, conditions, and degrees—to go along on
Finch.

"If they would have voted with us, we would have settled for
second degree on Finch and freed Carole. We never voted on
second degree, though, we just voted on guilty."

Mrs. Lang said emotions between the jurors became so tense after practically living together for three weeks before the case was turned over to them on March 4 that two of the panelists all but divorced themselves from the others.

"The two ate together, talked together, and stayed off by themselves," she said.

Mrs. Lang said, "Racial prejudice was significantly present in the jury-room" causing an undercurrent of distrust and personality clashes. She did not elaborate.

Another juror said attempts at compromise with the two hold-out jurors fell on deaf ears.

"The rest of the jurors tried to explain the law to these two," said the juror. "But they just wouldn't listen. They were obstinate throughout."

Juror Louis Werner (a seventy-year-old retired sales manager) identified the two jurors who refused to vote for conviction as (Mrs.) Dolores Jaimez, a postal clerk, and Eddie L. Lindsey, a postal employee—and the only Negro on the panel. Both declined comment.

When all this smashed into the open on front pages from coast to coast, District Attorney William B. McKesson said an investigation would be made of the turbulent deliberations of the jury that was unable to reach the verdict. No word was ever received if such an investigation was made or, if it was, what was done about it. The jury, remember, is to a large degree untouchable.

These shenanigans, it should be kept in mind, were going on during a trial in which two human lives were at stake in the result. Both could have faced the California gas chamber if convicted of first-degree murder. Such actions among judges trying the case alone could probably have been good grounds for ousting them from office if not actual disbarment. Among citizen jurors, however, the matter was simply ignored and they went back into the unknown public from which they had been summoned.

It would be foolish, of course, to claim that many juries conduct themselves in this fashion. The thought that this could happen with regularity would surely bring frenzied calls for revision. Yet how are we to know in just how many instances events similar to those just described do happen? Unlike the actions of a judge alone, the official moves of a jury are carefully insulated from public scrutiny. To the outside world, all the jurors appear "compatible and smiling" as in the Finch case. Yet despite the shock and amazement the public experiences when such things are brought into the open, it is still hesitant in condemning the system of juries as it now exists. They deride it and then add a little pat of respect at the end as though worried about having disturbed something sacred by bravely telling the truth. For example, here is the editorial on that first Finch jury, typical of many across the country, which was published in the Cleveland *Plain Dealer* on March 16, 1960:

If it proved anything, the jury which failed to agree on a verdict in the Finch murder trial in Los Angeles merely reiterated the long-known fact that people are funny. In this case "funny" means odd, unusual, or even objects of derision.

As more and more of the jury's personal business during its deliberations becomes known (and the jurors are talking despite the presiding judge's order of silence) the more disgraceful its reputation. Here was a jury finally selected after 19 days of careful examination by attorneys and yet this group of seven women and five men, apparently, as a unit was unfit to serve.

During the deliberations one Lothario on the jury reportedly propositioned three women; one juror was sworn in under another name; one juror threatened to throw another one out of the courthouse window; a juror, angry at not being chosen chairman, changed his decision in the case to vex the others.

The final result of the antics was a mistrial, declared after the jury could not agree.

Our jury system, copied from the British code of justice but whose roots go back to ancient Rome and Athens, will continue to flourish and perform its intended function—but no thanks to the jurors in the first trial of Dr. R. Bernard Finch and Miss Carole Tregoff.

THE LADUTKO CASE

Another instance in which the actions of jurors, and the interesting reaction of a judge, became public knowledge was a sensational murder and subsequent trial involving personal acquaintances of this writer. It was Cleveland's famous John Max Ladutko Jr., murder trial.

Thirty-two-year-old John, six-feet-two and personable, and Nancy, his pretty twenty-nine-year-old wife, had been classmates at Cleveland-Marshall night law school. Nancy worked full time at a large law firm as a librarian; John resigned a good job with an automobile company when he passed the bar examination and launched himself on a rather precarious law practice. He switched associations a few times and, a couple of years after graduation, seemed to have the beginning of a regular clientele. I met him around Christmastime in 1960, and we spoke briefly. He appeared cheerful, but a few days later I learned from court documents that Nancy had filed suit for divorce.

In the three years of their marriage they had lived in a semi-Bohemian type of apartment above a garage. I had visited them there several times at their invitation. It appeared cozy and comfortable for a newly married couple. The garage was set well back to the rear of a large old house that had once been a mansion. It was on a shady street near a large university. They lived there with only a large, friendly boxer dog. They had no children, although John said he wanted some; but Nancy preferred to have her career. Witnesses at the trial later claimed that it was the other way around.

The Ladutkos, handsome couple though they were, apparently had two major difficulties : the first was that they did not get along with each other's families, and had not visited their in-laws for more than a year; the other was that John evidently was not forging ahead financially in his career as rapidly as he would have wished. He was a poor boy, apparently hungry for the riches he thought his profession held for him, and when they eluded him he appeared frustrated, sometimes moody and angry, according to friends who saw him often or worked with him.

All this, and probably more, blew up in a blazing climax one winter evening when John's shotgun blasts tore the life out of Nancy and her forty-two-year-old escort, Charles D. Johnson, married and a prominent attorney with the large law firm where Nancy worked. Police found Nancy's body in John's apartment; Johnson's body was found in his station wagon, which was parked in the driveway leading to the apartment, its motor still running. Johnson had managed to stagger to it from the rooms. In an expensive home in exclusive suburban Pepper Pike were the well-to-do Johnson's wife and invalid young daughter waiting for him to come home from work.

John was nowhere to be found. For days the newspapers carried heavy headlines of the murder and the flight. A double murder involving three lawyers was, of course, big news. Finally, John came in to surrender to the police, saying he was tired of running away. However, before he gave himself up, he engaged the services of another attorney, Phillip C. Barragate. Then he gave a long statement to the police, which was filled with accusations against both his wife and Johnson. He said they had been carrying on a romance; that he had once caught them kissing. He told of the pending divorce which, he said, had distressed him, and how his wife had moved away from their apartment. On the evening of the killing, he stated, he had been preparing to go to dinner at the home of friends. He was alone in the apartment he and Nancy had once shared, he said, when he heard his wife and Johnson drive up in the station wagon. He silently hid in the tiny bathroom adjoining the living room with the hope they would get what they had come for and leave without knowing that he was even there. Instead, they remained and, a little while later, he heard signs of sighing and love making.

This goaded him to the point where he ran out of the bathroom with the thought of running from the house when, he recounted, he found them in an intimate embrace, a "compromising position," as the newspapers later described it. In the full fury of his rage, he told the police, he lost the power to think, ran across the tiny living room to where his loaded shotgun leaned in the corner, and shot Nancy dead on the spot. Then, as Johnson tried to run, he swung the gun around and shot him. As Johnson continued in his flight, John attempted to re-aim, but smashed the weapon against the low ceiling. The gun was so badly damaged, he said later, that it would not fire when he tried to kill himself with it. (Evidence was brought out at the trial that John had bought the shells for the gun — a gun that he had never before fired in his life — on the afternoon of the killing. His answer for this was that he had heard there were prowlers in the neighborhood and he had purchased the shells to protect himself.)

In checking through the possessions of the dead Johnson in the station wagon, the police came upon two letters in his brief case. One was from Nancy to him, strongly professing her love for him. The other was an equally warm love letter from Johnson to Nancy but which, however, had not been mailed.

That was the picture when, in March, John Max Ladutko Jr., came to trial for a double murder in the first degree, which could bring the sentence of execution in Ohio's electric chair. Common Pleas Judge Joseph H. Silbert presided and a jury was picked with reasonable dispatch.

The state's case, presented by two very capable assistant county prosecutors, Harvey R. Monck and Thomas L. Osborne, claimed that the killings were deliberate and planned. They argued that John had parked his car at a distance from his home so Nancy and her lover would not know he was lurking in the dark waiting for them. They said he had bought the shells that day as part of the planned murders. The couple had come to John's apartment in the belief that he had gone to the dinner engagement he had made with friends. The state further argued that the visit to the apartment was perfectly innocent; the purpose was simply to pick up Nancy's clothing and other belongings that she had left behind when she walked out on John. But the enraged husband, they emphasized, had set a trap for them and had waited in the darkness like a hunter for his prey.

However, the prosecution refused to let the defense attorney see the two letters that had been picked up near Johnson's bloody body. Despite the fact that the letters were public knowledge, and had even been partially quoted in the newspapers, they said it was not part of the state's case and they had no obligation to introduce them into evidence. At the last minute, however, they agreed to let the letters go with the jury in its deliberations. The judge also agreed, but with the provision that they would be sealed immediately afterward.

The stunning surprise of the trial came when John refused to take the witness stand in his own defense. Despite the pleas of his attorney, John sobbed and adamantly refused to step up to the witness stand. His attorney had no choice but to rest his case on John's lengthy statement to the police immediately after his arrest. Finally, the case was given to the jury for deliberation.

All through the trial every move had been followed with extensive publicity. Newspapers carried daily stories of its progress and television presented pictures of the jurors going to lunch, or going to the jury room. Guessing started in the court corridors as to what the result would be. Some predicted the electric chair, but most thought it would be second degree murder carrying a life sentence. The lightest verdict possible, short of complete acquittal, would have been manslaughter and it was rumored that the accused had offered to plead guilty to that, but had been refused by the prosecution.

At long last, after seven and one-half hours of deliberation, the jury was ready with its verdict. It was a little after noon when the panel came down and the courtroom became hushed to hear what had been decided.

"Guilty—of manslaughter."

John's maximum sentence could be only one to ten years on each charge. Nancy's brother, a key witness at the trial, was outraged at the result. Nevertheless, Judge Silbert politely thanked the jury of eight women and four men for its services and dismissed them. Then he sentenced the convicted lawyer to serve his terms consecutively.

Then, making very clear that he did not intend to criticize or take issue with the jury (he had many times stated to me that he was a firm believer in the jury system) Judge Silbert proceeded to make public statements for both the newspapers and television which flayed the verdict of the jury as had rarely been done before.

"I am satisfied he intended violence against Nancy," Judge Silbert told Fred Mollenkopf, a reporter for the *Plain Dealer*. "In my judgment he had made up his mind long before he killed her. The court sees no justification for these homicides. In the opinion of the court there was no justification even for assault and battery; these were deliberate and premeditated killings. He took two young lives for no reason. He did not know of the existence of the letters. It was cold-blooded murder."

The judge said that the jury apparently believed John's story that he killed in a rage when he saw his wife and Johnson in a compromising position and that the letters corroborated the claim. "But," he added, "as a judge and a lawyer I must view it differently."

How had the jury reached its verdict?

Mollenkopf reported that one juror, Mrs. Mary Ann Baxter, said: "We thought the whole case was based on his story. After we read the letters then you could really believe it. We thought it could very well have been the truth. Any man would have done that, finding his wife in that position." Another juror, Howard J. Krause, said: "The letters sure helped to make us believe that they could have been in a compromising position."

It was reported that none of the jurors voted for first-degree murder. The voting was ten to two favoring a verdict of manslaughter against second-degree murder. The next two ballots were eleven to one for manslaughter and the last was unanimous for it.

That was the story immediately after the trial. However, a few days later, other versions of what actually went on in the jury room began to slip out. The Cleveland *Press* headlined a story that told of alleged pressures by others on one member of the panel, Mrs. Catherine Kane, who said that she did not willingly agree to the manslaughter verdict, but that she had really favored a second degree conviction which would have carried a life term. Reporter Bill Tanner wrote that Mrs. Kane said she joined in the verdict only because the eleven other jurors refused to adjourn for lunch until she had agreed to the manslaughter conviction. She said she had a stomach ulcer and required frequent nourishment. When she became ill in the jury room and pleaded for a break for lunch, the others said: "Not until we get this thing settled."

"I finally went along with them," she said, "but that was not my verdict. If I could have had something to eat, I would be holding out for second degree even today." She added that when the jurors were asked if arrangements should be made for lunch, "they all said 'no' except me. I said I wanted to go to lunch and I asked twice more, but they wouldn't listen."

"I believed that Ladutko deliberately killed Mr. Johnson," she told the reporter. "He walked all the way across the room to get the shotgun and then held it to his shoulder to shoot. I think the normal thing to do, if he caught them as he said, would be to want to get his hands on the man, to beat him up; not to go after a gun to kill someone." She said she had been bothered by her decision ever since the verdict was returned and that she had talked about it with the judge but "he told me not to worry about the case any more."

The next day Tanner turned up another juror who, he said, compromised on the verdict and said that she reluctantly agreed to manslaughter. It was the same Mrs. Baxter who earlier had said the letters had convinced her. Now she said that "I believe killing two people is more than an unlawful act (as manslaughter was described). I think that Ladutko after killing one person must have known what he was doing." Nevertheless, she agreed to the unanimous manslaughter verdict, "Because I didn't want to go through the ordeal of going to lunch." She said she and other jurors became upset after discovering that each time they left the jury room they would be besieged by television cameramen with bright lights "who followed us everywhere we went. I hated to see a circus made out of something serious. We were all mentally and physically exhausted, and they took our pictures every time we went up or down the stairs."

The judge's comment to all this was: "Every juror should make every effort to consider the arguments of his fellow jurors. However, if after such consideration he cannot agree with the

rest, he should stand on his convictions. We cannot have compromise verdicts, or verdicts made under stress. All verdicts
must be individual and freely arrived at." He concluded, however, that the Ladutko case was now closed and that the
disclosures by jurors that it was a reluctant verdict could not
reopen the case. Here, again, was the conflict between the ideal
and the realistic in a jury trial. The judge blithely quoted the
ideal and blandly proceeded to accept the realism of pressures
and compromises that go into a jury action. It was once more
as it had been described by Jim Bishop: It comes down to
creature comfort.

But what of the public, the masses for whom the judges
are simply the administrator's of the public's laws; what did
they think of the strange jury situation that was once more
displayed in the Ladutko case? Here is an account from the
press of a suburban council meeting soon after, where Mayor
Robert E. Willeford of Bedford Heights criticized the jury in
the Ladutko murder trial:

After Councilman Zelma E. Monahan had suggested a state
law jailing jurors who vote against their convictions, the mayor
said:

"We have very learned judges. We have fiery prosecutors. We
have good and able defense attorneys. But we have twelve idiots
deciding the fate of a man." This came after Mrs. Monahan had
said she was "ashamed to belong to a sex that has no stomach."
She explained that she was referring to two women jurors who
were quoted as saying they were pressured into voting for a
manslaughter verdict.

Mrs. Monahan said jurors should have the courage of their
convictions, otherwise they should not sit on juries. The mayor
agreed with her, but when Mrs. Monahan proposed the state
law, Mayor Willeford said: "We cannot invade the courts." And
the subject was dropped.

This is the normal procedure when a jury's action comes to light. There is a momentary buzz of protest. Some voices are raised in indignation, and calls come "let's do something about it." Then the old tradition comes into play. The juries are believed to be sacred. The system, weak though it may be, must remain inviolate. And the subject is dropped.

It may be because of situations such as these that the Cuyahoga County (Ohio) Bar Association called for the end of the death penalty altogether. The jurors are sometimes motivated by color, religion, geography, or whatever inborn prejudices they might have, a committee said. It added: "We do not always get the best intellectuals to serve as jurors at our murder trials." The committee noted that many who would be more suitable evade the unpleasant task of serving by declaring they are against capital punishment and "what is left in many instances is something less than the intellectual cream of the cross section of our society."

THE PETRO CASE

While a glimpse at the inner workings of a jury is unusual, due to the traditionally well-hidden nature of the proceedings, and comes out only in such rare situations as just shown, many times the confusion and uncertainty of a criminal jury can be seen in the results it brings forth. Such an instance was the murder case of a well-known hoodlum by the name of Julius Petro. He was unanimously found guilty of murder in the first degree without recommendation of mercy by his first jury. This meant he was condemned to death in Ohio's electric chair. But the second jury, which heard exactly the same case a little over 18 months later, just as unanimously found Petro completely innocent and freed him.

Obviously, one of those two juries committed a grave—an unforgiveable—injustice. Facts in both trials were exactly the same. The defense lawyers were the same men in both trials and their arguments were the same. Improving this even more as a clinical study was the fact that the same prosecutor appeared both times and did an equally vigorous job each time.

Who was wrong—the first jury that sent what could have been an innocent man to his death, or the second panel which may have freed a cold-blooded, vicious menace to society? The purpose of this illustration is not to decide which did right and which wrong. It is to show that through the vagaries of the jury system a gigantic and horrible wrong can be committed in the name of justice—an obvious and clear-cut inexcusable wrong.

This case started at 2:00 A.M., February 26, 1946, with a simple, small-time robbery by two shadowy figures. John Bush, an aged porter, was alone in an insignificant little neighborhood café when two men came up behind him, threw a towel over his face, gagged him with adhesive tape, and tied him to the pipes in the men's lavatory. He said later that for just a moment he could make out the forms of two young men in the darkness. It was reported to police that a total of $4,117 had been hidden around the café in a number of places. Part was in drawers, the balance under a steam table and behind a shelf. It was a usual precaution against total loss by the owner, Mrs. Marie Estrate. The robbers, without hesitation, went to all the hiding places and made their escape with all the cash.

That was not all. They also took a St. Francis medal, a valve spring and cap, a key ring, and some Canadian coins from the cash register, which had been used as payment over the years by the café's patrons. Through all this a hostile Spitz dog, which slept in the café, did not even bark once. Police concluded from all this that it must have been an inside job.

Main target of suspicion was the twenty-one-year-old son of the owner of the café, Theodore (Bobby) Knaus. Linked with him was a friend he had met while they were both inmates at the reformatory, the twenty-three-year-old Petro. Both had been sent up for auto theft, burglary, and larceny. A police teletype message therefore went out to pick up the pair for questioning in the robbery.

However, there was one little problem : Bobby Knaus did not come home the night of the robbery. The next night his mother thought she saw him sitting with Petro in a car parked in front of her house. She said they drove away together. The next day, February 28, at 5 :00 A.M., the police grabbed Petro in his home. In his jacket police said they found a St. Francis medal, a few Canadian coins, a valve cap and valve spring, and a key ring. All were identified with the robbery. Only two things were still missing, the $4,000 — and Bobby Knaus.

While detectives could not find Knaus, two small boys did. The barking of their dog attracted them into roadside shadows, where they discovered Knaus' body lying in a snow-covered ravine. Bullet holes were in the back of his head, in the small of his back, and in his left shoulder and arm. Fifty feet from the body police found an empty .32-caliber shell with a peculiar mark made by a revolver's firing pin. Three .32-caliber lead pellets were recovered from the body of Knaus.

Although Petro flatly denied knowledge of the robbery, and made very clear that he had not seen Knaus in a long time, police, after locating Petro's car, found in the right front door behind the upholstery two .32-caliber lead slugs. Under the back seat were three empty .32 shells, each with the same peculiar firing-pin dent as in the shell found near Knaus' body. Ballistics tests also showed that bullets from the body and from Petro's car had been fired from the same gun.

In addition to the St. Francis Medal and other things found with Petro, a university expert testified that spectroscopic analysis revealed the mud found on the floor of Petro's car was identical chemically with samples taken at the murder scene. The county coroner testified that the victim was killed between 8 : 00 P.M. on February 27, and 2 : 00 A.M. on February 28. Petro only argued that he did not do it and that the killing must have taken place some time after 5 : 00 A.M. when he had been picked up by police. In other words, he said, he was already in jail when the murder took place.

But the jury did not believe him. Their unanimous verdict was guilty with no mercy. Petro was condemned to die in the electric chair, and the verdict was upheld by the Court of Appeals, the intermediary reviewing court; Petro was placed in Death Row to await execution. However, as a matter of routine in execution cases, the matter was taken to Ohio's Supreme Court. Here, to everyone's surprise, after Petro had been in Death Row 18 months, a new trial was granted. The ground was a mere technicality : it was held that proper procedure had been violated when the prosecutor had failed to give the defense attorneys a bill of particulars before the trial.

The case came back for retrial in the original court. The same prosecutor, aggressive and capable Victor DeMarco, threw himself with renewed vigor into the new hearing. The same evidence was gone through again; the same arguments given. Again the case went to the jury — but this time a different jury. This was the only thing that had changed thus far. But that brought about the second big change — exactly the opposite conclusion was reached. Petro was found to be completely innocent of any wrongdoing; he was freed.

The result stunned DeMarco. He told newspapers that the acquittal was "shocking" and accused the jury of not being able to present tangible reasons supporting the verdict. (But, of course, they did not have to give reasons. As a jury they were only required to give the verdict, and then melt back into the anonymous masses from which they had been summoned.) The usually good-humored DeMarco snapped that "this was a bad jury; it didn't measure up. Scientific evidence went over juror's heads. They didn't understand what was going on."

He emphasized that the nine-woman, three-man jury had freed Petro on "exactly the same evidence that another jury weighed to convict him almost two years ago—the defense arguments were exactly the same in both trials. There is no doubt in my mind that this jury freed a guilty man." But defense attorneys, Edward C. Stanton and Michael Picciano were, of course, quite happy at the new turn of events and, presumably, with the jury system.

No matter what frustrations the prosecutor might feel, no matter how deep his anger, the matter was completely over for him because in an acquittal the jury, in effect, makes law. The prosecutor cannot appeal a loss because the defendant cannot be made to face double jeopardy on the same facts. The only one who could appeal an unfavorable verdict was the defendant, as was done here and in the Sheppard case. He, in effect, waives his right to protection from double jeopardy. If he is freed, however, no matter how damning the evidence against him, the case is ended and the state is powerless to press an appeal against him.

Petro was jubilant at the final outcome. (Although he was a strong suspect in another murder, the slaying of a city transit employee, that case against him was weak and was not pressed.) He had seen five men go to the electric chair while his appeal was pending, proclaimed that he was "going straight from now on," and that he intended to enter business. A short time later he was captured in a small-town bank robbery, brought to trial, convicted, and sent to the Federal penitentiary.

CASES ARE PLENTIFUL

It is not hard to find numerous cases where criminal court jurors have expressed confusion. This confusion comes in the imperfect understanding of their role, in the application of the law which they are given, in the actual results which they themselves have brought about. It gives a discouraging picture of justice and shows why more and more the accused are asking to have their cases heard by judges alone who, at the least, will not place them in the execution chamber purely by accident.

Take the case of the two women jurors who told the Ohio Pardon and Parole Commission that they did not know they were sending thirty-one-year-old Lewis B. Niday of Belpre (Ohio) to his death when they convicted him of first degree murder; their joining in a guilty verdict, without a mercy recommendation, carried an automatic death penalty.

Niday had been convicted in a gunshot killing of Mrs. Florence Cowdry in a tavern. He also had wounded the woman's companion, who had died a few weeks later. Conviction of this deliberate and premeditated killing could, with good conscience, carry the execution verdict. It should, however, carry the verdict actually intended by the jurors rather than come as the mistaken result of a misunderstood law. That apparently is what happened in this situation, because the Pardon and Parole Commission later heard from two jurors, Mrs. Dorothy Wilson and Mrs. Hattie Parks, that most of the six-man, six-woman jury was against sending Niday to the electric chair but that they misunderstood the death verdict.

Still another case was that of Mrs. Betty Downey, on trial in Cleveland for the fatal shooting of her husband some time after she had been beaten by him. Her trial was complicated by the death of her attorney during the first hearing and a long delay before the second trial came to be heard. She had been charged with manslaughter and had admitted that she aimed the gun at her husband and fired the single shot that killed him. Thus, under Ohio law, her defense was not in denying her guilt but in admitting her act and showing she had a legal reason for doing it. Her reason was self-defense, due to the earlier beatings by her late husband. Since she admitted she had shot him, the burden was upon her to prove that it was in self-defense.

But hear what a juror said after the panel ruled she was innocent in the killing : "We decided the state did not prove that it wasn't self-defense." Told of this comment, the county prosecutor, John T. Corrigan, angrily said that "under the law the state does not have to prove it was not self defense. The defense has to prove that it was."

It can be seen here that it is an easy matter for juries, in the secrecy of their deliberations, to ignore the law so carefully made by the proper legislators and substitute their own law of the moment — made as non-elected quasi-legislators — for what is actually on the books. The jurors, arbitrarily without telling the prosecutors, shifted the burden of self-defense to the state.

Questionable activities of many juries in southern states during the civil rights uproar of the middle 1960's are too well known to require repeating in detail here. All-white juries again and again freed fellow townsmen charged with beatings, and even murder. Once freed, the accused could not be brought to trial again, and the rest of the world criticized the juries in vain. The accused, often guilty of vicious crimes, were thus encouraged to repeat them. Civil rights workers, fighting for justice for the Negroes, were fair game. Juries, reflecting the climate of their own communities, twisted justice again to their own convenience.

One example, typical of the many of its time, was the acquittal of Thomas L. Coleman, a part-time deputy sheriff, near the end of September, 1965. The trial was held in Hayneville, Alabama. Jonathan M. Daniels, a twenty-seven-year-old Episcopal seminary student from Keene, New Hampshire, had been killed with a shotgun blast outside a Hayneville grocery store. The Rev. Richard Morrisroe, a Roman Catholic priest from Chicago, companion of Daniels, was critically wounded by a second blast. Both were civil rights workers. Coleman, a fifty-five-year-old highway engineer, was accused of the murder. His lawyer conceded he did the shooting.

Sarcastic editorials across the nation noted that the jurors believed Coleman's story, backed by white witnesses, that he shot in self-defense, that the young churchman was toting a knife, and that the Roman Catholic priest was packing a gun! Newspapers commented that the jurors—most of them workmen or farmers—disbelieved five Negro witnesses who denied this and ignored the fact that no such weapons ever were found.

Alabama Attorney General Richmond M. Flowers' denunciation of the verdict was reported widely. He was quoted as calling it a triumph of "irrationality, bigotry, and improper enforcement of the law." He added, almost needlessly, that "now those who feel they have a license to kill, destroy, and cripple have been issued that license."

The Rev. John B. Coburn, dean of the Episcopal Theological School at Cambridge, Massachusetts, which Daniels attended, said the decision was an "utterly shocking travesty of American justice." New Hampshire Governor John W. King also said he looked on the verdict "as a travesty of justice." These gentlemen appear to have been sheltered from previous activities in various courts.

One editorial concluded: "The nation is going to have to consider what other means are at hand to ensure fair and impartial justice in cases such as this. It was trial by jury itself which was on trial at Hayneville."

The United States Attorney General, then Nicholas D. Katzenbach, said that acquittals in cases like Coleman's "are the price you have to pay for the jury system."

In the same courtroom in Hayneville, Alabama, a few weeks later (on October 22, 1965) another jury found a Ku Klux Klansman, Collie Leroy Wilkins Jr., innocent of the killing of Mrs. Viola Liuzzo, a Detroit civil rights worker who was shot in her car while driving in Alabama. Wilkins had been named as the killer by Gary Thomas Rowe Jr., a paid informant and underchover FBI agent who said he was in the Wilkins car when the fatal shot was fired.

When word of the verdict reached Dr. Martin Luther King in Paris, the Nobel prize winner and civil rights leader called the jury verdict "one of the most dastardly crimes against justice that the South has performed to date." He said the acquittal of Wilkins "threatens all of the progress that we have made in the south." In New York James Farmer, national director of the Congress of Racial Equality, said the acquittal meant "the jury system of the state of Alabama has shown itself incapable and unwilling to render justice."

The jury, representing the community, included six self-described white supremacists and eight members of the Citizens Council. Efforts to keep them from the jury had been rejected by the state Supreme Court.

Despite the outcry of injustice, nothing could be done. The Alabama juries had ruled, declined comment, and vanished back into the community from which they had come. The acquittals could not be appealed no matter how unfair the trials may have been. The American jury system had once more acted in its wisdom as representatives of democracy.

They were only two of many such juries.

TROUBLES OF JURIES

It is apparent that a juror often is influenced not only by the facts in a case but also in the relationship of those facts to the juror's personal attitudes toward certain crimes. For example, a juror in a trial of a youth accused of throwing rocks through a neighbor's windows may recall an incident in his early years when he had done the same thing. The reaction could easily be one of sympathy for the accused. Or the juror may come from a neighborhood where such happenings were a normal practice and regarded as such by the residents. He would find it hard to see crime in such a situation even though the law clearly calls it such. He is reflecting the moral views of his own narrow status rather than the broader aspect of actual law. Professor Charles L. Newman at Florida State University's department of social welfare flatly stated in a paper published in the *Journal of Criminal Law* that the jury's attitude toward the accused could vary with the type of criminal charge:

If the indictment is for the violation of one of the multitude of regulatory statutes, it is not impossible that the jurors can see themselves in the dock and sympathize with the defendant . . . where the defendant has pulled off a fraud on big business, the jurors may regard him as a hero. But woe to the defendant who is accused of the crime of robbery, rape, or something in that category. Whatever the law says, it may well be that the jury puts on the defendant the burden of proving his innocence. After all, is not the sanctity of the home and the chastity of woman-hood at stake?

In other words, a juror, being an average man and an amateur at trials, would find it hard to adopt a clinical mental attitude in a trial, in order to divorce as much as possible his personal bias and prejudice from the facts in the case and the law that must be applied. This brings us to another problem common to criminal court. It is understood that the accused is innocent in law until proven guilty. This premise, however, can encounter difficulties: when a jury sees an accused for the first time, he is in close custody; his hands are often hand-cuffed, and he will likely have a disheartened, hang-dog look about him.

Emotional cards are stacked against the defendant even if he is innocent. The truth is that he is too often presumed

guilty, in the uninformed eyes of the jury, until proven innocent. It is not unusual to see defense lawyers taking a great
deal of time to establish that their client should be considered
as just another ordinary citizen — in other words, trying to overcome the presumption of guilt rather than trying to preserve
the presumption of innocence.

JURIES BOW TO PUBLIC PRESSURE

In his book, *The American Legal System,*[1] Professor Mayers
notes somewhat conservatively that "the present tendency is
toward increasing the use of the waiver of jury trial. Students
of criminal justice are inclined to believe that the extensive use
of the waiver would, on the whole, greatly improve the
efficiency of the trial process."

Avoiding a jury trial in criminal court, while often desirable,
is not always possible. Many states make the guarantee of a
jury trial something so absolute that no one can waive it. This
often, in effect, places a millstone around the neck of justice
rather than serving as the idealistic safeguard against injustice
it was intended to be.

Professor Mayers describes this danger vividly when he
writes:[2]

"In a setting of violent public hostility, also, a defendant
may well prefer to trust his fate to the judge, rather than to a
jury. In the celebrated Scottsboro cases in the early 1930's, the
Alabama prosecutors found no difficulty in procuring conviction
by the jury in each of the three successive trials, despite growing
weakness in the evidence; it became apparent that in the
atmosphere of community hostility to the Negro defendants, and
to their counsel, it was unlikely that any juryman, whatever the
evidence, would vote for their acquittal. Quite possibly, however,

[1] Pp. 114–115.
[2] *Ibid,* p. 117.

a judge, sitting without a jury, particularly one assigned from a distant county, might have acquitted one or more of the defendants.

"In a number of states, however, . . . the constitutional provision is so framed as to require jury trial, no waiver being permissible. Thus in an inflamed condition of public hostility, a constitutional provision which not only guarantees the accused the right to jury trial but goes further and compels him to be tried by a jury when he would prefer to be tried by a judge, may actually guarantee the accused not a fair trial but a lynching by jury. And in the situation, recurrent in our southern states, in which community hostility to the accused is racial as well as individual, the further constitutional command . . . that persons of the accused's own race be not excluded from the jury is quite worthless; for a Negro on the jury could hardly be expected, in an explosive state of community hostility to a Negro defendant, to brave that hostility by holding out against his white fellow-jurors.

"In *Shepherd v. Florida* in the U.S. Supreme Court, Justice Jackson, in a concurring opinion said that under these circumstances, for the Court to reverse these convictions upon the sole ground that the method of jury selection discriminated against the Negro race, is to stress the trivial and ignore the important . . . this trial took place under conditions and was accompanied by events which would deny defendants a fair trial before any kind of a jury. I do not see, as a practical matter, how any Negro on the jury would have dared to cause a disagreement or acquittal."

It is evident from the foregoing that the criminal juries in state courts leave a great deal to be desired in man's quest for a more nearly perfect method of dispensing greater equality of justice. Juries can be seen as biased, capricious, and blundering in their brief tenures of dealing with the affairs of other men; in their short experience of "playing God" with the lives of others.

It must be remembered that into the hands of these very average private citizens are placed many years of prison confinement for others — and, in fact, the right to take the lives of others. Where else in modern society, running the gamut from hospital operating rooms, to social service agencies, to mental hospitals, is such extraordinary power deliberately and repeatedly placed into the hands of unskilled and inexperienced strangers?

9

Jurors and Bastards:
Quasi-Criminal Law

PROBABLY ONE OF THE MOST DIFFICULT OF TASKS GIVEN TO
juries is to determine the paternity of an illegitimate child.
Unfortunately, difficulty does not provide a barrier to volume,
and these cases are coming through the courts in ever-larger
numbers. Rarely do they make newspaper headlines. Unless
the participants are particularly well known—such as movie
stars, sports figures, or civic leaders—newspapers tend to stay
away from such matters.

Making such cases emotionally difficult for jurors is the
fact that a bastardy suit usually involves three persons who
are particularly appealing to sympathy. There is the accused,
usually a guileless-appearing young man, apparently innocent
in the ways of the world. And there is the mother, looking like
a naïve child herself, yet having gone through the tortures of
society's shame. She does not come seeking vindication, as in

other law suits, but very real financial support for the result of the misdeeds of the young man, while shamefacedly admitting she played an integral, and often willing, part in the doings. Then there is the key figure : a charming child, usually about a year old. It is the innocent victim of this tragedy, and the jurors look on appalled and sad, as it happily plays with its mother.

In this setting are told the most amazing tales. Intimacies are stripped bare; stories that would make a veteran judge blush are told with straightforward candor and in great detail — almost as though the participants relished their role. In the strong light of personal embarrassment, befuddled by conflicting scientific testimony, the jury must come to the difficult decision that it knows can wreck the life of a young man, particularly if he is really innocent but misjudged by the jurors.

These problems faced by juries can best be illustrated by incidents heard by this writer in open court. Take, for example, the story told by a sweet-faced girl of eighteen; it took even her own lawyer by surprise and dropped a bombshell in the courtroom :

The girl had gone to the witness stand, simply dressed and soft of voice, to tell the story of her own seduction. While she spoke, the boy she had accused stared awkwardly at the floor. Under questioning of her own lawyer, she told modestly how she had gone to a midsummer dance with the young man on the night she was supposed to have conceived the baby. She faltered demurely as she told how during an intermission the two had gone for a walk. Their stroll took them to the parking lot and they had sat in his car and kissed. She noticed, she said, that he was getting more passionate, which in turn aroused her. When he pushed her down on the seat, she said, all her power of resistance had gone. She felt him pull off her underclothing and go through sexual intercourse to its completion. No, she said to her lawyer's question, the youth did not wear a contraceptive.

Her lawyer had established his case. Now he let the boy's lawyer cross-examine the girl. She stuck to her story. This was clearly the boy who had done it. She had not been under the influence of alcohol. She remembered everything clearly, every inexperienced fumble he had made in his passionate disrobing of her. Yet she stumbled a little when asked the color of her escort's automobile in order to test her memory of that night.

This led the boy's lawyer to a new trail: Had she gone out with other boys who also had cars? Her answer was yes. Had she been intimate with others in their automobiles? She hesitated slightly before she admitted she had, but made clear very quickly that she did not do that with any boy. The lawyer, hot on a new aspect, pressed further. Had she been out with some-one else the week before? Yes. The night before? Yes. Had she been intimate with them? Her answer was a disappointing (to the lawyer) no.

The lawyer's face fell. As a last desperate stab in the dark, he asked had she been intimate with anyone else anywhere around the night of the dance? She furrowed her brow before she answered yes. The lawyer's next question was almost shouted—when? Her answer stunned the courtroom. "About an hour after" the boy she accused of fathering her child. Under more questions, she told how the first boy had appeared to lose interest in her after he had been satisfied. Another boy who she also knew had escorted her home and, in his car parked in her driveway, he also had sexual relations with her.

The face of the boy's lawyer was a mask of amazed relief. The rest of the trial was routine. The girl's lawyer went through the usual measures of placing the baby next to the youth to show a resemblance of features. Finally the jury went out to deliberate. The girl appeared to have some difficulty with her lawyer when they were gone. He was seen to wave his arms in agitation as he spoke with her and her face flushed.

Finally, the jury returned. With great deliberation, the foreman turned in his written verdict. The jurors had found without a doubt from the evidence they had heard that the accused was indeed the father and should be made to support "his" child. The boy's mouth dropped open in amazement as the jury filed out.

What had inspired the verdict? Observers could only speculate. Here was a child, the jury apparently reasoned, which needed support. The young man had agreed that he had intercourse with the girl. He had been brought to court by her and she apparently must have some reason to believe he was the father. And so, in defiance of all scientific possibilities, this young man was saddled with supporting the child for the next 18 years.

SCIENCE OR EMOTION

Bastardy juries are notorious for their ability to discard scientific evidence; they fly in the face of proof and bring back verdicts that evidently stem from sympathy or other emotions. One such case, often cited, is that of *Berry vs. Chaplin* (75 California Appellate 2nd, 652) in which a well-known movie star was sued for allegedly fathering an illegitimate child. Here a jury returned a verdict in the face of uncontroverted and unimpeached scientific testimony that the defendant could not have been the father of the disputed child.

In this case, an infant girl, Carol Ann Berry, suing through her mother, Joan Berry, claimed that famed movie comedian and producer Charlie Chaplin was her father and should be declared so by the court. Her petition also asked that he be required to pay for medical care during the pregnancy and birth, as well as support for the child. Needless to say, this case made newspaper headlines across the country. Joan Berry testified she had the child which, she said, was begotten by Chaplin on or about December 20, 1942. Chaplin denied that he was the father.

Even before the birth, the two parties entered into a stipulation, or agreement, which was officially approved by Superior Court Judge William S. Baird. Under this, they agreed that Chaplin voluntarily would pay Miss Berry the money necessary for medical care and for her support, and for all hospital and medical expenses necessary for her proper care during the period of her pregnancy and confinement and attendant upon the birth of the child. But there was a condition that she would voluntarily submit the child after its birth to medical tests for the purpose of determining its paternity. Miss Berry must make herself and the child available at all times so tests could be made by competent medical experts.

Also under the terms of the agreement, one physician was to be named by Chaplin, another by Miss Berry, and those two medical men would select a third "who shall be especially skilled in such matters, who shall make a blood test or other tests accepted by medical science for the purpose of proving and establishing paternity and who shall report their findings and conclusions."

All this was done and, as the Court of Appeals later reported: "The qualifications, competency, and integrity of the physicians designated to make the blood tests are not questioned. After the tests were completed, they made a report that Chaplin had group "O" blood, Joan Berry, group "A," and Carol Ann Berry, "B.""

"The conclusion reached as a result of the blood grouping tests is that in accordance with the well-accepted laws of heredity, the man, Charles Chaplin, cannot be the father of the child, Carol Ann Berry. The law of heredity which applies here is 'The agglutinogens A and B cannot appear in the blood of a child unless present in the blood of one or both parents.' "

Two of the physicians testified at the trial that the report truly represented their findings from the tests made. They and one other physician testified that by reason of the tests, defendant was not and could not have been the father of the baby.

The reports and evidence of the physicians were not controverted by any scientific evidence, but went before the jury to be considered with all the other evidence in the case. The physicians were unanimous in their report from the test that Chaplin was not the father of the child. Despite all this, however, the jury rendered a verdict that Chaplin was the father of the infant. It was decided that he must pay $75 a week for the support and education of the child during her minority, or until further order of the court, and the sum of $5,000 in attorney's fees.

On what information did the jury reach its conclusion? No one knows, since it was done in secret. Here, however, is some of the testimony they heard: Miss Berry said herself that she and Chaplin had four acts of sexual intercourse, on the 10th, 23rd, 24th, and 30th of December, 1942. This was denied by Chaplin, although a butler said he had seen her in the home those nights. There was also testimony that Miss Berry had said a soldier then serving overseas had fathered the child. As the reviewing court said: "This evidence alone was sufficient not only to constitute a prima facie case, but to sustain the verdict although denied by the defendant."

Another hint of what influenced the jury is seen in the protest lodged for Chaplin on appeal when he complained of the order of the trial judge directing him to stand in front of the jury in close proximity to the mother, holding her child in her arms, in order that the jurors might study and compare the physical features of the infant with those of the defendant. This has been known in bastardy trials as the kiss of death for the defendant, however innocent he may be. What jury can resist the appeal of a chortling, happy infant, nestled in the arms of its sad-faced mother, as against whoever may be alleged to be the father? And what jury cannot see some slight resemblance in a child with any man, so long as they are at least of the same race? This is a devastating emotional obstacle for any defendant to attempt to overcome and before it is defeated scientific evidence such as blood tests.

A WOMAN'S REVENGE

Sometimes a jury becomes what is apparently an instrument of revenge. It has been said that there is no fury like a woman scorned and sometimes this becomes all too clear in trial testimony. Even despite this, however, the woman can emerge the victor. In one case I covered, a girl of about twenty took the witness stand to point the accusing finger at a former boy-friend who had parted company with her. In a voice fairly seething with anger, she described in precise detail how her erstwhile friend had seduced her in his flashy new car:

"Oh, he used to think he was a big shot alright driving around town in that bright red convertible," she said through clenched teeth. "He thought he could pick up any girl and when he got tired of her he could drop her like nothing, but I warned him he couldn't do that with me like I was any other girl."

She would have gone on that way, but her lawyer's warning signals from the trial table finally caught her eye and she subsided. At last the boy's lawyer got his chance to cross-examine her.

"Did you ever have sexual relations with other boys?" he asked.

With a stare of vengeance at the defendant and an angry toss of her head she said that she had done it with many other boys and that they had all liked her. Again, her attorney's warning signal cut her off.

Then how could she be certain that the child was begotten by this particular defendant and not someone else?

She hesitated a moment to gather her thoughts and then explained that all the others had worn contraceptive protection but that the accused had not.

Then the boy's lawyer apparently took his fatal step. How did she know that his client had not? he asked. And the young lady proceeded coldly to give the jury a discourse on exactly how it felt to her when the defendant reached the climax of his intercourse.

After that, all that was necessary was for her attorney to place her and the baby beside the young man in front of the jury. It did not take the jurors long to reach a verdict that he was indeed the father, even though he had vehemently denied not using protection and had practically wept from the stand that he had been intimate with her only once and that this had been at her urging and with her assurance that she also was wearing protection against conception.

Thus it is that attorneys, particularly those representing the man, are far from eager to accept bastardy cases before juries. They feel that the emotional cards are unfairly stacked against them, particularly if their client appears to be fairly wealthy. As an alternative, some have suggested a panel of three medical men to hear testimony and decide on the facts, leaving the actual setting up of financial arrangements in guilty cases to judges as now, or to a referee if the economic investigations become too burdensome on the court's time.

These physicians, being men of the world, would be less swayed by the emotional problems and more prone to give more exacting weight to scientific testimony — or the absence of it — brought out in the trial. And this panel would still carry all the freedom ·envisaged in the original meaning of a jury to decide the facts in contested cases.

Such a proposal, or any form of it, would serve to reduce doubtful accusations, since victory would not seem almost assured to the woman and would, at the same time, encourage more guilty pleas of men who are really the culprits and who will realize the difficulty of confusing this precise jury. It would, in short, bring more of a semblance of justice to what is admittedly a difficult situation in a type of case that is becoming an ever increasing problem in the courts.

10
Big City vs. Small Town

OTHER TROUBLES WITH JURIES ARE SOMEWHAT MORE SUBTLE than the specific problems just described. Although they are more general, they are no less fundamental. One such is the wide divergence in results brought by similar fact situations to which identical law is applied. The inscription on the Supreme Court Building in Washington, D.C., reads : "Equal Justice Under Law." In one way or another, that thought is repeated in courthouses across the country. Without doubt it is engraved on the minds of those who make a career of administering justice. Why then is it that courts with such virtuous goals come forth with such widely divergent concepts of the meaning of equality, of justice, and of law?

One reason lies in the very strengths of the jury system that many lawyers extoll. This strength, the lawyers say, is the power of juries to temper the law, to soften its harshness, and to breathe human warmth and understanding into the coldly phrased statutes. In short, to give the law the ability to adjust to the needs of society. These same men look at you bleakly,

191

however, if you bluntly ask them whether they would rather go through great inconvenience to file a personal injury suit in a distant big-city "high verdict" court or if they would not mind bringing it to a small-town court where the defense lawyer steps across the square from his office to the courthouse and faces a jury of sympathetic fellow townsfolk.

The answer should become obvious as this chapter progresses. It raises the uncomfortable question, in turn, of just how equal is justice across the country — or even across your own state — when in the prejudiced palm of the local jury, which adjusts the law casually to meet the needs of its own particular segment of society.

A splendid example of this can be seen in the experience of a personal friend who now, to his own gratitude, is a judge and no longer has to face juries as an advocate. This friend had a personal injury case in which he was the defense lawyer. There were, in fact, two suits growing out of a single accident: two men had been slightly injured in about equal degree as the result of an automobile collision in which they had been involved as passengers. The defense had estimated their damages at about $500 each and was prepared to settle for that.

The plaintiffs, however, would not hear of it. They insisted on going to trial with a jury — in their own community, of course. In fact, they had two juries, one for each suit.

My friend defended the first suit personally. He used all the energy and resourcefulness he had developed in serious big-city cases. His cross-examination of local witnesses was most thorough. His opponent at the trial table barely seemed to be listening. He had marched stolidly through his own array of witnesses earlier, without dramatics or imagination, and let it go at that. He rarely even looked at the jury.

He did not have to.

When the case was finished, the jury went out, elected a foreman, and quickly returned with a verdict of $6,500, to the amazement of the big-city lawyer caught in a small town.

As the second of his cases was being called for trial, the big-city lawyer saw the need for a rapid change of strategy. He pleaded with the judge for a two-week continuance of his case so he could attend "to some urgent business" back in his office. The judge amiably agreed to that.

It developed that my friend's "urgent business" was to contact acquaintances at the local bar association. They helped him find another lawyer, a native of the town where the trials were being held, whose father had been a well-known local lawyer before him. He was to serve as co-counsel on the case. My friend explained details of the case to his new associate during the two-week respite.

When the case was called for trial, my friend suddenly "learned" he was needed for an emergency back in his own office and begged the other to handle the entire trial of the case for him. He even doubled the $250 fee he had originally promised the local lawyer for his help.

As this second trial started, my friend slipped into a small hallway behind the courtroom to hear how his new strategy worked. Again, the plaintiff's lawyer stolidly marched through his set of witnesses as he had in the earlier trial. The lawyer my friend had hired hardly bothered to cross-examine in an effort to shake their testimony. Questioning of his own witnesses was purely perfunctory. My friend began to doubt the wisdom of his desperate strategy.

At last closing arguments were reached, much more quickly than they had come in the earlier case that he had handled himself. My friend felt the time had come for his co-counsel to distinguish himself with a powerful plea to the jury. Instead of the sound logic and appeal to reason used by the big-city lawyer, however, the local attorney's closing went something like this:

"I am going to finish this case in a hurry. I know you people have to get back to work. Now I agree that man had some injuries. Nothing serious, mind you, but he should get some money. I think about $500 would be a fair amount that would take care of all his damages."

It is hardly necessary to tell the ending of this incident. The jury came back with a verdict of exactly $500. The local lawyer knew his jurors; he knew how to handle the small-town person, having a high estimation of the value of the dollar. More than that, he was a fellow townsman that the jurors could trust, rather than the big-city lawyer who was unknown to them. Thus, by paying a local colleague a total of $500 in fees, my friend had gotten around his stiffest legal problem and had saved the extra $5,500 he had lost in the first case.

Trial of a case in a small town can be an illuminating experience for a lawyer. In an important case I covered as a newspaper reporter, the lawyer was visibly shaken when, right in the middle of one of his more dramatic cross-examinations, a juror suddenly stood up and asked of his fellow members which of them wanted soft drinks and which wanted coffee from the courthouse canteen. The big-city lawyer watched in stunned disbelief as the juror took the orders and left to make the purchases.

He turned to the judge in amazement and was politely told to continue with his questioning, since fellow members of the jury would "fill in the absent member" with what had happened while he was away. As the lawyer falteringly continued, the juror returned and, amid a flurry of whispers, he passed out his purchases. The jurors settled back to refresh themselves while the lawyer went on with his case.

VERDICTS REFLECT COMMUNITY

In many small towns, a juror might almost be termed a professional fact-finder. During winter months, nearby farmers who have time off from working the land are eager to pass that time away in the court house and make a few extra dollars besides. They constitute a continuous jury, serving in case after case throughout the cold season. When the weather changes, their places are taken by housewives whose children have grown up and by the older men who are retired and have time on their hands.

The small-town jury is known for small verdicts; small, at least, in the eyes of a big-city lawyer. Reason often given for this is that jurors have little contact with big-money deals. They are a frugal people who must of necessity live on funds that are small in contrast with their more wealthy metropolitan neighbors. Their conditioning is toward smaller sums because that is their normal daily contact. That is why successful personal injury lawyers working for plaintiffs make every effort to keep cases out of the small town. They prefer the more "equal" justice of a large city.

An example of this may be seen in the experience of a successful lawyer I know who was forced to come to trial in a distant small town. His case happened to be a wrongful-death action, and he represented the surviving widow and her children. He thought of how much money he would ask in terms of what he had been accustomed to in the big city. Then he adjusted it downward for the psychology of the small town. He finally arrived at a figure of $65,000 which, to him, was highly deserved in view of the facts of the case. Just before the case was ready to start, the lawyer was called aside by the friendly judge and told : "You know, the biggest verdict a jury ever gave in this town for a wrongful death was $7,500." This startled the lawyer a little. He grudgingly revised his estimate of the case down to $45,000. He found out later he should have believed the judge.

When the jury came back, the verdict for his client was $3,500.

Since exactly the same case, built on the same facts and damages, could probably have received around $65,000 in a large city, one feels ready to inquire as to the whereabouts of the equality of justice spoken of by those who have little to do with the courts or their administration.

A case of merely cosmetic nature bringing scars to a woman's face, but leaving her alive and in full possession of all her limbs, brought $175,000 in a big-city case I covered. Here, too, the jurors reflected the conditioning they had received in a community where large sums of money are bandied about by the local newspapers and in casual discussion much more than in smaller areas.

GROWTH BRINGS CHANGES

Interesting to note in this connection is the fact that as communities change in size, or in their contacts with larger cities, it is reflected in the size of their juries' verdicts. One such example is Lake County in Ohio, not far from Cleveland. For many years it was made up largely of small towns and farm land, and their jury verdicts were typical for such a community. In recent years, however, more and more industry has located there; talk of money in large figures has become more common. Also, with the improvements of highways, more people who work in Cleveland have taken to residing in Lake County's more spacious suburban countryside. With juries now being picked from among these semi-commuters and neighbors with whom they have become familiar, jury verdicts have shown a continuing increase and are nearing the levels set in the larger cities.

It goes without question that there are certain communities known as "big verdict courts." Lawyers don't even have to guess at them. Their names are available from associations of plaintiffs lawyers. A capable lawyer who wants to win "equality" on a high level will take his case there when possible. If he emerges successfully, it is with richer rewards.

A striking example of the vast differences which different types of jurors consider to be justice can be seen in the basically similar trials of appropriations matters. These cases are simply an attempt by jurors to place a dollar value on parcels of land that an arm of the government wishes to appropriate for a public benefit, such as a new road or housing development.

Lawyers who represent the government are often the same men. They travel from one community to another, using the same argument and approach in each instance. Thus they may be regarded as the comparatively constant factor in our little experiment. These men are amazed at the widely varying results which they achieve. In a large city, jurors come back with fairly reasonable estimates of the value of a parcel of land. They apparently achieve this by picking a middle point between what the owner is asking and what the government offers. In the small town, however, the verdicts are over-whelmingly in favor of the local landowner. Explanation of the lawyers to this is that "we know we are going to get skinned in a small town" because the jurors are close friends of the landowner and in deep sympathy with him. They may know the land in question is no good for either crops or for pasture and is worth only a small fraction of what they award for it. But they know, for one thing, that the government may some day want a piece of their property and the litigants in the present case may well be sitting on a jury deciding this. Also, it is a question of a neighbor versus the elusive big thing called government, which is composed largely of city folk — and they are well able to pay.

It can be seen from these few examples that "Equal Justice Under Law" has a wide variety of meanings within one country, or even among neighboring communities within one state. Actually, however, it is not the law that varies. Once a state statute is written, it is, of course, law for the entire state; but it is the strange interpretations placed on that law, and wide differences of understanding of similar facts, that makes the law mean one thing in a big city and an altogether different thing in a small town.

That interpretation is placed upon it to a large degree by the jury. It is obvious in the marked variances between nothing more complex than the sizes of communities that juries make the logic of law something altogether unpredictable and unrelated.

How can a lawyer tell a client with any degree of certainty what the outcome of a legal action will be in view of this? How can an ordinary citizen have the least conception of his rights under a law that is bent and turned by a multitude of interpreters as they may see fit without any relation to precedence or legal responsibility?

11

Foolish Uses of Juries

Too often juries are dragged into courtrooms for meaningless actions. They are necessary, however, because they are required to be in attendance by the foolish demands of laws or of lawyers. One such instance may be seen in a law that was on the books of Ohio for many years. It made it imperative that a jury be present to sign the results of a will contest suit even though the matters contained in it had already been settled to the satisfaction of the attorneys representing each side.

I was once a participant in such an action, and this is how it worked: One summer morning in the courthouse, a bailiff I know called me in desperation from the corridor to sit on a jury. In answer to my objections that I had not been properly summoned, he said that was unnecessary and that I was needed only to fill a chair. My pay would be five dollars, paid by the taxpayers of course. When I took my place in the box, I was surrounded by courthouse friends. There were bailiffs from other courtrooms, clerks from judges' offices, and visiting attorneys. We solemnly went through the formality of taking an oath to listen to the evidence and to judge the facts as we heard them. Then we were told that a will had been contested and that the opposing parties had reached agreement. We learned that all sides were satisfied with the agreement and that we were to sign a unanimous verdict upholding this mysterious will. We each laughingly signed this strange verdict, accepted the five dollars for service as jurors, and walked from the courtroom.

The great democratic function of the jury safeguard had once more been fulfilled to the satisfaction of the law.

On other occasions I have seen similar procedures gone through when minors have filed suits in personal injuries and then have reached a settlement before the scheduled time for trial. This time the lawyers want an "official" jury verdict as protection. Each juror is paid by the state for his efforts in reaching this "verdict."

Another type of suit in which jurors have looked especially foolish has been that which attempts to decide on the value of a parcel of real estate which an arm of the government seeks to appropriate for some public use such as a new highway or a housing development. This was touched on in the previous chapter. Here jurors are picked on the special basis that they know nothing at all about the value of real estate. They are then taken to the scene of the property and trudge through the land while women jurors snag hose on protruding nails or twigs. Replacement of these stockings is, of course, part of the cost of the trial. But the jurors have officially taken a view of the premises, which usually adds very little, if anything, to their knowledge of its value.

Then they are ready for the trial. They sit through a court routine that quite often becomes exceedingly lengthy. It can last a couple of weeks. By the hour, they hear experts for each side testify to the value of the property. An attempt is made to give the jury an intensive training in methods of real estate appraisal in a short time. High-priced expert appraisers take the witness stand to tell how much the land is worth to developers of homes, to industry, and its value in relation to nearby similar parcels. The land is evaluated by the square foot and by the linear foot along highways.

After awhile, the other side gets its chance. Again witnesses are called to testify what they think of the land's value. Of course, each expert speaks in behalf of the side that called him. The owner's men indicate under oath that the land is worth, let us say, $20,000 and not one cent less. The government's expert, equally well qualified, says it is worth at most $10,000 and not a dime more. Then the jury is sent out to deliberate and come up with the real value of that land. In a large city, the outcome is almost predictable. Most of the time, the jurors agree on a midpoint compromise, and, in our hypothetical case, come back with a verdict of $15,000. On what do they base their verdict? No one knows, except to guess that it was only a compromise on something of which they admittedly knew nothing.

How much more sensible it would be to have evidence such as this given to a panel of three real estate experts who could study the facts and, from their own knowledge, come out with a much more realistic figure.

Then there is the time when the jury signs its appropriation verdict without even knowing what the case is all about. This is a time in real estate appropriations that is similar under law to the settled will contest just described. In the land situation, a jury is summoned; but the parties think they are near an agreement on what the one side will offer and the other side accept as a fair price. So the jury is simply kept waiting while the two parties continue to dicker. This may go on for a couple of days, and for those two days the jurors are paid to sit, do nothing, and keep themselves available.

Finally a settlement is reached between the negotiators. The jury is summoned and marched into its jury box. It is then told, after being given the oath, that an agreement has been reached. The amount on the printed verdict, of course, has not the least meaning to the jurors. They are simply told to sign the official verdict, which they do, and then are disbanded.

In the eyes of the law, the jurors have officially reached an agreement after duly considering and weighing all the evidence on both sides. The jurors themselves, however, just giggle a little self-consciously at the foolishness of their work in court while other more important tasks at home or work go undone. Sometimes it is the lawyer who demands this fruitless signing to have an "official" verdict on record.

One good thing can be said for the foolish uses of juries — the time when they are brought in to sign a verdict only for the legal formality. It is one situation in which they can do the minimum of harm as a fact-finding body. They are not permitted to weigh evidence, and so their decision is free of any bias or prejudices they may have. It is not in their power to do damage to either side, and they preserve the cherished fiction that the jurors are indeed a great display of democracy in action.

Some wits around the courthouse have been known to say it might be worthwhile to maintain them in all procedures in the same fashion. The lawyers in a personal injury case, for example, could present their evidence and arguments to the judge and a panel of experts to reach an area of agreement on liability and what the judgment is worth. Once this is done, it could be presented to jurors as an accomplished fact and they would be asked to sign. Thus, say the courtroom observers, could be maintained both the democracy of the juries and the efficiency of the law. That is, of course, only a fanciful dream, and jurors continue to be summoned for the more important, as well as the trivial and meaningless, aspects of modern courts and trials.

12

Juries Breed Delay

A STORY, WELL-KNOWN IN COURTHOUSE CORRIDORS, GOES TO the effect that one Monday morning two similar personal injury trials started in adjoining counties. In one case, a jury was waived and the parties agreed to have it heard by the judge alone. In the other county, however, the attorneys preferred to assert their full rights and have a full jury trial. By the end of the first day, the first judge had finished hearing the case and had given his decision from the bench, telling how he had weighed the evidence, which facts had influenced his thinking, and what law he had applied. The attorneys had a complete picture in their minds of what had been done, and all that remained was for the winning lawyer to draw up a proper journal entry. In essence, the case was finished and the court was ready for the next matter. As he was going home, the judge passed the neighboring courthouse and learned that the attorneys had just tentatively seated the tenth juror and had adjourned for the day to return the next morning and resume questioning of the remaining panel in search of the last two jurors so that they might be ready to start their case.

This is not unusual.

In the first Dr. R. Bernard Finch trial, described in Chapter 8, the reader will recall it took a full 19 days to select the jury that finally ended the trial in as complete a legal fiasco as had ever been seen.

Not too long ago, a trial of seven boys on charges of murder was held in New York before Judge Irwin D. Davidson. They were charged with having jumped on Michael Farmer, a fifteen-year-old polio victim, who was stabbed, beaten, and kicked to death at a swimming pool. Here the job of picking a jury went on for more than two weeks and had an official record that took up more than 900 pages of typewritten transcript. The judge described it as the longest, most tedious ordeal he had ever endured on the bench. Allegations were made which, if proper, could later have ruined the entire lengthy hearing. By creating a mistrial, they could have forced the entire proceedings to be gone through again. One claim, for example, was that persons of Puerto Rican origin, or women, or Negroes, were deliberately, systematically and intentionally excluded from the jury. Since the defendants were of that nationality and race, it was claimed this was prejudicial to their rights. This problem, needless to say, would never have arisen but for juries as they are today.

It goes without saying that clogged courts and lengthy delay between filing cases and the time when they come up for trial are major problems in our courts. These problems are regularly reported in newspapers and are the continuing concern of judges and bar associations. Yet rare is it that lawyers have the courage to stand in the face of tradition and point to juries as a major factor in the delay.

Litigants turn pale when they are told that it will be at least three to six years before their case comes before a jury.

Stories of hardship are legion. It no longer is news that the injured party sees his medical bills pile up without payment, his family in financially desperate circumstances without money coming in, and waits while his suit languishes in the dusty courthouse files awaiting its turn in the slow, cumbersome system of jury trials.

In one case I covered, the plaintiff fell victim to cancer after the accident for which she sued, and still her original case lay awaiting its turn. Finally, her lawyer desperately pleaded that her case be advanced on the docket—pushing back other cases which had been waiting even longer—and it was. As she lay in the hospital, the lengthy process of selecting a jury began. But she grew constantly weaker. Finally, just as the jury was picked and the trial ready to proceed, word came to the court that she had just died of cancer.

Such cases of hardship are far from rare. The persons involved are the direct victims of the system which others glorify. The old phrase that "justice delayed is justice denied" is so trite that it has all but lost its meaning. Yet its truth can sometimes be all too accurate : even the young and healthy dread the tiresome long delay before their rights are adjudicated.

EVIDENCE FADES AWAY

Of great importance in this problem of delay is its effect on the case itself. Many things can change in a very few years while the case is waiting. Important witnesses die, or move away to distant parts of the country where their key evidence is not available without a great and needless expenditure of money. Or, should the plaintiff be lucky and all his witnesses remain close at hand, the passing years dull their memories. While they could state with certainty within six months the details of the incident they saw, if the time is prolonged to three years or more they are no longer so certain. Their testimony can be more easily shaken by the opposing attorney; the witnesses fail to convince the jury as they would have if they recounted an incident still fresh in their minds.

Of course, it would not be fair to say that the entire blame for delay in the courts falls in the lap of the jury. Some can be attributed to rapidly growing metropolitan areas and the failure to increase the number of judges to keep up with the burgeoning business. It is fair to say, however, that the jury system can properly take a great deal of this blame since much more than a simple increase in the number of judges is needed to handle this situation.

ENGLAND SPEEDS JUSTICE

A friend of mine, a prominent attorney and former president of the Cleveland Bar Association, Wendell A. Falsgraf, has long been sincerely concerned with this problem of delay in justice. While head of the bar, he led a survey of civic leaders into causes of this problem. Here is what Mr. Falsgraf had to say about the situation in a major court of the country, behind in its docket by some three years:

A large segment of the trial bar believes that entirely too many cases are tried to juries, and point to the fact that, commencing with an experimental period during World War I, the British have generally abandoned the use of juries in civil cases. It appears to be the consensus of the British bar that as a result justice has been improved, delay in reaching cases for trial has been eliminated, and substantial economies have been effected.

In England the average time required to try a simple personal injury case in the county or high courts is five hours. These would be cases of either motor accidents, or under the Factory Acts, where no interpretation of law is involved and where the medical reports have been agreed upon. If there is a disputed point of law or disputed medical reports, about seven and a half hours are required to try the case. A case of considerable complexity might be expected to take ten and at the most fifteen hours. The time required to try cases on circuit, otherwise known as 'assizes' court, is about 35 per cent less.

It is interesting to note that in England, where a minimum of cases are tried by jury and where the judiciary is appointed, contested cases involving personal injury may be tried between six to nine months after the commencement of the action. I have been advised by London barristers that whenever the barristers in a case are ready any case may be tried six months after filing. In divorce actions uncontested cases may be tried in six weeks after the filing of the petition, and on an average are tried in from three to six months. In contested cases, the trial takes place within from six months to a year after the filing of the petition.

The federal courts have provided an opportunity to compare the time consumed in the trial of a case before a jury and before a judge without a jury.

All claims under the Federal Tort Claims Act are tried before a judge. There is, therefore, no determination by counsel on either side as to whether or not a jury shall be waived. The average number of hours consumed in court for a trial under the Federal Tort Claims Act is 3.9 and the average time in chambers is 2.3, making a total of 6.2 hours average per case.

In personal injury cases tried before a jury, the average number of hours consumed in court is 9.6 and in chambers 2.8, making a total of 12.4 hours per case. The average number of hours consumed in a personal injury case in which a jury has been waived is 5.4 hours in court, and 2.4 hours in chambers, making a total of 7.8 hours. Where all of the cases are tried without a jury, just half the time is required by the trial judge for the disposition of the cases as against the time required for cases tried to a jury.

It is safe to assume that jury trials on the average take more than twice as long to try as non-jury cases.

As in all legal matters, it is difficult to reach agreement. There are those of the academic side—a few professors whose careers are devoted to theorizing about the law but whose practical experience is limited—who question the value of restricting the use of juries.

They agree that juries take a great deal more time, but they feel that the value of their efforts are such as to make it a more worthy project to add to the ranks of judges in an effort to cut the time lag. This view has found faint support from men who are daily involved with courts, from the newspapers which are concerned with soaring costs already in existence, and from the taxpayers who must pay those costs. Adding more political judges is rarely a popular move with the general public. Its heaviest weight of value rests largely in the minds of the ivory-tower theoreticians.

Should the argument of adding more judges to the bench as a complete solution to the delay problem have any real merit, the lag in cases would also be as pronounced in trials involving equity and the handling of estates where an equal shortage of judges exists. The fact, however, is that the real delay is almost entirely in the jury trial of cases. They constitute a bottleneck and are a real cause in much of the delay.

Judge David W. Peck of New York has bluntly said that the cause of delay is the jury system. It is the inherent slowness of trial by jury—a pace which cannot keep up with the flood of cases coming into court—which creates a bottleneck and prevents timely dispositions. Thus, while the country in its early formative years went at a pace slow enough to absorb jury delays, the movement of public affairs today are such that juries are an unfair drag.

HOW JURIES ARE PICKED

Why do jury trials consume so much valuable court time? Let us step through the courtroom doors to see what happens in a typical civil case. The robed judge is already on the bench and before him are the legal papers of the case. They contain detailed information about the claims of the plaintiff and the answers, or denials, of the defendant. The parties in contention sit at the trial table before him with their lawyers. To one side of them is a vacant jury box.

There are preparatory whispers among them as they await the jury panel. Finally, about 30 persons file into the back of the room and are seated by the judge's assistant, his bailiff. This assistant then calls the first 12 names on his list and they take their places in the jury box. The judge may give all the prospective jurors a preliminary statement in which he cautions them to speak up loudly when answering questions. He advises them briefly on their functions as jurors who must decide only the facts to be presented in court.

The judge then questions to see if there are any jurors who have served on previous cases and whose term may be nearing an end. This is so they will not be carried over into the following week at an inconvenience to them and their families. Other questions of inconvenience are also raised as to those who have pressing business or family problems at home. Those who have valid excuses are dismissed. This may amount to half of the panel in the jury box and they are replaced from those in the rear of the room.

Finally, the attorneys have their chance at the tentative jurors. First the plaintiff's lawyer has the right to question them individually. He asks questions about the juror's job, his wife, his children, his involvement in accidents similar to the one on trial. If the lawyer feels a juror has strong feelings about the pending case, he tries to get the judge to dismiss him for "cause." This means mainly at the behest of the court. If this fails, the lawyer may dismiss the juror himself without any reason. This is the well-known peremptory challenge. Each party to a case has a certain number of peremptory challenges, the number varying among the states. The new juror who ascends to the box to replace the one dismissed then goes through the same process of questioning.

When the plaintiff's lawyer is finished, he takes his seat and the same process is gone through by the defendant's lawyer. By the time the second barrage of questions is completed, several more members of the original panel may have been dismissed and replaced by others from the back of the room.

After the defense lawyer is finished, the questioning then goes back to the plaintiff's lawyer. Somewhere during this process, all the waiting potential jurors may have been used up and the entire process grinds to a stop while the call is sent out for more prospective jurors. When they arrive, the process is resumed. Thus it can be seen that the example given at the start of this chapter is far from unusual. It can be understood, too, how it took 19 days to seat a jury in the Finch murder trial.

Sometimes, in a particularly important trial, jurors are questioned out of the hearing of their fellow panelists so that they may not be influenced by answers given to questions asked of those summoned earlier. This, too, adds a great deal of time consumed. In one instance which I observed, the lengthy process of picking a jury was practically completed. All that remained was the selection of the last juror. The man who was called survived all the questioning. Then came the final routine question : was he personally acquainted with any of the lawyers in the case? His reply was properly negative — and then he beamingly volunteered an additional statement. Although he had never met the plaintiff's lawyer, he had read of him frequently in the local newspapers and he was a great admirer of his courtroom dramatics and the large verdicts they won for him. Opposing counsel was on its feet immediately with objections that this admiring comment had unduly influenced the rest of the jury which had already been agreed upon. The judge reluctantly conceded that this was a good possibility and dismissed the entire jury which had been impaneled and the lugubrious, time-consuming process was started all over again.

FINALLY THE CASE STARTS

All this, it must be remembered, takes place before the case really starts. Let us say that all the hurdles are overcome and the hearing is ready to proceed. The plaintiff's attorney starts with an opening statement. In it he tells what the case is all about in his estimation and outlines what evidence he expects to present to prove his case. This can vary in the amount of time consumed, depending upon the complexity of the case and the skill of the lawyer. Unfair statements here, too, can be the basis for a mistrial and a need to go back to selecting a new jury. When this attorney is finished, counsel for the other side then takes time to present the opposition view and to sketch out his case. When this is all done, the case is ready to be properly launched with its witnesses and other evidence. At its completion, each side is given time for its final arguments to the jury, or the summation as it is sometimes called. Time for this can vary from a half hour to a day or more, depending on the length of the trial and its importance. Then comes the charge to the jury, or the reading to it of the law that is applicable to the case, by the judge. This, too, can vary in length, but it is not unusual to have it last a couple of hours. Finally, the jury is sent to its room to deliberate. At this point, the judge can call for the next case if he wishes, but quite often he relaxes in chambers instead and chats with the lawyers while they await the jury's return. If after a reasonable time, however, the jury cannot reach agreement, it is dismissed as a hung jury and the case is set for retrial at a later date and the same procedure is repeated.

Now let us take the same case without a jury. It will be heard by the judge alone or, if it is a major criminal case which could carry the death sentence, by a panel of three judges. The judge has had a chance to read all the legal papers pertaining to the case before the lawyers come into his room (often he does this at home at night). These tell the claims of the plaintiff, outline the damages, and allege the negligence of the defendant. The written answer of the defendant gives his denials and briefly tells his side of the story.

Thus, when the lawyers come in, the judge already has a firm grasp of the case. When the lawyers give their opening statements, therefore, they are shortened considerably because both sides know what is already in the judge's hands. There also is no need to waste time with dramatics because it is known they will usually not influence the judge. If a lawyer should launch upon such actions, the judge will interrupt him and tell him to confine himself to the basic questions. As the case proceeds before the judge, he may interrupt at various times to clarify a point being developed or to cut short an unnecessary line of questioning that has no bearing on the legal issues involved. He would hesitate to do this before a jury for fear of influencing them by his actions. Once the case is completed, the summation by the lawyers will be short and direct, held to the issues of the case. In all this there is, of course, no chance of mistrial through errors on the part of jurors or misconduct of attorneys in an effort to influence them. There obviously is no chance of a hung jury, since a judge clearly cannot disagree with himself over his conclusions. In the case of a panel of three judges, in most instances agreement by a majority of two judges is enough to reach a valid verdict. In the meantime, no time has been wasted in a lengthy reading of the law which too often has no meaning to the jurors and is ignored by them.

CUTS TIME AND COST

So it is that valuable time is cut from court trials by proceeding without a jury. This is the time that can be used for the next trial, according to those who favor elimination of juries. Some will say, however, that the verdict is quicker in coming from a jury since they must reach a conclusion before they are allowed to disband. A judge, on the other hand, may take a matter under advisement and it may be months before his decision is issued. This is rare — although an instance has been known where a judge has died before being able to issue his verdict — and outside pressures usually push a judge into disposing of a case before others which follow pile too high upon him. Also, it has been known that judges work on these decisions in their evening hours at home rather than take up court time for such efforts.

Not only does this save valuable court time, however, but it is also a major factor in cutting costs. The cost of jury trial in dollars is much higher than anyone could imagine. It has been estimated that in the trial court of New York County, the cost is more than $750 a day for each courtroom. This includes the cost for court facilities, clerks, attendants, judge, and jury. It can be seen, therefore, that the very average jury trial which lasts about four days will cost the taxpayers some $3,000. Often this is more than the amount involved in the case being heard, so in those instances, the taxpayers evidently would be money ahead if they just paid the claim without going through the trial.

Added to this should be the fees paid to lawyers since the more time they spend in court the higher their charge will be. It is not unusual to hear a personal injury lawyer, whose fee is contingent on victory, accuse the defense lawyer of using delaying tactics, thus increasing the latter's fee, which is paid on a per diem basis.

These excessive delays and high costs are among the reasons why other countries have abandoned, or never adopted, the jury system. They are factors in influencing litigants to settle their cases out of court, sometimes at amounts lower than they are actually worth. They show why many litigants prefer arbitration and other means of avoiding juries, with their attendant delays.

PART IV

Roots Of The Trouble

13

Ideal–and Real

PROBLEMS FACED BY JURIES IN THE VARIOUS AREAS JUST discussed are a natural product of fundamental difficulties inherent in juries. Now we turn to the fundamentals themselves. The ideal of a typical American jury presents a handsome picture. It is seen as a broad cross section of society, composed of persons wise in the ways of the world. They are capable of detecting fraud; they are rarely deceived by untruth; any prejudices they have are either discarded in the performance of their functions or, at worst, are balanced out among twelve divergent views to reach a distillation of honesty and justice. It is presumed that their conclusions are reached through open-minded discussions of differing views until the twelve independent judgments reach an equitable common ground. Although all of this is fine from the ivory-tower level, from the practical point of view it leaves many disturbing questions.

The first fallacy arises in the thought that the jury indeed is a broad cross section of society: any trial lawyer knows that certain classes of people just never appear in a panel of prospective jurors. An Illinois congresswoman, Marguerite Stitt Church, once noted that litigants and prominent attorneys have often complained that many well-qualified prospective jurors are being excused from that important service with the result that important cases are frequently tried by jurors of somewhat limited capacity for understanding and judgment. There are, in fact, in some states extensive exemptions for prospective jurors, which may include not only lawyers, but school teachers, staffs of colleges, undertakers, all persons over sixty-five, and physicians and dentists. At least one state exempts judicial, civil, naval, and military officers, as well as National Guardsmen and local government officials. Also, chiropodists, optometrists, and druggists; officers of prisons and jails; employees aboard boats and ships on navigable waters; express agents, mail carriers, and employees of telephone and telegraph companies; keepers of ferries and toll gates; firemen, brakemen, motormen, and conductors of railroads. As one wag commented, "apparently all are kept out except the halt and the blind."

Making the trouble even worse is the fact that in addition to those excluded by law, officials are willing to excuse citizens who wish to escape jury service for financial reasons and because of inconveniences. The classic example of this is the case of *Thiel v. Southern Pacific* (328 U.S. 217) where an entire class of citizens not exempt by law was automatically excused. Facts in this case were that a passenger on the train had jumped out the window of a moving train. His claim was that the railroad knew he was out of his normal mind and should not have accepted him as a passenger and should not have left him unguarded. An objection was raised to the makeup of the jury. It was argued that the jurors were mostly business executives and did not present the required cross section. The only question reaching the United States Supreme

Court was that of the makeup of the jury. Evidence showed that both the clerk of court and the jury commissioner testified that they deliberately excluded from the panel all persons working for a daily wage. The clerk of court was quoted as saying: "If I see a name John Jones and that he is a long-shoreman, I do not put his name in. If a juror is called on a venire and says he is working for ten dollars a day and cannot work for four dollars, the judge has never made one of them serve." The jury commissioner had purposely excluded all the iron craft, bricklayers, carpenters, and machinists because, due to the financial hardship involved, the judge ordinarily let them go anyhow.

Thus it may be seen that the ideal picture of a jury composed of a fair cross section of society, bringing to bear the views of divergent personalities on a problem, is not in reality always the case despite the widely held assumption that it is.

Even in those instances where certain valuable types of jurors are not excluded by law and are pushed through by jury officials, they face another obstacle in the careful screening by lawyers in the selection of favorable juries. It is not at all uncommon in a case involving mechanical failure due to flaws in engineering, for example, for a lawyer to have dismissed from a panel a professional engineer who might understand the technical facts to be presented in evidence. Those excused even include former engineering students who have since turned to other work. The reason given for releasing a person who, in good logic, should make a particularly capable juror is the argument that their knowledge prejudices them to the facts and evidence to be presented. It is said that by reason of their training they already hold opinions on certain points which might come up during the trial and would not view them with the cold objectivity of a person completely devoid of knowledge on the subject. However, what the lawyer means, too often, is that he fears his arguments may not be able to influence in his direction the mind of a person who is able to understand the information given to him in court. The same reasoning holds true for objections toward physicians on a jury hearing a medical or personal injury case and of other examples of a similar nature.

ARE JURORS REALLY INDEPENDENT?

An argument of the legal idealist is that a jury verdict is the product of the equal interaction of independent judgment of facts by the various jurors. In other words, each person has reached his own conclusion and, by a reasonable averaging out of these conclusions, a true group verdict is reached. The hollowness of this argument is quickly grasped by anyone who has ever participated in group activities. He knows that practically any group will divide itself into a leader and followers; one person dominates and offers the most persuasive argument, whether on which restaurant to go to after a theater — or what verdict should be returned. Others in the group may offer token suggestions in an attempt to show a form of independence, but that is as far as it goes. Once their show of independence has been made, they are ready to follow the leader and agree with his verdict.

Thus it can be seen that quite often what is described as a joint verdict of all twelve minds on the panel is in reality the decision of one strong mind and the passive acceptance by those who are weaker and easy to influence. In most instances, it is good for the efficient administration of justice that a powerful mind can lead the weaker. Were this not the case, many juries would be hopelessly deadlocked by the insistence of several strong, independent thinkers that their views were the only valid ones. There would be a sudden surge of "hung" juries. Such cases then face another costly, time-consuming retrial to the unhappiness of judges, counsel, and litigants.

Enough independent jurors and cases might never be finally decided.

As far back as 1875, when life was much simpler, William Forsyth said in his book *Trial by Jury* (p. 206):

Possibility that a few "unreasonable" men, or even one man, may hang the jury inclines courts to exalt the passive virtues for the few rather than the active virtues for the many. So a proper "deference" to others' opinions is continually urged upon juries. Obstinacy and stubbornness is condemned. But obstinacy may be in fact the result of sincere conviction and the court must not by instructions discourage proper independence of mind. As a matter of fact, there is probably much less danger in obstinance than there is of too ready compliance. Few men like to appear obstinate and unyielding. It is an ungracious thing to stand out against numbers, especially so when by so doing many others besides one's self are put to inconvenience. Under these circumstances a man will often be persuaded to give way although he remains unconvinced.

While such juries may lead to the good administration of justice, as reflected in a court's statistics of the number of cases resolved in a certain period, it is highly questionable whether such decisions lead to good justice. And, after all, good justice is what litigants have come for in their attendance at court.

Compare the practical operation of juries if the courts are to step ahead with their dockets with the idealistic views voiced by the courts themselves. In the case of *Richardson v. Coleman* (131 Indiana 210) the court saw the jury verdict in this idealistic light:

The law does not expect any compromise on the part of jurors. It expects every juror to exercise his individual judgment, and that when a verdict is agreed to it will be the verdict of each individual juror. . . . The law does not expect, nor does it tolerate, the agreement by a juror upon a verdict unless he is convinced that it is right. . . . To say that jurors may compromise on a verdict is to say that twelve jurors, all differing in their views as to what verdict ought to be returned, without any of them changing their views, may agree upon a verdict which is not believed to be right by any considerable number of the jurors, but agreed to as a matter of expediency in order to dispose of the case without the approval of the consciences of any considerable number of the panel approving it.

To those personally acquainted with the actual operation of a trial, these words seem a little quaint and far-removed from harsh realities. It is not surprising to court observers to see judges exerting a modest pressure upon their jurors to reach compromise and avert a retrial. I have seen judges, with agreement of counsel, keep jurors at work long past their normal quitting time with the apparent hope that jurors beginning to weaken in their views might be pushed into agreement by sheer weariness. This, in effect, would bring about a surrender of individual judgment and the acceptance of a compromise.

While compromise has usually been a key factor in reaching agreement in a jury room — and quite often that means compromise with justice — it is nonetheless a known fact that a judge may without fear of reversal urge his jurors to come to an agreement. This gentle pushing from the keeper of the court is often enough to bring over the recalcitrant ones. In fact, even a more insistent attitude by judges has rarely been grounds for reversal by a reviewing court.

The pressure from the bench quite often joins with the more virulent pressure from fellow jurors to wilt even some of the more independent minds, bring about an end to lengthy debate, and effect a compromise of justice. It has been said that it is hard for one man to stand out permanently against eleven others locked up in one room with him and clamoring to be let out.

JURORS FOR JUSTICE OR VICTORY

Ostensibly, a jury is selected for the primary purpose of seeking justice. Therefore, lawyers, as officers of the court, should ideally present all pertinent evidence in the forum of justice with the hope that truth will prevail. If this were so, any jury would be proper so long as it could objectively and fairly listen to both sides and, in the end, render a just verdict. Unfortunately, the practice of law forces those who wish to survive in the continuing contest to be much more realistic. It is not enough just to present a good case effectively; the payoff comes in the winning. In the harsh reality of life, a lawyer gets paid for a victory—and he knows it. With this thought in mind, the successful trial lawyer bends every effort to achieve victory. It is not enough just to have a good case, a good preparation, and good ability. He must also have a good jury. This means a jury good to his cause, having inherently a tendency to favor him.

In lawyer's talk, there is a plaintiff's jury: one which will show a high degree of compassion for the person bringing the suit and a certain freedom with the money of others, such as the defendant or his insurance company. And there is a defendant's jury, which is cautious and conservative: it must find strong proof of wrongdoing on the part of the defendant before it awards anything, and if it should finally be convinced would be tightfisted in the amount it awards. It is the practical task of the attorney for each side to pick a jury which will best serve his needs. This is a talent all to itself and it comes naturally with a capable trial lawyer.

Although jurors cast suddenly into the unreal world of a hotly contested law suit are usually not aware of it, they are nevertheless being studied as they are being selected with much more attention and cold analysis than a professional psychiatrist gives to a highly troubled mental patient. Their every move is observed; their gestures are noted; even the lines of their faces are read for any hint they might give of the owner's attitude toward life, money, or anything that might have a bearing on the pending case. Lawyers are estimating which man might be the strong one in the jury—the one who might sway others—and what his convictions might be; they are guessing which ones might be tough and hard to convince; but the jurors need not fear, because it is all part of the game of justice in which they are suddenly cast as star players; and they will be treated royally—as long as they are in a position to grant what the lawyers seek.

One close friend of mine, one of the most capable trial lawyers I knew, a man of rare talent and an incredible string of high-priced victories, was to the day of his death candid about this very practical side of the law. His name was Abe H. Dudnik and it was he who won the $625,000 record-setting verdict in the insect-bite case noted at the beginning of this book and which will be described in greater detail in the Appendix. Mr. Dudnik was once asked how he picked juries that were so favorable to him that his victories had become legendary. His quick answer showed the result of many years of studying personalities as reflected in faces. These were years of persuading twelve persons that his client of the moment was entitled to large sums of money in damages. His conclusion, quite naturally, was that it was not wrong to attempt to get jurors who have sympathy, compassion, and the capacity to be moved deeply for others.

Asked if he could give specific examples, he turned to famous persons in history whom he had never met but whose faces he could study at length from their photographs or paintings. In each of these faces he read a message that was tied directly to the possibility of a favorable verdict: the target of his profession. For example: Mr. Dudnik said he would not want Mona Lisa on his hypothetical jury; he felt Mona Lisa's features were elusive and difficult to categorize. "She has lips that show kindness, but could also be bitter. I can't judge her and when I can't judge a person I stay away."

On the other hand, Mr. Dudnik thought he would accept Whistler's Mother, although he was at a disadvantage in not seeing her whole face. He said he liked what he saw in her profile, which to him displayed such attributes as sympathy, peacefulness, refinement, kindliness, and sweetness. But he would accept her as a juror with some reservations, he said, because "I realize she would not lead a fight for what she thinks. She might be for my client, but she would not be a strong factor on a jury."

When it came to going out of his way for a juror, however, the one Mr. Dudnik would choose was George Washington. He admitted he was fascinated by Gilbert Stuart's oil paintings of Washington. To Mr. Dudnik, Washington's entire face indicated strength : "If he were for my plaintiff, he would go all the way for a high verdict and take many of the jurors with him." He added that Washington's face "shows the battles he had been through in war and politics. He experienced the agony of Valley Forge with his men, and so he would not be likely to turn down the claim of a man who had been through pain and suffering."

Another juror who would find a warm welcome on the Dudnik panel would be Rembrandt due in large part to the Dutch painter's self-portraits. Here is what they meant to a veteran trial lawyer : "I am especially fond of four self-portraits, the first done in 1634 when he was thirty, happily married and with lots of friends. That picture shows a nice intelligent face, round full lips that don't go up or down, and soft eyes. The next, in 1650, shows a reflective, troubled countenance. He had financial troubles. Within a few years his wife had left him and he had been accused of fathering an illegitimate child. The emotional wounds are in his visage. By

1660, Rembrandt had had it and his self-portrait showed it. There was pain, but no trace of cruelty. He was not blaming anyone for his troubles and he didn't want to see anybody else suffer."

However, not all artists would remain on this imaginary jury. The Spanish painter Goya, for example, would be dropped immediately with a peremptory challenge because, to the eyes of the lawyer, Goya's self portraits from nineteen to eighty-one tend to show him as a hard, cynical man who elbowed his way through life. The plaintiff's lawyer prefers a person with a full, "liberal" face; but a smooth, unlined one hints at lack of feeling.

Others who would be acceptable to this jury for the plaintiff included such persons as Alfred E. Smith, former governor of New York — who, according to the lawyer, was a nice guy who came up from the sidewalks of New York and who never lost the touch of the common man — and New York's baseball strongman, Lou Gehrig, "a smiling, thick-lipped man of conviction who would be wonderful on my jury."

Among other "favorable" jurors would be: Justice Oliver Wendell Holmes (" 'The Great Dissenter' would be an ideal juror because he had the courage of his convictions"); Florence Nightingale ("She did so much for humanity during the Crimean War and afterward that she would have to be a woman of compassion and courage"); George Washington Carver (because "I like what shows in his eyes"); Will Rogers (because "His face shows both strength and softness").

Since Mr. Dudnik could not pluck his jurors from museums, however, he had a special philosophy for those who poured through the courtrooms where he worked. He prefers the factory workers and the waitresses, the bartenders and the cab drivers. His reasons were blunt: "They have the feel of the man in the street — the common touch — and are more likely to give a higher award than an engineer, accountant, or chemist. Technical people are more interested in the factual than in the future of the injured party."

Mr. Dudnik's views of his successful juries were honest and straightforward. There was nothing devious about them; they were spoken as the facts of life and the realities of law. He gave his views openly in a night law class he taught and recounted them just as openly for a Sunday supplement article. This practitioner's evaluation of juries is much more believable than the abstract reasonings of their value given in the academic views of the theoreticians.

Make no mistake about it, Mr. Dudnik was wholeheartedly in favor of the jury system as it is now. It had been good to him and he found worth in it. But to those who seek the ideal of equality in justice for both parties to a lawsuit, whether or not their respective attorneys have this talent with juries, the present system leaves an uncomfortable feeling that there is something to be desired.

This feeling stems from the belief that courts are meant to provide justice for litigants rather than a dramatic display before a hand-picked jury with a verdict as the prize. There is the disquieting thought that jurors are supposed to be calm evaluators of the facts, instead of ones whose emotions are captivated and guided by a capable attorney. Part of the fault may lie in the fact that lawyers have a wide latitude in selecting their jury, whereas the judges play a secondary role, merely sitting back and seeing to it that the lawyer, in picking the panel, does not go beyond the bounds of propriety arbitrarily set by the judge in that particular courtroom. Should one lawyer step beyond the bounds, it is fully expected that this will be made up by his adversary since, after all, one side is supposed to offset and correct the efforts and zeal of the other.

In England, however, the judges perform almost the entire selection of juries, in those rare instances where they are still in use. Barristers have little chance to select and weed out jurors because of the way they tilt their heads or smile. Here, perhaps because of the very fact that jurors are more objective and less under the influence of the lawyers, the juries are rapidly fading away, with constantly larger numbers of cases being heard by the judges alone. After all, what sense is there in going through the complicated procedure of selecting a jury if it cannot be conditioned in your direction?

JURORS AND THE LAW

Probably the most discouraging part of a trial is the time when the judge tries to cram into twelve non-legal minds all the law applicable to the case at hand. The blank expressions on the faces of the citizen-jurors is pitiful; it is matched only by the bleak look on the judge as he plods through the legal terminology that he knows is making little, if any, impression on his listeners. Take, for example, this segment from the law, better known as the charge to the jury, in the previously mentioned insect bite case which brought the $625,000 verdict:

By a safe place to work the Court instructs you as a matter of law, that in this case that means the railroad must maintain its tracks and premises in the same manner as a reasonable man ought to maintain them in the circumstances there prevailing, having in mind the standard of care must be commensurate to the dangers of the business, and is measured by what is reasonable and ordinary care and by what is reasonably foreseeable under the circumstances.

Imagine that quote being given orally — and without a pause or a chance to take notes or ask questions for clarification — to a group of average citizens untrained in either the law or rapid abstract absorption.

But that is only the beginning. Specific phrases in that paragraph have a special meaning in the law. For example, what exactly is meant by "ordinary care" in that very small portion just quoted from the 32-page charge? Here is what it means to the law:

"Ordinary Care" means that degree of care which persons of ordinary care and prudence are accustomed to use and employ, under the same or similar circumstances, in order to conduct the enterprise engaged in to a safe and successful termination, having due regard to the rights of others and the object to be accomplished. Ordinary care, therefore, requires in different circumstances different degrees of watchfulness, so that what would be reasonable or ordinary care under one state of circumstances would not be such in another. By the term "Ordinary Care," as here used, is meant such care as ordinarily prudent persons ordinarily exercise, or are accustomed to exercise, under the same or similar circumstances, in conducting and carrying on the same or similar business, and this applies to the defendant so far as the negligence complained of is concerned, as well as to the plaintiff in regard to contributory negligence on his part.

Try that one out on a jury! And, by the way, the term "ordinarily prudent person" also has specific meaning in law.

Thus it may be seen by these small examples that the task so casually assigned to citizen jurors is indeed gigantic; for all but a few exceptional jurors, it can even be practically impossible. Yet the law continues to go under the assumption that this type of material is clearly understood and properly applied in trials that are of the utmost importance to the participants.

The law, however, is in the hands of practical men. They are often fully aware of its shortcomings. Sometimes they become questioning men, as was a Federal Judge, the late Jerome Frank, in his article "What Courts Do in Fact," pub-

lished in the *Illinois Law Review*.[1] He noted that the usual
method for describing the verdict in the jury system can be put
down as a formula : $R \times F = D$. Spelled out, this means Rules
of law (the court's charge), times Facts (what the jury hears
from the witness stand or sees in exhibits), equals the Decision.

But, Judge Frank went on to say :

No description could be more misdescriptive of what really
happens. In truth, a "contested" jury trial goes thus : The jury
is exposed to testimony, to the sight and sound of witnesses, to
the dramatic performances of the lawyers; then the judge intones
in the jury's presence a treatise of law-in-discourse. This treatise
is largely unintelligible to the jury. Most jurymen tell us that
the judge's rules are ignored in the jury room. The jury's verdict
is often a result of gambling technique—or worse. No attempt
is made by juries to separate out the R [rules] and the F [facts].
They bring in a verdict—their D [decision]. . . . That D becomes the judge's D . . . unless he grants a new trial. If he
does so, then a new trial is had before another jury which goes
through the same performance. . . . No one knows—and no one
is allowed to prove—what was the jury's R or the jury's F.
Indeed there is no jury R or jury F—there is only a jury D.

It would seem evident from this that the ritual of going
through a fought-over, complicated, and precise jury charge
has little practical meaning. It is a ceremony tied to nothing.
Apparently the normal procedure for a jury is to reach a
conclusion—largely based on emotions rather than solid fact
and legal procedure—and then see if it can make up reasons
to fit that conclusion, and make it appear logical. Although
it is not really even necessary to make up reasons since in the
general verdict the jury does not have to write them down or
explain them to anyone.

Yet it must be remembered that in the curious ceremonial

[1] *Illinois Law Review*, Volume 25 (1932), pp. 645, 651–652.

of a trial, these rules—or charges of law—have been long labored over by the judge and argued over by the lawyers. The counsel fought hard over prejudices or dangers to their client in nuances they saw in the wording or the emphasis.

But why the strong desire to retain this meaningless ritual? Charles C. McCarter, an assistant attorney general of Kansas, said that some people answer that it upholds one of the basic principles of our government, that we have a government by law, not by men. By preserving the legal rules and enunciating them to the jury in the form of instructions, it is made to appear that these instructions are the law and that our government truly is one of law, not men. It provides mental comfort for those who crave logical and legal justice in form.

McCarter wrote in the *University of Kansas Law Review*:[2]

I have read that the profession [of law] knows and even applauds this myth. The proponents of the myth think greater justice is rendered in those "hard" cases when the instructions are forgotten and justice is found according to the "general ideas of what is best under the circumstances." They feel the general rules of law are often too harsh for one particular situation. The right and duty of a jury is to mitigate these general rules to avoid harshness. Thus it is proper for the jury to render a verdict that is contrary to law.

I must confess that all this to me is most singularly an example of government by men, not by law, and breaks the very ideal which the ritual itself seeks to establish. Furthermore, if such ignorance and illogic are attendant of our jury system, there should be some changes made.

PITY THE POOR JUROR

It should again be pointed out that all this is not meant to be critical of those honest citizens summoned from their homes

[2] Volume 4 *University of Kansas Law Review* 1956, p. 425.

to give up time for jury service. They are in many instances, indeed, to be pitied. The conditions under which they labor are far from the best. In the eyes of the idealist, jurors have ample time in which to ponder the important questions they must decide. Their surroundings are imagined to be conducive to deep concentration and free discussion. They are believed to be given every opportunity to reach the best possible conclusions.

But then there is reality.

The jurors, themselves the most naïve neophytes to this bewildering judicial process, are herded together, made to wait tedious long hours with little to do, suddenly pushed into situations for which they have little ability, less training, and no interest whatsoever, and ordered to take temporary command of the judicial ship. The situation exists across the country; few areas are exempt. Listen to the words of a perceptive observer who is not a spokesman for any legal interests. The voice is that of James Rowe, an editorial writer for the Corpus Christi, Texas, *Caller-Times*. His views were reported in the April, 1961, *Journal of the American Judicature Society* (p. 211) in an article "The Plight of the Juror."

He opens with the discouraging — but highly realistic — view that Corpus Christi lawyers and judges have come rather lately to the realization that public confidence in the administration of justice in state courts has continued to decline through the years. One of the most disturbing manifestations of this crisis in confidence is the growing reluctance of many people, especially business and professional men, to serve as jurors. Rowe depicts the atmosphere of the court house as "completely alien and forbidding" to the outsider. In this he is in accord with the majority of first views of citadels of justice across the country. The usual atmosphere is that of drab walls, and behind them a small army of public servants toiling in a veritable rabbit-warren of offices, busily performing work that is too often deadly routine in nature.

Here is how Rowe describes what happens to the unwary citizen suddenly forced to administer justice:

He is directed to a courtroom where, after some delay, he answers to his name as the clerk calls the roll. Then he takes an oath (often heard imperfectly) "to true answers make concerning such questions as may be propounded to you touching upon your qualifications and service as a juror. . . ." The braver men, or those with prior experience, rise to explain to the judge that they would suffer extreme hardship if forced to serve as a juror—they may or may not be excused, depending on the number of jurors available and the mood of the judge or his ability to detect shirkers.

Once he is accepted as a prospective juror he becomes something of a prisoner. After the usual delays he may be excused and ordered to report back the next morning, or he may be ordered to report to a specific court. There he may be selected as a juror in a civil or criminal case, or he may be excused with an admonition to return at some later date.

If he is selected as a juror, the individual in both civil and criminal cases is introduced to another ordeal. He may spend much of his time outside the courtroom, walking the corridors aimlessly or, if he is lucky, finding a seat on a hard bench, while lawyers argue points of law before the judge. If he is a civil case juror he may go home for the night. But if he is selected for the trial of a criminal case he is herded by the bailiffs to hotel rooms at night if the trial lasts more than one day. For this he gets $4.00 a day and a free hotel room, but he must pay for his own meals.

Many, many jurors complain bitterly about the time they "waste" in trying "piddling" cases, or of the inexplicable delays or the interminable waiting in hallways while something they do not understand takes place in the courtroom. In all too many cases the individual makes a mental vow never to serve as a juror again if he can possibly avoid it.

Even this picture, however, dark though it is, is only part of the entire problem. It shows only the physical discomforts of jurors. Equally as important are the frustrations to conscientious citizens, eager to do a good job, who find themselves helpless in the mental manipulations as described in the preceding section. They are sincerely eager to understand both the evidence and the law and to perform their functions properly, but they are overwhelmed by the obstacles.

As the time for decision approaches to act on a final verdict, they suddenly find themselves under pressure of time : pushes from fellow jurors, requests to speed up action from the judges. Time comes to eat and some are reluctant to leave in the middle of a discussion that is becoming heated. Others become angry at the discomfort of their enforced hunger. The very heat of the talk leads to other pressures for the more sensitive person, who may be pushed into reaching an agreement which does not coincide with his own views if for no other reason than to get out of an unpleasant situation.

Even veteran judges often find it difficult to reach agreement on facts. In several situations with which I am acquainted, defendants in first-degree murder cases waived juries and were heard by three judges. The highly experienced judges had no difficulty in reaching agreement on what the law was in these cases, but they ran into great areas of disagreement when it came to the facts and found it most difficult to reach unanimity. Yet this is exactly the area in which we ask citizen jurors to operate.

14

Problems of
Putting a Jury Together

A MAJOR QUESTION WHICH THOSE FAVORING WIDE USE OF
juries have been unable to answer is that of how should a jury
be put together. They have the glib academic answer, "From
a broad cross-section of the community," but run into difficulties when faced with such practical issues as the placement
of Negroes on juries in southern states, or of trying to use
women in states where they are not required to serve under law.

As pointed out earlier, juries in state courts are selected
largely by the lawyers in the case. They naturally try to pick
those they feel would be most sympathetic to their causes. This
quite often rests on sex, religion, and race, each carrying its
own prejudices which the lawyer hopes to exploit.

This was emphasized in an incident I observed when, after
a trial, a lawyer shouted at his jury that they had returned a
low verdict for his Negro client because they were "bigoted

and prejudiced against the minority group for which he stood."
This is a situation with which academic supporters of juries
have probably never been confronted and which they would
find hard to understand.

The effect of women on juries has often been discussed
informally by lawyers. Their acceptance or rejection rested on
the type of case at hand. For example, in one case where the
woman victim had to wear a wig briefly, after a minor accident
to her hair from a home hair spray, the lawyer was wise in
selecting a predominantly male jury. Every one of the men
voted in her favor. The minor opposition came from the
women. Yet in another case, where a woman shot and killed
her husband, who had a record of beating her, a majority of
women was deliberately picked with the thought that they
would have greater sympathy for the mistreated wife than for
the dead husband.

Despite these views of practical trial lawyers whose reputation hangs to a large degree on their ability to select proper
juries, the ivory tower of academic research persists in attribu-
ting to women a strange aura of calmness and ability to pacify
the heat of debate. In an article published in the April, 1961,
Journal of the American Judicature Society, page 206, for
example, Wallace M. Rudolph, of the Chicago bar, formerly
assistant editor of the *Journal* and an instructor at the University of Chicago Law School, wrote:

From a study of the transcripts of the jury deliberations (in
mock trials), it was determined that the women play the role of
mediators. In the sociologist's terminology, they show solidarity,
tension release, and agreement. Men, on the other hand, tend to
delve into the issues of the case and express their opinions. Again

in the terms of the sociologist, men give suggestions, opinions, and orientations. Such activities, necessary as they are, lead to tensions and antagonisms. This was borne out in the study which showed that men had showed more instances of tension and antagonism than women.

The role of women, then, was to break the tension and help the group come to some agreement. The importance of this role in jury deliberations cannot be over-emphasized in a system that requires a unanimous verdict. The cost to society and to the parties of a hung jury is so great that any reasonable method of avoiding hung juries must be preserved and extended.

Probably the best analogy to the functioning of women on the jury can be drawn from everyday experience. Everyone is familiar with the normal social discussion of politics and religion. In such cases it is usually the men who go to the issues and become heated and antagonistic while the women look for a way of breaking the tension and stressing areas of agreement. This is the same process that occurs in the jury room when men trying to find a solution come to different conclusions and become antagonistic.

This is indeed a pleasant picture, and is apparently acceptable in academic circles. But compare it with the realities in the Finch case, for example, which were discussed in Chapter 8. Far from serving as mediators, their presence helped stir up antagonisms that brought about exactly the opposite result, and the nation was shocked with the carryings-on in the jury room. From this one case that was revealed, it can only be guessed at how many others go unpublicized.

But what of the "equal justice for all" desired of juries in the objective application of criminal statutes? Mr. Rudolph noted that the major differences in voting preferences between men and women came in cases involving the home and juveniles (an expected situation, since women should have a greater knowledge and interest in these areas of litigation):

Thus in the deliberations concerning the recording of the Durham case involving a plea of not guilty by reason of insanity of an eighteen-year-old boy, women in each socio-economic class voted to find the defendant not guilty in significantly greater numbers than men of the same class. It is clear from these votes that women on the whole are more sympathetic than men to young offenders.

On the other hand, it was found that in an incest case involving a father and a daughter, the women divided into two groups. One group was more hostile to the defendant than the men, while the other group was less hostile. The first group of women were the mothers while the second group was made up of single women and working wives. The desire of mothers to protect the home with criminal sanctions could not become clearer than evidenced by this vote. A practical result of excluding married women with children through the volunteer system of choosing women jurors deprives the community in cases involving the family of the views of the group most vitally interested in preserving the home—the mothers.

A lawyer defending a man accused of incest would, quite obviously, be foolish to accept mothers on his jury. The prosecutor would fight to get them on. As a result, the case might well be won or lost in this battle of selection—before a single shred of evidence was brought into court. It is hardly to be imagined that this was the result intended by those who founded the jury system, but it is the practical reality of a modern trial.

Impressive though academic arguments may appear, they are in marked contrast to the problems of practical life. This is illustrated by the opinion of an Arkansas court where women were still being excluded from criminal trials. In *Bailey v. State*, the court in refusing to reverse a conviction for rape because women were excluded from the jury said :

Criminal court trials often involve testimony of the foulest kind, and sometimes require consideration of indecent conduct, the use of filthy and loathsome words, references to intimate sex relationships, and other elements that would prove humiliating, embarrassing and degrading to a lady . . . while the right of the commissioners to call women unquestionably exists . . . a defendant who complains that due process was denied must show something more than the continuing failure of jury commissioners to call women for service in a division of the court where the innate refinement peculiar to women would be assailed by verbal expression, gestures, conversations from which most would recoil.

It can be seen from this that at least one court is not completely convinced of the necessity for talents of women as mediators in the criminal courts.

OTHER BENEFICIAL VIEWS MISSED

If the benefits of women's views are often missed in jury rooms, the ladies are hardly alone in their exclusion. Missing even more are the level-headed views of business executives, professional people, and Negroes. These people are not seen on juries for a variety of reasons.

For example: when the call for jury service comes, the leading businessmen suddenly find they have other things to do which are much more important to their well-being. They discover a multitude of reasons for their non-appearance, not the least of which is the financial hardship and damage to their business brought about by their absence. Therefore, it would appear as though clerks are more easily spared than their supervisors; so the former often sit in judgment on cases involving thousands of dollars — or the lives of men. This, despite the fact that executives are accustomed to handling large sums of money and that their daily tasks may well involve the analysis of personalities.

Then there are those who find the patriotic way out. In Ohio, for example, members of the National Guard are exempt from jury service — and not only members, but those who contribute funds to the guard and are thus given a type of honorary membership. Thus, the patriots also have the benefits of their views denied to the litigants.

Finally, there are those whose beneficial views are denied by virtue of their race. This is most obvious in the case of Negroes, where an appalling lack of them is found, particularly in juries of southern states; and they are often kept at a minimum in northern courts also. Their appearances on juries thus appear to be far less than their population ratio in the community would indicate.

Not only is a large portion of the "cross-section of society" that supposedly comprises a jury generally absent from the panels, but in the comfort of summer living, that remaining sliver of cross section becomes even smaller. A newspaper, for example, reported recently : If you had been on trial you'd have had a time of it pleading your case before a jury of your peers. They were "gone fishin." More than two-thirds of those called for jury duty stayed away. Only 104 of 340 jurors appeared.

"It happens every summer," commented court officials. They added dryly that citizens who did not report for jury duty when summoned may by law be arrested and fined. Also, the sheriff is empowered to round up jurors, haul them bodily into court, and place them in a jury box. [How these jurors would act on cases before them could well be imagined.] Only 32 of the 75 jurors called for a first-degree murder trial showed up. Only 18 of 115 petit jurors appeared.

This did not include the great numbers of prospective jurors who telephoned to say they could not appear. Their service was politely put off for a time when it would be more convenient for them. Their excuses included such things as vacations coming at about the same time as their call for jury duty, children home from school who needed parental care, and those who complained that they normally could not work hard in the hot weather ! As he excused them with the reminder they might be called at a later time, the jury commissioner commented that even if they appeared for a trial, their minds obviously would not be on the cases and that it was better they be excused.

It can be seen, therefore, that the mere absence of women from juries, together with whatever benefits they may be expected to add, should not be one of major concern to those interested in a more perfect system of justice. The real problem is in getting *any* jurors to appear who might be qualified to handle the difficult and delicate job which is forced upon them against their will. Anyone who is aware of juries, and particularly those who advocate them, know that the verdicts are molded by the personalities and emotions of those jurors who do appear. From this it would seem a fair conclusion that one of the troubles with juries is the difficulty in getting citizens to appear in court.

15

Pursuit of the Jury Mind:
And so to Trial

A RECENT NEWSPAPER CARTOON SHOWED A YOUNG ATTORNEY smiling gallantly at a jury box filled mostly with middle-aged housewives and saying : "Gentlemen and *young* ladies of the jury . . . ." The intent of this eager young salesman was obvious. He was trying to sell the jury on himself and, through that, to win his case. This pursuit of the jury's mind is well known. It goes on avidly and with little shame. The reason is simple : there is no way around it. It is more important to our system of law in too many instances than is the law itself. One judge, also the author of a popular novel, put it this way, speaking through one of his characters :

Gambling on what a jury will do is like playing the horses. The notorious undependability of juries, the chance involved, is one of the absorbing features of the law. That's what makes the practice of law, like prostitution, one of the last of the unpredictable professions—both employ the seductive arts, both try to display their wares to the best advantage, and both must pretend enthusiastically to woo total strangers. And that's why most successful trial lawyers are helpless showmen; that's why they are about nine-tenths ham actor and one-tenth lawyer.[1]

Of great interest to everyone concerned with justice is the mental process of the dozen citizens selected to rule on the facts in a trial. On the twists and turns of their minds rest the reputations of two lawyers, the future of two litigants and, for the judge, the status of the law.

Lawyers, in particular, are interested in tracing this process, for from it can be learned methods for future arguments and appeals. All they can usually do, however, is question individual jurors after a verdict has been returned, thereby receiving only a mass of conflicting statements.

An example of a jury's reasoning thus should prove interesting. This one, of course, is not supposed to exemplify all juries. It merely illustrates how a jury in one particular case reached a rather baffling conclusion. I pierced the veil of secrecy surrounding the usual jury deliberations by unabashedly eavesdropping with the help of a sympathetic court attaché. The sounds of juror arguments came clearly through a thin wall.

The case they were discussing loudly had been a particularly strongly contested libel action. Bits of evidence were discussed at random without any attempt to relate one to the other or to the case itself. Jurors' reactions to what had been published were emotional and personal — "how would I have felt if someone had said something like that about me?" — rather than concerning themselves about the actual plaintiff.

They finally agreed that the plaintiff "was not entitled to

[1] Robert Traver, *Anatomy of a Murder* (New York: St. Martin's Press), pp. 39–40.

a damn cent," that he had only brought a nuisance suit to annoy the defendant. They were ready to return a verdict for the defendant which would, in effect, rule that he had done no wrong and had not broken the laws of libel. Just then a feminine voice suggested that the plaintiff would probably have to pay his lawyer a fee for handling the case and that he looked like a person who could ill afford that. On the other hand, the defendant looked like a comparatively well-to-do publisher.

"Oh, yes, we never considered that fact," said another voice. Others chimed in that the hour was getting late and questioned about how much a lawyer would charge. Someone guessed about $500 would be a fair fee. And thus it was agreed that the publisher was really guilty of libel under the facts they had heard and the law they were instructed to apply. The amount of damages to the now-injured plaintiff came to exactly $500.

So it was that to help a person pay for his attorney, a new set of standards had been set up to determine what facts constituted libel. While to the jury a matter had been settled equitably to their minds, to the judge and lawyers a new precedent had been established to determine future libel, and to publishers a new guidepost set up as to what could or could not be safely written. Thus did the jury in its own way fashion law without the help of a legislature.

Such jury-made law is most unusual by normal standards. There is no useful reasoning to map the path for the next lawyer; it is neither written into textbooks as a lesson for prospective lawyers, nor is it found in published decisions for those already in practice. Nowhere can it be found in codified form, for it is actually interpretation of law rather than the setting down of clear-cut rules. While the lawyers enter a problem with a good knowledge of what judicial rulings have been on previous cases bearing similar facts — and not only in their own jurisdictions but in comparable ones as well — the jurors,

strictly amateurs at law, come in with practically no knowledge
of what has been done before. Nor do they care what will be
done after as a result of their decisions. Nonetheless, jury-made
law is very real law.

It would be very easy to place the entire blame for this
situation on the shoulders of the jurors and feel that we have
accomplished our mission. But the facts are not as simple as
that : much as with the litigants and the courts, the jurors, too,
are victims of a variety of circumstances over which they have
little control; and they are ordered to make the best of it. Most
of the time they are simple people, taken out of familiar surroundings and placed into those which are strange and often
perplexing. They are suddenly thrust into a mysterious routine
of oath-taking, mountains of petitions and cross-petitions, leading questions, cross-examinations, objections, and whispered
conferences with judges out of their hearing. They are made
to sit through hours of meaningless questioning. Their utter
boredom is quickly apparent to anyone who strolls in during
the trial. The jurors' eyes snap from the witness to the person
who has entered the room as though in welcome relief.

Juries are required to perform feats of memory in the
relation of facts that are staggering. What is worse, they are
often beyond their capabilities. In most states, for example,
they are absolutely denied the right to take notes even during
the longest of trials. At the same time, surprisingly enough,
veteran judges, long experienced at handling trial facts, are
permitted to take copious notes throughout the hearings. They
refer to those notes continuously and make decisions based
upon them.

The lawyers, who have lived with the case so long that they
are thoroughly intimate with both their own facts and those
of the opposition, are constantly busy at the trial table scribbling notes of testimony and evidence. They, too, refer to
their notes constantly during cross-examination and closing

arguments. Even with all this note taking there arises constant debates over exactly what a particular witness said or what was contained in a specific piece of evidence. Yet all parties concerned seem to feel that a jury can absorb all this information and apply the law accurately to its most minute details without being allowed to take a single note.

Arguments judges use to prohibit note taking are interesting. They say that all jurors do not have the same capacity to take accurate notes. Thus the juror with the most complete information will have an undue influence over his colleagues. Their verdict, then, would not be an agreement of all twelve but would tend to follow the expert note taker who has the most information on hand. Another pet argument is that juries decide via the psychological gestalt theory. This means that they reach a conclusion based on their insight and on their general view of the case as a whole rather than on specific words or points of evidence. This is immediately negated by the wrangles of counsel over the wording of certain questions, strong objections to minor bits of evidence, and efforts to discredit even weak witnesses whose testimony is at variance slightly with the massive tapestry of the trial.

THE MEMORY GAME

The method set up for the handling of a court trial leads to a major problem in memory. All the evidence is not presented to jurors in a continuous thread in the way events happened. Instead, the jury hears first only the side of the plaintiff. For long hours, often days, at a time, the jury hears and sees only one side of the issue. By the time this phase is concluded, the jury is convinced that the plaintiff deserves all he has sought, because the defendant has been deliberately kept from presenting any of his story. All he can do during this time is attempt to discredit the plaintiff's witnesses.

Finally the defendant's turn comes. He, too, takes hours to present his story, and quite naturally shows only what is favorable to him, leaving out large pieces of the story on the theory that the opposite side will have presented it in its turn. His train of evidence, too, is interrupted with numerous objections from the other side of the trial table and further whispered conferences with the judge.

Through all this, the jury is supposed to keep a reasonably clear picture of the events as they actually happened, remembering previous pieces of the jig-saw puzzle and fitting them into place where they belong. What is more, everything is further complicated by the use of legal terminology, with which jurors have only the most remote acquaintance.

It must be remembered, too, that when jurors view the evidence they have not the faintest idea of what was legally unimportant and what was crucial in the law. They have no way of knowing what aspects of the trial deserved the most of their attention and what was merely legal window dressing. The foundation of many a trial rests on evidence which a jury, in its honest naïveté, may consider insignificant, while other more emotional and dramatic incidents, which may have little to do with the issues at hand, lodge firmly in their minds.

It should not be forgotten that the average trial is heavy with emotion. Conspicuously lacking is the calm so necessary for dispassionate deliberation and the absorption of large quantities of fleeting oral testimony. As the late Federal Judge Jerome Frank has said: "Jurors hear . . . evidence in a public place, under conditions of a kind to which they are unaccustomed. No juror is able to withdraw to his own room, or office, for private individual reflection. And, at the close of the trial, the jurors are pressed for time in reaching their joint decision. Even twelve experienced judges, deliberating together, would probably not function well under the conditions we impose on the twelve inexperienced laymen."[2]

[2] Frank, *Courts on Trial* (Princeton University Press), pp. 119–120.

STREET PSYCHOLOGY PAYS OFF

So much for hurdles placed by the law before efficient mental operation of jurors. Another important aspect is the mind of the individual juror, which is expected to handle those hurdles. Here is the spot where the trial lawyer's quick eye and understanding of street-wise psychology pays off in big money dividends. Great trial lawyers I have known — and they are men of undoubted talent — tell me there are a few little signs to show whether a juror will be generous or tight-fisted. This, of course, has not the least application to justice. It aims entirely at the business-end of law: the business of winning cases.

Very often the subject matter of the case to be heard gives an important clue to the type of person who would be valuable for a winning "plaintiff's jury," as it is called by callous practitioners. A splendid example of this was recounted by Francis L. Wellman of the New York Bar when he described a libel case that he won. He had been representing a fellow attorney who, in addition to being prominent in the legal profession, was also a fine husband and father. A newspaper, in what was clearly a case of mistaken identity, falsely accused him of misconduct with a woman of doubtful morals. The plaintiff had rejected a retraction because he felt it would be buried among the want ads in the rear of the newspaper. All he wanted was a verdict of sufficient size to clear him with his social friends and business colleagues.

During the selection of the jury, one man was called who immediately got into a quarrel with the bailiff for mispronouncing his name and who became even more angry when, on challenging the man, that clerk even went so far as to misspell it. Obviously, to one of less talent than Mr. Wellman, this juror would have been too troublesome to keep on a jury. But to this expert trial lawyer, a man so precise with his own name would surely be shocked at a newspaper for damaging another person's name, even though done inadvertently. Wellman therefore decided to take a chance with this juror. His gamble paid off most handsomely when the jury returned a verdict for $10,000. What is more, Mr. Wellman recounted that in an adjoining courtroom a similar libel case was tried against a different publication. In that case the facts were practically identical. In fact everything was the same except two things: the quarrelsome juror who was so precise with his name was obviously not in the second case—and the verdict there was for only $500.[3]

While the selection of a jury is supposed to be only for the purpose of picking out an impartial panel which can hear the matter at hand without prejudice, that definition is accepted by only the most naïve and innocent. It might more accurately be described as the beginning of a subtle conditioning process, a pursuit of the jury's mind. The attorney for the plaintiff smilingly asks each juror if he would oppose the awarding of a specified large verdict—say, a half-million dollars—if he were convinced it is deserved. Waiting jurors hear this sum tossed about casually. Gradually their awe of its size diminishes. In its place comes the notion that a person who would ask that much must indeed have been badly hurt. The jury does not know it, but it is gently being brainwashed in favor of the plaintiff.

Then the defense attorney takes over in his questioning and tries to prod the jury's mind back with the question if it would have the courage to deny recovery if it were proved not to be the defendant's fault. So here, before a shred of evidence has been given, adept hands are already at work trying by words, gestures, smiles, and frowns to mold the foundation for this all-powerful arm of the law: the citizen jury.

[3] Wellman, *Luck and Opportunity* (New York: Macmillan Company), pp. 118–119.

The most successful trial lawyers have told me that this was not altogether their purpose in the selection process, but if it could be done, so much the better for their cause. The way they put it, the personal intimate little questions with the jurors establish a rapport with the attorney, a sort of cozy communications system : an understanding upon which a canny lawyer can capitalize when the proper moment arrives.

In all truth, however, it must be admitted that the conditioning process began long before the prospective jurors ever stepped into the jury box. The teary tales they witnessed in the movies, or the soap opera of television, has left its residual effects.

A powerful conditioner, as was touched upon earlier, is the daily newspaper. Here, large verdicts are played up as important page-one stories. This is surely not meant as criticism, because when a member of the community suddenly comes into a large fortune in such dramatic fashion it certainly is news. By the same logical reasoning, when a verdict is small, the story is given little space—if it is used at all. And if the verdict is for the defendant, which means no money is given, of course there is no story, because nothing has happened. (There have been exceptions to this, I have participated in a few, but these were due largely to strange circumstances surrounding the verdict. Suffice it to say that this is most rare and victorious defense lawyers usually do not get the publicity they deserve.)

Thus it can be seen that jurors, who come from a newspaper-reading public, are made strikingly aware that large verdicts are normal happenings and they are conditioned by this half-told precedent, the other, and losing, half of which is usually known only to the judge and the small number of persons in his room who participated in it.

PRESUMED TO BE CAPABLE

Courts, in the little fictitious dream house they have built up, proceed on the assumption that a juror performs his important obligations not only on a high judicial plane, but very morally as well. To make certain of this they have set up certain qualifying standards for the citizens who serve on this fact-finding panel, and those who do not measure up to them are dismissed. The presumption is that those who remain are capable of handling the difficult task placed before them. How erroneous this presumption can be, to the detriment of litigants and their hopes of justice, can be seen in the qualifications which have been set up.

The law generally holds that to disqualify a juror there must be a situation by which he is personally affected in such a manner as to render him basically prejudiced in the trial of a case. This is the law's vague attempt to safeguard litigants from jurors. Yet the law takes no notice of the fact that a juror can be prejudiced against a litigant's race, his sex, his manner of dress, or habits of speech or walking, whether the defendant is an individual or a presumably wealthy corporation. It is obvious here that law is not a maiden blindfolded to superficial flaws and balancing justice equally on her scales, for jurors are rarely students of the law and respecters of its majesty.

What courts think a juror should be is shown in the Texas case of *Dallas Railway and Terminal Co.* v. *Kurth* (247 South West 2d, 930), in which the fact that one juror's son had a claim against the streetcar company which the juror did not disclose did not require reversal. The case was reversed, however, and sent back for a new trial on the grounds that another juror had failed to reveal during the process of selection that he had obtained a settlement for a collision with a truck, and that the chest injury that had resulted still bothered him at times.

A basic test for a juror is simply to ask him if he honestly thinks he can decide the facts in the case before him without favor or prejudice, but simply on the evidence as he hears it from the witness stand. It is surprising how easy it is to answer that question in the affirmative in all honesty, yet to find that factors creep in which one never expected. For example, even though a juror may be positive he is not biased, his untrained subconscious holds unsuspected prejudice in readiness to mislead every attempt at justice. This is obviously a mental or emotional status, yet who is to decide that this exists when the person himself denies it.

How can anyone predict that a juror who sincerely believes he is free from bias will not become angry during a trial if a young motorist in dirty, wrinkled trousers and run-down shoes fidgets on the witness stand and tries in his own awkward fashion honestly to prove that he is actually innocent.

When a juror's ability to be impartial is in doubt, how does the court reassure itself? It simply asks him and, on his own word, it accepts him without further doubt. After all, a juror is an historical fact and who can dare to doubt him? So he is taken, bias, prejudice, and all, to be absolute judge of the facts.

AND SO TO TRIAL

Finally the jury is selected to the satisfaction of both sides. The show is ready for the road. As with all shows, it starts, as we have seen, with a condensed overture. Here it is called an "opening statement by opposing counsel." The lawyer speaks directly to the jurors, ostensibly to give them an outline of the trial which is starting so that they may follow it more easily and fit the pieces of evidence together.

Among trial veterans, here is where the performance gathers momentum. The lawyer speaks intimately, trying to capture each juror with his eyes. He warns them that what he is saying is not to be considered evidence, all the while knowing full well that what he says sinks into their memories and makes as strong an impression as if it were full evidence properly admitted before the court. Here is the gestalt theory in full swing. The speaker knows that at the beginning of the trial the jury is most alert. It is in a new situation and grasps all that is given to it. Smart lawyers use it to place the thoughts into the jury's mind that they know later will not be permitted into evidence. The pursuit of the jury's mind is in low gear, beginning its first big push toward the desired end.

How much more efficient, and eminently more fair, would it be if this introduction were presented by the judge? He is fully familiar with the facts by now and could present them calmly and in proper sequence in order to really aid the jury. But lawyers do not want to relinquish even that much control over their jury to the court. It is clear to the lawyers that by the very nature of their selection, the jurors lack a number of important attributes. Among these is a knowledge of the psychology of testimony. It takes intensive training, such as a judge receives, to develop the ability to hold a number of facts in mind, to weigh their relationship to each other, and then to render a verdict as a result of this admittedly difficult mental process.

So it is that the experienced lawyer, knowing well this weakness, passes lightly over facts he would have stressed before a judge alone, and instead puts his emphasis on the dramatic aspects of his case. Here is where the orator takes over and leaves the lawyer behind: he knows that each juror is influenced by his own background, training, and heredity; that the listener, as in all audiences, can be led about by his emotions and prejudices. So the lawyer hits these hard. He puts aside his professional desire for objectivity in justice and instead attempts to capitalize upon the whimsical excesses that juries are known for.

These very emotions which a lawyer tries to grasp firmly are a major obstacle in the way of a jury sincerely seeking to find the facts about a case before it. Whenever a jury is emotionally opposed to the power of a large corporation—or to a member of a minority race—it is blinded toward the facts as they are and twists them to what they would like to believe them to be. It is well known that many of our most successful damage lawyers often indulge in acting and by-play which have little to do with the facts, but are employed for the very purpose of arousing sympathy or prejudice.

Sometimes the lawyers themselves are carried away by their own dramatics. It is a common occurrence, which I have witnessed many times, to have an attorney, arguing a point of law before the judge with the jury absent, suddenly leap to his feet with a resounding hand slap on the trial table and a shouted objection to a point made by his opponent. Then the judge smilingly chides him with : "Now, now there is no need for that, Mr. Counselor. There is no jury present to be impressed by that, you know." And the lawyer subsides shamefaced to the chuckles of the court attachés.

LAWYERS ON TRIAL

This naturally leads to the question of the amount of influence the personality of the lawyer has on the jurors. In other words, does the jury really evaluate the facts, or does it simply judge the lawyers for each side? Of course, this is impossible to determine accurately, but it is clear from the tactics employed by top trial lawyers that they are convinced their personality and mannerisms have a great deal to do with the verdict.

One lawyer I know, when opposing the slick appearance of a corporation lawyer, emphasizes his own normally slow, shuffling walk. He sometimes appears to be confused at the actions of his opposition, although the trained eye perceives he is quick to notice their faults and moves in skillfully and effectively to capitalize on them.

Another lawyer confided in me he takes care to note the jury's attitude toward a witness and guides his own actions accordingly. For example, his opponent called a kindly, motherly-looking, elderly lady to the stand. Her testimony was most damaging to his cause and, at the same time, was evidently exceedingly untruthful and contrary to what she had said at an earlier informal hearing. Had he been appearing before a judge alone, he would have dispatched this witness quickly by showing her changed story. Before the jury, however, he had to walk gingerly to prove her a liar, but without angering his twelve citizen judges.

He therefore smilingly complimented her appearance, and solicitously asked if she wanted a glass of water. He suggested that possibly the passage of time had dimmed her memory, as it does with all persons. He reminded her gently that she had given him a previous statement under oath and hinted what it contained. By this time, she was obviously stumbling in her answers and perspiration was showing on her face. With a sidelong glance at the jury to note they were also squirming in sympathy with her, the lawyer suddenly excused her from the witness stand without further embarrassing questions. He graciously extended his arm and helped her down. In full view of the entire room, he tenderly gave her his own glass of water.

The collective sigh from the jury reassured him that he had won his case. His tactful moves had made him a hero to the jurors. They had practically forgotten the unfortunate lady's damaging testimony in their warm feelings toward the kindly lawyer.

Examples such as this are endless to veteran court observers. One group of law students noted after a visit to court that lawyers seemed to be putting on a show for the jury, and that as soon as the jury was dismissed for any reason, the histrionics would be dampened, the facts clarified, and the argument would be transformed into off-the-record discussion between judge and counsel. While it is obvious that lawyers deliberately put up a show to capture the naïve minds of jurors, it should be equally clear that experienced judges are perfectly aware of these tactics. Observation of these specialized trial lawyers in operation during case after case soon renders a judge familiar with when lawyers are sincerely presenting important information and when they are simply going into their dramatic routine to impress their clients and earn their fees.

This is, of course, lost on jurors innocent to the methods of the courtroom. They accept the dramatic lawyer at face value. (If they were acquainted with either of the two lawyers, and their personalities, they would automatically be dismissed from the panel as prejudiced.)

As the trial proceeds, the capable lawyer paces his case to the jury mind. He knows full well that jurors are alert and receptive in the morning, so this is when he offers his most important evidence. As the long day wears on, he sees jury eyes stealing to the windows, their thoughts wandering back to more familiar areas. They think of tasks at home, undone because of their absence, and of problems awaiting them. This is when the wise lawyer knows it is time to sit down and let his opponent cross-examine the witness. He hopes his competitor for the jury mind will continue in the same droning tone with which he himself has just ended, so that he will not disturb the jurors' reveries.

At the end of a mentally fatiguing day, the judge indulges in one last legalistic fiction before sending the jurors on their way for the night. He warns them not to discuss the case thus far with each other or with anyone else, including their families. The wistful theory is to keep their minds untouched by outside opinions, indeed to have no opinions at all until every last particle of evidence is in and the law is read to them. All the time the judge is going through these motions required by the academic law, he knows full well that the jurors cannot wait to get home to the dinner table to discuss it with their spouses, children, the neighbors, or anyone who will listen to them. This is often their lone moment of importance to the world and they are eager to exploit it to the fullest.

Then the judge tells them to be careful not to read any accounts of the case in the newspapers so that they may not thereby be prejudiced. Sometimes judges have been so gracious as to point me out as the newspaper reporter, standing near his bench, who would probably write something about the matter at hand. Some jurors have been grateful for his thoughtfulness, because the next day they were kind enough to call me aside during recess and compliment me on the nice story I wrote about the case and how fair I was to the poor plaintiff because they felt the same way.

And this on stories they have been specifically and emphatically warned not to read! Judges to whom I have spoken of these incidents have smiled, and noted that jurors were only human and had understandable weaknesses; besides, they were too far along in the trial to start all over again and they had carefully warned the jurors—their words were safely in the trial record—and they had every confidence the jury could disregard what they read. Besides, I had been nice enough to get the judge's name in the story and the news account was really very accurate and fair.

THE IDEAL IS FOLLY

By their very words, the judges acknowledge the folly of trying to live up to the ideal of a trial by jury, and having realized its limitations, they were content to live within its dream world as practical men. These rules were evidently set

up long before modern rapid communications, before a newspaper account of the trial could be on the street even before
the jurors left the courthouse. Those who made these rules
never contemplated that a jury could relax in easy chairs at
home and watch a litigant tell a news commentator what he
thought had been proven that day.

By the third or fourth day of an average trial—and trials
of that length are far from rare today—the jury is running
into amazing mental problems. First is memory : they find they
have forgotten many important facts given them in the early
days of the long, boring trial. Being left to listen to an array
of facts in which they usually have little interest, it is little
wonder that their mind fastens on the angle of the lawyer's bow
tie or the way his adam's apple jumps when he swallows. It
surely is not the jury's fault when this happens—any more
than it is the fault of the judge or the lawyer.

It is also interesting to examine exactly what information
actually penetrates the jury mind. Is it actual facts—which the
jury is by law supposed to evaluate—or is it merely the interpretation of facts as seen by witnesses? It is apparent that all
viewers of a factual situation see it differently. In the comparatively simple situation of an automobile accident, one
person testified he distinctly saw the offender cross the road's
white center line. To another witness, at another spot, it was
equally clear that the auto never touched that center line. Each
speaks most truthfully of what he saw from his particular angle
in the road. Whom shall the jury believe?

In other words, it is often opinions and not facts which
reach the jury's ears in the courtroom. To one surgeon, the
plaintiff is so seriously injured he will probably never walk
again. To another, equally well qualified by training and
experience, it is only a matter of time before the muscles and
bones heal to the point of usability. Which "facts" can a
conscientious jury truthfully believe? It is evident that a really

heavy burden is being placed upon an exceedingly slender reed in this fairly common type of jury trial.

It is obvious that a witness's preconceived ideas condition what he sees. So does his background, his bias, his training, and his environment. Now put that together with another bias in a juror toward the witness, the plaintiff, or either of the lawyers. It is evident that it takes a cold and dispassionate eye to handle such a situation; an eye that has seen a parade of similar witnesses can begin to distinguish between what is fact, what is opinion, what is a wide streak of imagination, and sometimes what is perjury.

Still another hurdle the jury must overcome is the problem of lack of communications, and here again the judge is at an advantage. When a witness lapses into slang which has little meaning to him, the judge can stop him and question him on the exact meaning. He can probe until he is satisfied he understands perfectly what is being told. The same holds true for areas wherein the continuity of the testimony seems to lack cohesion. Again the judge can stop and question the witness. The jury cannot do either; it has no choice but to sit silently and listen, passing over parts it does not fully understand and hoping that it will all somehow make sense by the time the case is completed.

The story is told around courthouses of the young attorney in his first trial. His presentation was confused and rambling; all his evidence was objected to by the opposition and ruled out by the judge. Finally, in his closing argument, a mass of unfinished sentences left the jury completely bewildered. Yet, within a short time, the jury returned with a verdict for this young man's client. Astounded newsmen questioned the jurors after they had been excused. Among the reasons for favoring this young lawyer was that he appeared to be trying to tell them something and, if they could only have questioned him, they might have clarified it. Since they could not, however, they had merely injected their own thoughts into the areas that he had left incomplete. Naturally, the jurors liked their own ideas and, thus, favored the young lawyer.

It is clear that if the jury dislikes a man it is almost impossible to win a verdict for him, no matter how right his cause. It is equally obvious that if a lawyer is liked, it would be most difficult for him to lose.

The usual jury trial is divided into two distinct "acts" once the opening statements, or "overture," are completed. In the first half, the plaintiff has the stage. He presents his evidence, and his witnesses : persons who will support his cause completely. The opposition has almost no way of showing its side, but can only object to what he considers improper questions and cross-examine his opponent's witnesses in an attempt to discredit them.

But even in this the defense lawyer is limited by the presence of a jury, although his rights are perfectly legal. For example, a lawyer knows only too well that if he objects too often, even though his opponent's questions are completely illegal, jurors through their lack of knowledge of these technical improprieties will begin to wonder what he is trying to "hide." To them, knowing nothing of the rules of evidence, an objection means simply that a lawyer is fearful of a damaging truth. Too many of these and the jurors begin to look at him with strong doubts; the lawyer picks his objections carefully, ignoring those that he might have used but which he considers not too important. Thus the jury can be seen to be hampering the due process of law rather than helping it.

Finally the end of the first act is reached. The plaintiff rests his case. The defendant, in a purely routine action, seeks a directed verdict with the hope that the plaintiff has not made out a case. The usual response from a judge is that the motion is denied and the defendant may proceed with his case. Here the amateur jurors raise a collective eyebrow at this seeming defeat suffered by the defense, generally unmindful of its routine nature.

At this point, too, the judge usually takes a moment to admonish the jury to keep an open mind. It should not reach a conclusion, he says, until all the evidence has been presented from both sides and the law is given to it. He emphasizes that at this point they have heard only one side of the matter and the defendant is yet to present his views.

It is well known among trial lawyers, however, that this is an almost worthless admonition. The juror is, after all, only an average man, having almost no knowledge of court procedure. Quite often his judgment is almost completely formed at this point. Either he is impressed with the plaintiff's view and resents attempts of the defense to reconvince him, or he has been irritated by the plaintiff's lawyer to the point where he welcomes almost any excuse from the defendant to upset him. In any event, the juror hardly possesses a calm judicious view, holding one set of facts in abeyance until he can merge it with the coming second set to reach a just conclusion.

The second act of the performance is similar in form to the first, being an attempt by the defense attorney to sway his audience. He now presents his side to the exclusion of his opposition's best facts, and now the plaintiff's lawyer must content himself with trying to throw doubt on opposing witnesses through cross-examinations and objections.

Finally the third act of the production is reached. This is the important act: the payoff. Here is where all stops are pulled by the lawyers and full dramatics are put on for the benefit of the jurors. Here, again, the lawyers speak directly to the jury as they present their closing arguments. But here is where they, in effect, pour the blood on the floor and tear at the open wounds of the litigants.

The closing argument is supposedly simply a last review of the evidence which has been presented. Yet who is to object if it is polished up a bit? Here is where the attorney speaks shudderingly of the "bits of living flesh that were left on the bumper of that cruel automobile." He notes to the jury that the injured person was a member of "your community, practically a neighbor," and tries to convey the impression that the accident could have happened to any one of the jurors. He speaks in a horrified voice of the excruciating pain. He walks to his client and places a friendly hand on his shoulder as he says in choked tones that his man—"your own neighbor"—may never be able to play a good game of tennis with his own son again. And who is to deny the lawyer the right to shed a few honest tears at a proper moment if it dramatizes his case? After all, this *is* the high spot of a dramatic trial; what matter if it goes a little beyond the actual evidence in the case?

An opposing attorney who has the bad grace to object at this point might well feel the outrage of a truly touched jury. Besides, the defense attorney will have his turn to bask in the dramatic limelight as he proclaims the innocence of his client in ringing voice and calls upon the jury to defend this man—who, in turn, could easily have been any one of them— from the obviously unjust demands of the opposition which is seeking its pound of flesh for the purely accidental spilling of a few drops of blood.

CLUTTER WITH EMOTIONS

Observances of a few such closing arguments, once the dramatic spell of the competing lawyers has been shaken, makes it clear that they too often have little to do with the facts of the case at hand. They are evident attempts to take the matter away from the clarity of pure law and justice, and to clutter them with emotional issues which have nothing to do with the facts in the case. Attending a few closing arguments before the court alone in equity matters, and then watching the same lawyers performing before a jury, makes the difference painfully clear. The calm reasoning and logical arguments in the former stand in marked contrast to the dramatics of the latter. Finally, the noisy acting has subsided and the last earnest, almost-whispered "thank you, ladies and gentlemen of the jury" has been said.

That is when the judge steps into his sole prominence in this play of justice. He clears his throat and takes front-center of the stage to launch into a lengthy, dull recitation of the law. He rattles along about the "determinative issues" in the case. He tells the jury to consider what an elusive, fictitious "reasonably prudent man" would have done in similar circumstances, although it is difficult to find even one judge who successfully can define the actual meaning of such a person.

I once heard a judge take pity on his jury and attempt to define what he meant by "determinative issues." He said: "Since I have used the phrase determinative issues, I will attempt to explain it to you. A special or determinative issue is a statement of ultimate fact controverted in an answer. Therefore, in coming to a conclusion as to what a determinative issue in this case is, you, the jury, must find facts from the evidence which have been presented in this courtroom." The judge was lucky his face was buried in the sheaf of papers from which he was reading this statement or the look of blankness that swept his jury would have dismayed him.

It has been said that the law poured out by a judge at the panel of citizen jurors in an hour is enough to make a third-year law student turn pale. But of course the student has been inculcated with the history of justice and the meanings of terms which in law carry implications far different from those in general use. That this is known to members of the legal profession is abundantly clear. Arthur F. Triplett, a half dozen years back when he was president of the Arkansas Bar Association, expressed it this way in behalf of his colleagues :[4]

A juror is, of course, not expected to know what the law is except as he is advised by the instructions of the court. Many cases involve fine distinctions and splitting of hairs which would make them difficult to decide even when placed in the hands of a judge who has been trained in law. How can it be expected that jurors totally unfamiliar with the law could have a few instructions read to them by the court and go out and apply the law properly to facts which are in dispute. In most cases there will be an average of possibly ten instructions and the jury would have only a hazy conception of the law from having the instructions read to them by the court. How many trained lawyers could hear the instructions read in a case with which they are not familiar and be able to grasp from the reading the exact meaning intended to be conveyed?

Question of just what instructions of law mean to jurors has disturbed conscientious legal practitioners across the nation. In Kansas, Charles C. McCarter, an assistant attorney general, said :[5]

I wanted to hear what the jurors themselves thought about the validity and efficiency of the system they were using. Twenty per cent of those questioned were willing to admit that they did not understand the instructions. A jury verdict in most states must be unanimous. With 20 per cent of the jurors I questioned not understanding the rules and thus not using them properly, 20 per cent of the verdicts rendered by these jurors could be wrong.

Probably the percentage would have been even higher if the

[4] *7 Arkansas Law Review* 222.
[5] *4 University of Kansas Law Review* 434.

jurors could have been asked for their opinions in a less direct manner than to ask: "Do jurors understand instructions?" It is not human nature to answer in the negative when in effect asked: "Do you, as a juror, have sufficient intelligence to understand the instructions?"

In Cleveland, Ohio, Common Pleas Court Chief Justice Emeritus Samuel H. Silbert told this writer many times that the jury system needed serious remodeling. He once tested the law by deliberately asking a jury to take notes during a comparatively unimportant trial as a test case. He was promptly reversed on that point alone by his reviewing court.

The chief justice also is convinced that juries are needlessly baffled and often led astray by the old-fashioned complexity of jury instructions. Here, as in the fight on note-taking, he was brought to a hopeless halt by the rigidity of the law which forbids him to simplify matters although after more than 40 years as a judge he says he found the evidence plentiful that such a change was urgently needed.

Finally, to return to our trial, the reading of the law to the jury is completed. The practical climax of the courtroom drama is reached: the jury, ostensibly filled with proper evidence and law, retires to its quarters to deliberate on the facts and to reach a just verdict. It is at this crucial point that the law drops an absolute curtain of secrecy around the proceedings. The public has to this point been welcome to the fair trial in open court. But now, when the matter reaches its point of decision, the methods used in reaching such a decision are locked away from all but the jurors. Banned from these sessions are not only the general public, but the newspapers, lawyers, litigants, and even the court itself. The much-feared star chamber trials could never be this secret.

This point is criticized by Arthur F. Kingdon of the Bluefield, West Va., Bar with this interesting comment:[6]

[6] McCarter, p. 425.

266

Juries and Justice

It is a fixed and universal rule of the courts not to receive proof of the bases upon which verdicts are rendered for the purpose of showing either error or bias. The rule rests largely on the theory that the jurors are, under the constitution, exclusive triers of the facts and that the courts have no right to inquire into reasons for their decisions. This rule could be changed and it should be. There is vastly more reason for requiring jurors to show how and why they reach their decisions than for judges.

What happens in these super-secret deliberations is an important key to the entire foundation upon which our system of citizen-jury justice rests. Unfortunately, little can be learned of this other than by rare instances of eavesdropping as recounted earlier. However, hints can be garnered from the rebellious comments of the dissatisfied. For example, one juror said : "I was called a fathead for holding out on an 11–1 vote on Thanksgiving Eve. Everyone wanted to go home. They said the decision meant nothing to me, so why should I hold out on Thanksgiving Eve when everybody wanted to go home. After several hours I gave in against my better judgment. I am sure that case was decided wrong." Another juror said : "Be damned sure that no one does jury duty who has an appointment in their mind. One day while I was jury foreman a lady had an evening engagement and said 'I want to get out early, so whatever you decide I will go along with, but many of the details are not clear to me.' "

Small wonder, then, that the jury room has been somewhat sardonically dubbed "the darkest corner of the law."

As Dale W. Breeder wrote :[7] "The striking fact is that no one really knows how well these supposed functions are performed. This universal public ignorance of the jury's deliberations, however, is not accidental. The 'jury tradition' has been the people's sacred democratic cow. Even judges have been induced to cover jury-room deliberations with legal shrouds calculated to protect them from close scrutiny."

He later commented that while the jury might be a popular symbol of democracy, it was in one sense the very antithesis of democratic government since it was responsible to no one; its membership was anonymous; jurors appeared out of the ranks of society and as rapidly disappeared back into them.

The grounds for a jury's verdict are unknown and, barring extreme error, disappointed suitors must cry by themselves. Small wonder, then, that a lawyer not given to the dramatics necessary for a successful jury trial hesitates seriously before plunging into the court room. He must weigh the possibilities of obtaining justice for his client from the jury. He must pause to reconsider when he realizes, for example, that he may have the correct side of the case in law but that it is lacking in the melodramatic or colorful attributes needed to excite a jury.

[7] "Functions of the Jury," 21 *University of Chicago Law Review*, p. 386.

PART V

Conclusion

16

Fading, Fading in America

DESPITE VIRTUES THAT ITS DEVOTED DEFENDERS SEE IN THE jury system, the flight from the jury by persons most directly concerned with the matter — the litigants themselves — is becoming embarrassingly evident. It is almost as though the lay persons are saying "if you like the thrill of the jury gamble, Mr. Lawyer, you stay with it — but we are primarily concerned with justice given promptly and we are going to get it our own way."

In effect, by refusing to modernize or to adapt the ancient jury system to present-day needs, the law is pushing the litigant away from it into more efficient methods on the outside. This can be seen in many areas: it is evident in the soaring use of arbitration before experts to settle differences that would otherwise take years of waiting in the courts; it is seen in the swelling number of settlements with the aid of a judge alone in pre-trial sessions; it shows in increasing numbers of instances where the privilege of a jury is deliberately waived so that the matter may be handled more quickly by a judge alone in his court-room; it is apparent in the greater use of boards and commissions to resolve disputes in rights created under new laws; it is manifest in comparatively new laws such as the Federal Tort Claims Act, which specifically denies use of juries even though the case is to be heard in court. In short, this is the answer to the arguments of those who say that trial by jury is a cherished right guaranteed by the federal and state constitutions and must be retained in full bloom as the bulwark of our legal system.

Admittedly, most of the boards and commissions created by law to settle differences are limited to commercial, industrial, and labor matters. This is the result of growing agitation by business leaders, who claim that the pace of commerce and the importance of legal results are too great to have such matters left in the hands of untrained jurors. It is equally clear, too, that dissatisfaction with jury handling of personal injury cases is growing rapidly. It would appear that one reason this type of case has not been removed from courts is because there is no organization of injured plaintiffs, similar to business organizations, to bring pressure for laws which would snatch such cases from the grasp of juries.

SETTLEMENTS BY PRE-TRIAL

If every case that is filed in court, and which has a right to a jury, were to go to such a panel, the result would surely be chaos: the entire legal system would be thrown into confusion from which it would be hard to recover — even if it overloaded the courts with hordes of additional judges and their accompanying masses of jurors to attempt to handle the giant load. The reason this does not happen is because a large majority of persons involved in law suits prefer to dodge the jury.

In the court which I know intimately — the Cuyahoga

County trial court which sits in Cleveland—of 7,929 civil cases disposed of in one year, only 291 went through a jury for their verdicts. In contrast, 1,567 were settled by pre-trial judges meeting in their chambers with litigants, another 2,131 were settled and dismissed in the court's emergency room, and 1,817 were handled in full trial by a judge alone, in that emergency room.

Of the rest of the cases, 948 were settled by efforts of the trial judges alone, 46 were settled in the middle of trial, and 234 were heard by a judge alone in a regular trial room. The rest were resolved in various ways without juries, such as, for example, by agreed judgments, agreed verdicts, or foreclosure decrees.

This hardly indicates a great enthusiasm among litigants for juries of their peers. Indeed, these days a judge is much more often seen sitting in shirtsleeves in the comfort of his chambers helping to negotiate a settlement than as a formidable robed figure on the bench running his courtroom with the help of a citizen jury.

The pre-trial session is an interesting form of justice, being a way of getting around a jury in many instances. In this procedure, the plaintiff's attorney sets out the amount of money he thinks his client deserves. He tells what damages were suffered due to the alleged negligence of the defendant, and describes what he thinks that negligence to be. He then gives a sample of the evidence he has available to prove his case. In turn, the defense attorney gives his view of the accident on which the case is based and gives a hint of what evidence he has to prove his points. Then he tells what his client is willing to offer to settle the case. All this is done before the judge alone, who can weigh both sides with objectivity. He notes the strengths and weaknesses which each party has and offers his suggestions for money settlements. He may bring the claim of the plaintiff down somewhat and, with logic and reason, raise the offer of the defendant.

Drama is absent : no blood is figuratively dragged across the floor; no broken bodies parade to the witness stand to influence jurors. The attitude is one of negotiation, law, and logic. Surprisingly enough, after a brief stand for their original proposals, attorneys are willing to settle down and approach agreement. When they finally reach a just figure, each steps aside to confer with his client. Part of this conference is, quite often, an explanation of the unpredictable nature of juries with the result still a great gamble on both sides; the high cost of litigating a jury trial will frequently be mentioned.

The fact that litigants are not eager to place their causes into the hands of twelve fellow citizens is seen in the high rate of settlements across the country as shown by the sample statistics above. To a large degree, settlement is extremely satisfactory to the participants. They feel that they have had a hand in their own affairs and have reached their conclusion voluntarily rather than been told what to do by a group of outsiders. It certainly makes the courts happy. Evasion of the jury cuts greatly the time required to handle each case; it does away with the tedious procedure of having to seat a jury with its attendant multitude of questions and maneuvers by lawyers. And it clears the docket of the case completely. There are no more motions to be heard for a new trial, no possibility of a mistrial, or countless appeals to higher courts by the losers. Thus it develops that those comparatively few cases which do go to a jury trial many times spring from stubbornness on the part of parties who cannot sit down and talk matters out. Or it may come from the fascination of the gamble of the jury trial with the bait of great victory at the end.

The importance of the pre-trial settlement can be seen in the emphasis placed on it in the Los Angeles Superior Court, where a presiding judge, Louis H. Burke, informed me :

"The personal injury pretrial program has exceeded our fondest hopes. In addition to the direct costs saved the litigants, since jury fees average around $90 a day, there is a saving to the taxpayers estimated at between $300 to $350 a day, which represents the non-recoverable court costs computed on an all-inclusive basis. We have had no protests from litigants or lawyers. Because of the fact that our latest program effects settlements right at the time of pretrial, it holds, we believe, even greater promise of economy and efficiency from the point of view of all concerned."

The special program for the settlement of personal injury cases of which Judge Burke spoke saw 451 cases settled out of a total of 742 cases heard in a four-month term of court. This showed a 60 per cent success rate as the program continued to gain momentum. About 25 per cent of all personal injury cases were being referred to the special calendar by request of the attorneys representing the litigants in such cases. (An extension of this, the personal injury non-jury panel, is described later.)

This plan was set up especially to handle cases in which the participants wanted the court to take the leading role of assisting counsel in working out an amicable settlement. Lawyers who agree to have their cases transferred to this calendar must comply with certain rules for special preparation for the hearing. These are calculated to facilitate the possibility of settlement. Included among these rules are requirements that the claims manager of any defending insurance company be present as well as the plaintiffs themselves. The rules also require the exchange of such items as medical reports, bills for medical expenses, and repair for car damages in advance of the hearing.

Success of this special program, which obviously gives the normal jury trial a wide berth, can be seen in the report of one of the participating insurance companies that out of 98 cases referred to the special calendar, 80 were satisfactorily settled. A second company reported that out of 67 cases handled in this special way, 54 were settled. The latter company estimated that $31,000 was saved in fees for medical experts and other preparatory and trial costs as a result of these settlements.

The procedure in Los Angeles may thus be taken as a good example to show the eagerness of parties to a lawsuit to sidestep the time-honored method of a duly empaneled jury, with all its cumbersome procedure and legal trappings. Justice is achieved more quickly and efficiently with a method never dreamed of when the jury system was founded, and when it flourished as a protection against tyranny and power of a ruling class. It shows that modern problems bring modern solutions no matter how sedate and resentful of change the more conservative legal leaders may be.

These solutions may now be regarded as a mere temporary side-path to a regular trial. With the usual slow evolution in law, however, they can eventually pre-empt the field until jury trials become obsolete and only of academic historical significance.

THE TREND TOWARD ARBITRATION

More and more the public is turning toward arbitration as a way to bypass clogged courts and their troubled juries. Under this plan, the two parties in a dispute agree on an outside person to hear the facts in the matter and to give a decision. Both sides agree to accept that decision as a final determination of the differences.

In a way, it can be argued, that is exactly what a jury is supposed to do. Jurors are, after all, selected to hear facts on both sides of a dispute and to give their opinion of who is right. But there the similarity ends, and a major difference arises; although jurors are picked from the general public — chosen because they know nothing about the case they are to judge — the arbitrator is selected for the opposite reason, that he is an expert in the matter to be before him. In other words, he is chosen not only for his admitted fairness and impartiality, but because of his special expert knowledge of the business involved.

Arbitration has long been used in the world of commerce. The American Arbitration Association is widely known for its settlement of labor disagreements. And it is becoming the common practice to employ the association to resolve differences in the interpretation of business contracts. Often, in fact, a clause written into the contract itself specifies that the parties should agree to arbitration if problems should arise over carrying out of the contract terms.

In a copyrighted article in the *Wall Street Journal,* it was reported by Axel Krause, a staff reporter :

Arbitration appeals to some railroads because it provides an opportunity for them to submit technical disputes to men well versed in the industry's affairs. "We've used it and favor it over courts because juries just don't know anything about our business or contracts," says Joseph H. Wright, general counsel for the Illinois Central Railroad. In matters of awards particularly, juries too often judge on the basis of "emotion and feeling," Mr. Wright declares, adding that experienced railroad men are better equipped to handle complex inter-railroad disputes and are less inclined to make what he calls "unreasonable" awards.

In one case, for example, a brakeman, John Noble Summers, was crushed against a switching engine while repairing a defective coupler on an Illinois Central coal car parked near a West Frankfort, Illinois, mine. While he was a regular employee of the Chicago & Eastern Illinois Railroad, he technically was also working for three other lines tied to the whole mining operation through a joint contract : The Illinois Central, the Chicago, Burlington & Quincy, and the Missouri Pacific.

The issue, Mr. Wright explains, was whether or not the Illinois Central was solely responsible because of the defective coupler, which brought Mr. Summers to the scene in the first place, or whether all four lines should share equally in his $51,000 injury claim under terms of their joint operating contract.

"A jury most likely would have tied all the blame to us on the basis of common sense," the I. C. attorney states, adding that Warren Newcome, retired assistant solicitor for the Chicago & North Western Railway Company, was instead agreed upon to arbitrate the dispute. "Mr. Newcome ruled that all four lines must share damage costs under terms of their joint operating contract; it was an expert decision based on more than 30 years experience in the rail law field," Mr. Wright says. "Lord only knows what would have happened to the award if a jury got hold of the case."

Increasing use of arbitration to settle disputes that formerly would have gone to the court to be heard by citizen juries also caught the attention of the *Wall Street Journal* in another article :

The number of commercial cases settled by arbitration topped 21,500 in a recent year. That was more than triple the total half a dozen years before and equal to nearly 15 per cent of the 300,000 civil cases tried to a verdict in state and federal courts of general jurisdiction. Insurance companies are the largest users of commercial arbitration but it's also employed extensively by railroads, textile manufacturers, construction firms, auto producers, and many other business concerns. They use it for everything from fixing responsibility in auto accidents to deciding whether a shipment of coffee measures up to the grade claimed for it.

There's abundant evidence of the recent rapid increase in the use of arbitration for non-labor disputes. Two organizations of insurance firms, the Association of Casualty & Surety companies and the National Association of Mutual Casualty Companies, arranged for arbitrators who settled 19,036 automobile insurance cases involving member companies in one year, 2,681 more than the preceding year and more than triple the total six years earlier.

The American Arbitration Association, a non-profit organization, provided arbitrators for 1,464 non-labor cases in one year, more than double the total only five years earlier. Nearly half involved insurance companies and their policy holders. Other associations arranging for arbitrators for commercial disputes include the General Arbitration Council of the textile industry, the New York Stock Exchange, the Green Coffee Association of New York City and the Association of Food Distributors.

The use of arbitration for settling automobile claims "could easily double within the next five years," says John S. Hamilton, general counsel for the National Association of Mutual Casualty Companies. Rising sales of auto insurance, the increasing number of accidents, and worsening court congestion should all help boost the use of arbitration, he says.

Arbitration is also being considered for entirely new fields. At least one medical authority sees it as the coming method of settling medical malpractice suits. "This is a highly technical matter better handled by medical experts," says Dr. Geoffrey T. Mann, head of the medical college of Virginia's Department of Legal Medicine. "We're already moving in that direction through a committee consisting of doctors and lawyers which now screens malpractice disputes in the state and recommends possible legal action." Similar committees are presently functioning in New York, California, Arizona, and Utah, according to the American Medical Association.

The rapid disposition of cases by arbitration contrasts sharply with the delay in many courts . . . after waiting a frustrating six months for his auto accident claim to come to trial in Cook County's congested Circuit Court, stocky thirty-seven-year-old John J. Conlong, a Chicago policeman, decided to take a short cut to settlement by submitting his case to arbitration. Seventy days later, the arbitrator awarded him $2,900. His case wouldn't have come to trial in the courts for at least four more years.

In addition, the time required for an arbitration hearing is usually much less than would be needed for a court trial of the same case. Viola Steptore, a fifty-five-year-old Chicago housewife, spent five hours at an arbitration hearing on her $10,000 personal injury claim. "Had the case gone to court, the trial probably would have required five days," Bruce S. Berry, her attorney, says.

It is clear that when those charged with administration of the law refuse to adjust to the pressing needs of the times, the people who are most directly involved in the maelstrom of jury cases will find another way out. The arbitration procedures just described are, of course, completely outside the court. However, arbitration may be appealed to courts if misconduct or bias of the arbitrator can be proven, but the number of such cases whch turn to courts is very small.

George Kerver, a past president of the insurance companies' Claim Managers Council, is enthusiastic about out-of-court settlement of claims by arbitration. He told me that the system had been set up to save a lot of time and trouble for policy holders. It grew from a need for good public relations, which had been stymied by old-fashioned court delay. Formerly the parties had to resort to long, inconvenient litigation; they would have to prepare volumes of papers, come to court, find their case postponed, and have to go through the whole process again.

Here is how this plan works: the Association of Casualty and Surety Companies and the American Mutual Alliance, representing almost all top stock and mutual firms, have organized a combined claims committee in New York. This committee appoints a local arbitration committee selected from members of the Claim Managers Council. If two parties in an automobile accident, each insured by a different firm, cannot agree on who is responsible for the collision, the facts are presented to the arbitration panel for determination.

High praise is given to arbitration by a veteran Cleveland trial lawyer, Harry J. Dworkin, who has acted as an arbitrator in many cases. He noted that most of his work had been in labor contract disputes:

We used to run to the trial courts and our cases flooded the dockets. Now 90 per cent of our union contracts have simple clauses calling for arbitration. There has been a very great increase in this effort as more and more cases became tangled in the endless web of courts. Parties involved pay for the arbitrator, so they speed the hearings to save money. This also takes the financial burden off the backs of taxpayers, who must support the "free" courts of the general litigants. The litigants come away from arbitration satisfied that they have received justice and happy that it is not long delayed in the courts.

Out-of-court arbitration still maintains a semblance of judicial handling. Both parties to a dispute file charges and countercharges, which go to one of 14 regional offices of AAA or to its New York headquarters. These statements of charges are similar to legal briefs: they outline the dispute, explain how it began, and indicate claims for damages. Then arbitrators are agreed upon out of a file of 12,500 businessmen, engineers, lawyers, accountants, and other experts. When statements are filed, the AAA mails the parties a list of some 20 persons, from which the arbitrators are chosen. This is followed by a hearing behind closed doors, conducted in an informal manner to save time. After the hearings, the arbitrator has 30 days to issue his decision, which is binding on both parties.

ARBITRATION IN COURT

Since arbitration has proved exceedingly effective outside court, an attempt was made to use it on court matters in Pennsylvania on small claims. Again, this move, which completely sidestepped juries, proved highly successful. The Pennsylvania statute vested the county courts with authority, by rule of court, to compel parties in all civil litigation involving less than $2,000 to submit to an arbitration board of three lawyers for adjudication. As a condition to obtaining a complete jury trial on appeal from arbitration, an appellant was required to reimburse the county for the arbitrators' fees. Experts have hailed the Pennsylvania Compulsory Arbitration statute as a bold and significant innovation in the civil law, enacted to eliminate jury docket congestion and its attendant evils.

This compulsory arbitration is, in effect, a system of trial by lawyer. A three-man panel is picked from a list of 2,500 lawyer-volunteers on an alphabetical basis. The case is heard in the office of the chairman of the panel rather than in court. The parties testify informally, complainant giving his side of the story first, then the defendant tells it as he believes it. To this extent, the proceedings are similar to a court except that they move much more quickly due to absence of archaic procedures that knot up the court's movement.

Dramatics and displays by lawyers are cut to a minimum; the panel of lawyers usually is less influenced by emotion than is the ordinary jury. Their decisions rest more often on a firm foundation of law. Thus, evidence is introduced more quickly, rules to keep out information are discarded — since there is no jury to be led astray — and the arbitrators get a more complete picture of the case than is possible with a court jury. Persons who use this system of arbitration usually come away amazed that this system was not put into effect a long time ago, nor can they understand why in many instances the litigants still drag along with all the long delays and discomforts of the usual court trial.

As in any new system, arbitration such as this has raised a hurricane of controversy among lawyers. Some have told me it is an unjust plan devised by insurance companies who are unhappy at the increasingly high verdicts being handed down by juries in court. At the same time, other lawyers have told me it was clearly a plot hatched by plaintiff lawyers to get their cases heard more promptly while witnesses were still available and memories of the disputed incident still fresh.

Either of these arguments may be right, but the fact remains that congested courts are pushing more cases into the hands of the arbitrators and litigants are walking away happy with the results. The much-hailed jury system, with all its tradition, is thereby weakened.

CALIFORNIA'S NON-JURY PANEL

Still another method used to bypass juries in personal injury cases has been tried in Los Angeles with some degree of success. It is the personal injury non-jury panel, called their "PINJ program." It was established by the presiding judge, Burke, who, after several years of its operation, indicated to me that "we average from one to two jury waivers a day in favor of the panel. Panel judges hear cases in from one-half to one day, as against an average of three to three and one-half days for juries."

This program recognizes the reluctance of lawyers to waive their right to trial by jury until a case is assigned for trial in a specific department. Often, after a case is assigned for trial, the mere fact that one side may then announce willingness to waive a jury would bring reluctance from the other side to join in such a waiver.

The new plan was placed into operation with the encouragement of many plaintiff and defense lawyers with whom it was discussed, and with approval of the court's advisory committee. There is no attempt by the court to force or induce attorneys to waive trial by jury. Success of the program rests entirely on its own merit and desirability.

Here is how the plan works: When a case is called in the Master Calendar Department, in which the attorneys have stipulated that they might be agreeable to waiving juries, the judge calls the attorneys to the bench and states the name of the first available judge on the special panel. If no objection is raised by either side's lawyers, the case is assigned to that judge and is heard by him alone. If, however, either side voices an objection to the judge mentioned, the presiding judge then names the second available panel judge. If the attorney who has kept silent on the first judge mentioned finds objection to the second, he says so and the name of the third available judge is drawn. By this time, each side has exhausted its objections and must accept the third judge.

Thus it is found that lawyers are more willing to agree to waiving a jury if their cases are assigned for trial by one of the ten judges, provided that each side has the right to note at least one objection to a proposed judge. The objection is in no sense a challenge of the judge and no affidavit or statement of reasons is needed and no record kept of such objection. The matter is entirely confidential between the lawyers and the court. The courtesy of allowing attorneys to voice an objection to a judge is in recognition of the efforts of counsel to cooperate with the court in expediting the trial of these matters.

A form of written agreement is provided at the preliminary hearings and, when signed by the attorneys, all jury fees are ordered refunded. Jury fees are also refunded if jury waivers in consideration of assignment to the panel are made at any time after the preliminary hearing but before the daily jury panels are actually ordered, or if they can be utilized for other cases.

When the panel judges are not hearing cases under this plan, their time is not wasted because they can be used in the trial of other cases, usually of short duration, to assure their maximum availability for the trial of panel cases.

A court day seldom passes when there is not at least one case assigned to PINJ and sometimes as many as four. As a sample, one month with 20 court days saw 30 cases transferred from the general jury trial docket to the special panel judges. Two were settled en route to the trial department and 28 were disposed of by trial judges. Conservatively, this meant that during the month, the plan saved not less than 56 court days, the equivalent of adding about two and one-half judges to the civil pool. This is because the average trial time for a personal injury case is three and one-half days if tried before a jury, and one day of trial without a jury.

Los Angeles judges who have worked on PINJ say it is impossible to estimate the beneficial fringe benefits which necessarily follow. It is rare indeed that an appeal is filed from any case heard by a panel judge. That means no retrials after reversals. It also eliminates the time-wasting procedural mistrials and the new trials after a hung jury or mistrial after the case has been turned over to the jury.

It saves time and promotes justice. What more can be asked?

Judges have also noted that it is impossible to estimate the valuable saving of attorneys' time, both in preparation for trial and during trials. Ordinarily, it requires less time to prepare a case for trial before a judge than to prepare it for trial before a jury. It would appear that in cases where compensation of plaintiffs attorneys is contingent on the amount of money he wins in a case, the actual gamble of lawyers' time is cut by more than two-thirds.

So it is that another slide of cases that have long been regarded as the property of juries has now slipped from their hands. These are personal injury cases, the "big business" of the trial lawyer, for which much shouting has been done over the claimant's inalienable right to have his cause heard and decided by a democratic jury of his fellow men. It shows at least a partial answer to those who ask what would one use to replace the troubled jury system. The replacements are already in operation in the Los Angeles courts, and working.

FEDERAL TORT CLAIMS ACT

In 1946 an extremely important bill was made into law by Congress. Before this law, relief for injuries caused by United States Government employees could only be obtained by private bills in Congress. No one could sue the government without its permission. This permission was given through special bills which passed Congress, one bill for each law suit.

In the years just before the act was passed, Congress was deluged by thousands of private claim bills. For example, in each of the Seventy-Fourth and the Seventy-Fifth Congresses, more than 2,300 private claims bills had been introduced, seeking more than $100,000,000. This method was slow as well as clumsy and added to the heavy burdens of the legislature.

In the hearings before the House Judiciary Committee for the Seventy-Seventh Congress, the following statement was made: "From the Committee hearings we learn that the previous 85 years had witnessed a steady encroachment upon the originally unbroken domain of sovereign immunity from legal process for the delicts of its agents. Yet a large and highly important area remains in which no satisfactory remedy has been provided for the wrongs of Government officers or employees, the ordinary 'common law' type of tort, such as personal injury or property damage caused by the negligent operation of an automobile."

In creating the law which allowed the United States to be sued for such actions, however, the framers of the statute did a highly significant thing—they provided in clear and specific language that "any action against the United States . . . *shall be tried by the court without a jury.*"

Thus the Government, despite the provisions of its own Federal Constitution, which guarantees right to trial by jury, unequivocally denied that very right in suits against itself. Here, again, is an answer to those who say the Constitution blocks any efforts at modifying the jury system. By creating a new right that was not in effect when the Constitution was written, Congress could specify under what conditions that right could be exercised and it chose to deny "democratic" juries.

Reasons guessed at for this major change in viewpoint are many. They even include the thought that this provision is to escape the huge jury awards that are the fashion of the day and that would probably be even larger when the Government is the defendant. Another guess is that the well-known cumbersome delay caused by juries would add even more to the burdens of the Federal courts. Whatever the reasons, it seems abundantly clear that the modern Congress both did not fully trust today's juries as they have been seen to operate in other areas and did not feel them a necessity to protect the rights of "defenseless citizens" against the "power of the ruling group," the tyrants of early days. This obviously is the newer view more in tune with the realities of the present rather than the sentimentality of the past.

Under this law, the facts are heard in court by a judge alone. He rules on those facts and applies the laws which relate to them. And he himself sets the value of the damages and decides the amount of the verdict. It is indeed rare when an objection is heard to the justice handed down in this fashion.

This method is similar to that set up by the new democracies that have recently come into being. It points the way to the courts of the future much as the first jury trials, born of the necessities of the times, sealed the doom of the superstitions of trial by ordeal or by battle. It ties in with the age-old equity and divorce trials which have long proceeded to justice without the benefit of a jury.

If this class of personal injury actions can be regularly tried in Federal courts to a judge alone, the same method can be transferred to state courts now clogged with jury trials and demonstrative antics of lawyers. Many FTCA suits arise out of accidents involving government vehicles, which obviously are not different from private vehicles. The accidents are the same; the injuries are the same. The only difference is the absence of the sacred, secret juries.

State courts would be well advised to examine closely this Federal situation, which has been operating long enough to demonstrate both its strengths and weaknesses, with an eye to adoption at the state level.

ADMINISTRATIVE AGENCIES AVOID JURIES

A major area that has never been allowed to fall into the hands of jurors involves disputes over such things as regulation of radio and television, railroads and motor carriers, labor, stock exchanges, and unfair business practices. Congressman Oren Harris, as chairman of the U.S. House Special Subcommittee on Legislative Oversight, said :

We live in an age when administrative commissions and agencies [of the Government] issue, interpret, apply, and enforce more rules, regulations, and policies than do Congress and the courts combined. The classic justification for government by commission is that the necessary flexible and expeditious control of "emerging industrial complexities and the regulation of their economic relationships" can best be accomplished by expert, impartial administrative bodies authorized to act according to standards enacted by Congress.

This has come about from the pace of today's commercial world. It cannot afford to be bogged down in lengthy court delays and it cannot risk placing important decisions into the hands of naïve and inexperienced jurors. Yet how much more important is the functioning of business than the protection of individual rights for the much larger general public?

Business finds many advantages in this system of administering the law by way of expert boards and commissions. Excessive delay and expense in procedures can be immediately investigated and set right. Alleged discriminatory enforcement of the law and regulations can be protested and corrected : something that could not even be attempted with juries, whose discrimination or bias cannot be questioned.

Most important of all, there is a logic and continuity to decisions that maps out a clear path to be followed. Formulating and publicizing policy and interpretations keeps the regulated industry completely informed of the rules of decision. Thus, application of the law does not wander and vary from one case to the next despite similar facts, as is true with juries ruling on caprice. Those businesses being regulated—even as individuals are supposed to be under a nation of laws—know exactly where they stand and what they are allowed to do : That is more than can be said for the individuals.

The last generation has witnessed a particularly rapid growth of administrative agencies, keeping pace with the expansion and increasing complexity of business. Evidently, now that an effective means has been found to handle such problems without getting tangled in the web of courts, it is being used to an always greater extent. Here are brief sketches of how the major such groups work to illustrate their method of increasing efficiency without loss of justice :

NATIONAL LABOR RELATIONS BOARD : Used in unfair labor practice cases to determine if rules (laws) have been abrogated and, if so, by whom. A case that comes in is assigned by the executive secretary to one of the members of the board. The record is sent to his legal staff. There is a staff of 18 : one chief legal assistant, three legal supervisors, and 14 legal assistants. One of these 14 legal assistants is assigned to the case; he works under the watchful eye of a supervisor and the chief legal assistant.

This legal assistant undertakes a complete and detailed review of the whole record. As a result of this review, a proposed decision is drafted. After this tentative decision has been cleared within the panel chairman's office, it is circulated among the board members who are part of the panel. There it is again reviewed, this time by the respective legal chiefs.

After this circulation, the case is considered at a meeting of the so-called sub-panel, made up of the chief legal assistants of the three board members participating in the panel. They have previously consulted with their principals and are fully informed as to the position of the board members. To assist this unit, this meeting is also attended by the legal assistant who has read the record, as well as his supervisor.

If this meeting reaches agreement, a proposed decision based on the principles is drafted and circulated to be assented to. If, however, one of the board members feels that the case should be decided by the full board, a memorandum is prepared and it serves as a basis of discussion among the board members themselves.

SECURITIES AND EXCHANGE COMMISSION : This is helped in its review of the record by the Division of Opinion Writing. This division prepares a digest of the record and this is studied by the members of the commission. Their deliberations are in the main based on this digest, considered in connection with the hearing officer's report, the briefs of the parties and, in some cases, oral arguments of counsel.

After examination of these materials, the commissioners further discuss the case with members of the staff of the Division of Opinion Writing and arrive at a decision. A draft decision is then prepared by the division and submitted to members of the commission. They may approve it or suggest changes. These changes are later agreed upon in a still-further conference with members of the opinion-writing staff.

FEDERAL TRADE COMMISSION: Oral argument, in those cases where it is had, is the first step in the consideration of the case. Since the commissioners, upon hearing oral argument, are at first unfamiliar with the case, counsel for the respondent must utilize his time to acquaint the members of the commission with the broad outlines of the case and with the general nature of his principal contentions. Thereafter the commissioner to whom the case has been assigned, on a rotating schedule, reviews and studies the record.

This commissioner has a legal adviser who may, and often does, assist in the review and study of the record. Then, on the basis of this joint study, a report and recommendation as to the disposition of the case is prepared. This report is then sent to other members of the commission for the benefit of their consideration as well.

The case is next brought up for conference discussion. At such conferences, one or more of the commissioners will frequently ask for additional time to review and study the case. When a majority of the members of the commission have finally agreed on a decision, the case is again assigned to an individual member for preparation of the formal decision. It may be the same member who prepared the original recommendation, if the decision is in accord with it.

INTERSTATE COMMERCE COMMISSION : In the usual course of a case, an assistant to one of the commissioners reviews the record and evidence, checks the pleadings, reads the briefs or legal essays that have been filed, and studies the transcript of the oral arguments. Then he prepares a proposed final report, which is circulated among the commissioners who are to vote on the case.

The report is also reviewed by a board composed of experienced examiners, who consider such matters as its consistency with prior commission decisions (here can be seen the effort to give equal justice to all involved in similar situations), its effect on the rate structure involved, and other similar matters. Comments of the board of review are also circulated among the members of the commission who are to participate in the decision of the case. The proposed final report and the review board's comments on them are then studied by each commissioner with the assistance of his staff.

If particular issues which have been raised by the objections previously filed appear significant, the assistants to the several commissioners, or even the commissioners themselves, may go beyond the staff report and comments, and make a personal study of some aspects of the pleadings or testimony. Very often the individual who prepared the report may be called in to answer questions regarding the facts of the case.

After this study by the commissioners has been completed, the case is placed on a conference list to be considered on a specified date. At that conference, the views of the various commissioners are brought forth and discussed. Sometimes this conference results in the making of changes in the proposed final report that had been originally prepared by the staff. In other cases, the proposed report is approved as originally drawn up.

It should be noted that the operations just described are

the equivalent of jury deliberations. This part is often preceded by a hearing at which arguments are presented and a record made for later study by the commissioners and their legal assistants. It is the businessman's way of stepping around juries and putting their matters into the hands of experts.

Judge David W. Peck, as presiding justice of the Appellate Division of the Supreme Court of New York, in a speech to a regional meeting of the American Bar Association, emphasized that although commercial controversies have grown greatly in the last three decades, they have not gone to court, because businessmen have set up their own tribunals. They feel the traditional judicial process is unable to handle their problems, is cumbersome and dilatory.

In view of all this, the eminent jurist concluded, it was understandable that when Congress was faced with the need of establishing procedures to carry out the mandates of new laws dealing with the complexities of modern times, where promptness was of the essence, that it should have turned away from the courts and created a more streamlined and efficient procedure for justice.

"How great the conviction and provocation must have been that, to overcome the slow motion of the judicial procedure, it was scuttled and made a part of the administrative—no longer a part of an independent branch of government, but a dependent branch of an executive department," Judge Peck said. "That a form of appeal is allowed to the courts is scant compensation or correction for the condition which has been created—it is a protection only against gross error and flagrant abuse."

It would seem evident that other victims of the wandering jury-and-court system are turning more and more in the direction already taken by their commercial brethren. They have already gone into the arbitration arena. The vast increase in settlements and pre-trial agreements is only transitional. It is the connecting link between the old revered jury trial and the more efficient and just "trial" by commissions and boards which would appear to be the juries of tomorrow.

Sad though this may be for those attorneys who feel their livelihood may be affected by this change, or that they may be deprived of that sharp edge of pleasure which comes from invigorating jury combat, it is even more ironic to contemplate that they themselves are a primary cause in this change, due to their pressures on the juries, their constant drive for ever higher—or lower—verdicts regardless of justice, and their development of skills to twist the citizen jurors to the advocate's advantage and to delay the prompt administration of justice.

17

Summary: What Experts Think

ATTITUDES OF ATTORNEYS TOWARD JURIES ARE, QUITE NATUR-
ally, often tempered by their successes or failures with them.
The newer, more progressive, view is that juries are a hold-
over from an outmoded era. These lawyers feel jurors take
law out of the hands of courts and make up their own as
they go along. They feel juries are extreme in their awards,
either giving verdicts far too high for the damages suffered,
or denying payment completely to severely injured persons.
They agree that juries are thoroughly unpredictable and that
going before them is a grim gamble at high stakes.

As interesting as the views of those opposing juries is the
reasoning of the group which defends them; it shows a dis-
heartening distrust of the American system of justice in which
they play important roles. For example, it is commonplace for
lawyers to use juries as a jockeying device in picking a
favorable position. Here is how this works: when filing suit,
the attorney automatically requests a jury, particularly in a

large community where there are many judges available to hear the case. The jury is then held as a defensive weapon. If the lawyer should happen to get a judge who he feels could lean in his direction, he dismisses the jury and goes before the judge alone. Should his judge be one who is strict in his views, however, the lawyer keeps his jury as a buffer against the judge and hopes that he can be more convincing to the lay persons than he could be to the experienced jurist.

This ties into the attitude most often expressed by lawyers: they admit freely they do not trust judges. They say judges can be influenced to favor lawyers who belong to the same social background as they do, or to the same church or fraternal lodge, or economic circle, or any of a number of influences.

This is indeed a sad commentary on the quality of American judges by the men who should know them best: the lawyers who practice before them. They say a jury is necessary to protect them from such politically minded masters of the courtroom. Nevertheless, these same lawyers proceed quite happily before these same judges in a wide variety of cases in which juries are often denied. Many of these cases are of the most discretionary sort in which a weak judge could be easily biased, yet rare indeed is the complaint raised to their rulings.

One type of these is domestic relations matters. Here judges often sit alone to rule on facts and apply the law on such elusive matters as bitterly contested divorce suits where each side accuses the other of the most devastating affronts. They rule without benefit of jury on such matters as who should have custody of the children in broken homes where each parent debases the other to prove him an unfit parent. Another type is probate cases involving such matters as the filing of wills, adoptions, determining if a person is mentally incompetent, and the appointment of guardians. Still another is the wide range of equity cases which include such hotly debated issues as injunctions in labor disputes, specific performance in contracts, balancing of hardships, and accountings in business deals.

It is clear that if judges sitting alone become the dangerous tyrants that many lawyers would have you believe, then a type of trial in which juries are specifically denied must continuously result in injustice. Yet case after case of this type has shown justice much more clearly and logically rendered than in the dramatic display of an emotion-governed jury trial.

Another brand of pro-jury sentiment claims that after years of hearing tragic trials, judges become hardened to them. The judges, the argument goes, become anesthetized to the human problems and rule too harshly on the human foibles which appear before them. It is much better to have a fresh group look at the same facts each time than someone who has become bored with them over a period of years, goes this argument.

This, too, points up a distrust of judges and seeks a way around them. It also ignores the many good rulings they hand down in cases outlined above, or in courts of appeals, or supreme courts—without juries—where they have heard the same problems many times. It ignores the fact that by listening to the same tales repeatedly, a judge can become expert at discerning what is truth and what is fancy, what is said merely for effect and what is real and goes to the heart of the matter.

The usual argument lawyers give for favoring a jury is the sentimental one that they are symbols of democracy and that we should be most careful before tampering with any part of our democratic system. This ignores the evidence that rather than being democratic and answering to the voters for their actions, jurors are the most despotic and arbitrary persons in a courtroom. They need answer to no one. They take the law into their own hands, issue a ruling, and then disperse into the public from which they came, leaving behind them a decision and no one to blame.

A judge, on the other hand, in many states must stand for re-election, and there his rulings come back to haunt him with the voters. He cannot take the risk of going too far wrong, too often, if he values his reputation and, through it, his job.

LAWYERS PICK JURIES

When top trial lawyers get to talking informally—off the record—their arguments boil down to the fact that they believe they can do more with a jury to win that unusually large verdict which will upset all precedent and set a new record, bringing them fame and wealth. Or, on the defense side, that they can convince a jury to return nothing. They are, in fact, relying on the inherent weaknesses of juries in the hope that they will render an extreme verdict. Their confidence in feeling they will win this big one rests on the fact that in America, alone, lawyers have almost absolute control in picking out the jurors. They are confident always that the next time they will pick a winning jury that they can condition to carry them all the way to victory.

This is evident to anyone who has ever seen the *voir dire,* or selection of a jury. The opposing lawyers question and badger prospective members until they have formed the jury into the exact mold they wish. They eliminate with peremptory challenges those they think will harm their cause —without regard to whether they will do justice or not—by simply telling the court they will excuse a certain juror, without having to give a reason. When they have used up their limited supply of peremptory challenges, they badger and push the unwanted juror into such a position with their questioning that the judge excuses him for cause.

Only when each side is satisfied with the jury "as presently constituted" is the matter settled. The judge has hardly anything to do with this procedure except mildly to reprove a lawyer if he becomes a little too aggressive in his efforts. In law school, and in many books by experts, it is stressed that the proper selection of a jury is the pinnacle of victorious trial lawyers and that cases are won or lost by merely the picking of a sympathetic jury. Nothing is said here of seeking a jury that will do justice. The emphasis is on one most calculated to win your case.

How different this is from the procedure in England. Rare it is that juries are used here, but when they are brought in, the selection is made almost wholly by the judge alone, in a minimum of time, and the matter proceeds to seek justice rather than victory for the one more adept at picking the right jury.

It is clear from talking with lawyers that they will not give up their control over jury selections in America. With it rides their hope to control the outcome of the trial. This is too often what they mean when they speak of the democracy of a jury. Albert S. Osborn wrote more than a generation ago, in 1937, that:

It is quite natural for those unfamiliar with the conditions to suppose that the presence of incompetent jurors on the panel would not greatly matter as they would not need to be called to serve, but experience demonstrates that in many cases they are the very jurors that one of the lawyers wants. They, in fact, constitute his only chance to win, or to secure a disagreement, which too often is an indirect way of winning.

It thus clearly appears why some men in these courts are not enthusiastic about improving the jury system. If it were suffi-

ciently improved they would be at least partly out of business.
Their reputation as trial attorneys would suffer if all members
of every jury were able to recognize sophistry and buncombe.[1]

An all-too-clear inference to be gained from this is that often
lawyers and their clients stake their chances of winning an
unjust, indeed an often utterly spurious, case on the known
weaknesses of the jury system. Thus it would be hard to
imagine them opposed to it. Lawyers, in fact, act aggrieved
when it is suggested that the jury system can stand serious
reform. They outspokenly see such thoughts as a threat to their
livelihood. Since it often takes three times as long to try a case
before a jury it can be seen that fees could sometimes play a
part in their interest.

Although some argue that the long delays before coming to
trial reduce the number of cases they may handle and thus cut
their overall income, a lively lawyer can make himself busy
with other profitable enterprises while awaiting his turn, thus
avoiding a financial loss.

WHAT JUDGES THINK OF JURIES

The opinion of judges toward their jurors is to a large degree
summed up by an off-the-cuff comment of one of the more
astute judges of my acquaintance. He said, with a wide smile :
"It is often such a comfort to know they are there."

Generally, however, a majority of the trial judges I have
interviewed are opposed to the jury system as it now exists
— but their opposition is emphatically "off the record," for
fear of treading on too many important toes. Their criticism
of juries usually began with the prologue : "You, of course,
know that I cannot speak my mind on this for publication,
but . . . ."

[1] Osborn, *The Mind of the Juror* (The Boyd Printing Company, Albany,
N.Y.), p. 18.

Their "but" went through the entire gamut of a jury trial from the time jurors were impaneled, while they were forced to sit as mere observers, through to the time when verdicts were returned, which bore little apparent relation to the evidence the judges had heard from the bench.

They noted, for example, that many trial lawyers brought the same expert witnesses to trial after trial. These consisted of doctors, engineers, psychologists, physicists, and others. These men, obviously in the pay of the attorney who summoned them, piously went through the same testimony in each case. To the judge, their words soon carried the sound of having been memorized. (He could almost tell at exactly what point during the proceedings the expert would be called to speak.) Yet the unknowing jurors (sitting on a trial for only a brief time and, usually for only once in their lives) listen to these experts with great belief and awe. The pain and suffering described by the doctors, the emotional upheaval recounted by the psychologists brings from naïve jurors a sympathetic understanding that later can be translated into dollars.

Judges underscore that this is surely not the fault of the jurors. Anyone placed in their position would react the same, and skilled lawyers count on that. The judges feel that such a situation could be counteracted, at least slightly, if they were permitted to comment on the credibility of various witnesses, as is done freely in British courts and to a large degree in some Federal courts here. Unfortunately, this would not eliminate the problem completely, because jurors — with sympathy in full sail — would still fall prey to the words of well-paid experts; but it might trim their belief a little and give them an insight into how lawsuits are sometimes handled.

By the same token, experienced judges not only become familiar with the bought witnesses, but become capable of seeing through the deception of those who testify for their cause with little regard for the truth. In divorce court, for example, after a few instances of watching the tears of a wronged wife quickly dry up when a hefty cash settlement has been made, the judge learns to distinguish such phony dramatics which flow past his bench in endless stream from the real emotions of a wife, or husband, who truthfully is torn by the prospect of a home breaking up and really seeks a means of preserving it.

Another problem, the judges feel, is that jurors are too often subjected to technical evidence that is far beyond their capacity to grasp. The surgeon, speaking in complex medical terminology of the effect of a fracture upon surrounding ligaments and nerves, leaves the jury far behind him and completely bewildered. The seasoned engineer, telling why a contract for involved machinery could not be fulfilled exactly as specified, leaves jurors equally baffled. Yet into the hands of these jurors is placed the all-important task of deciding if a wrong has been done and, if so, how much should be paid in damages.

I saw this problem solved in one courtroom where a case, centering around whether a highly technical contract for machinery had been correctly handled, was being tried. The two litigants agreed to the judge's proposal that a panel for arbitrating this problem be set up. The plaintiff selected one member of the panel from a society of machinists; the defendant, another man from the same society. The judge picked the third member, who was a patent attorney, well versed in technical laws.

The panel went to a vacant adjoining courtroom; they heard the evidence. After brief deliberation on the facts and law, they gave their written conclusions to the judge who, in the meantime, had been free to handle another case. The judge compared their findings with the transcript of the hearing and accepted them as his own. Both parties left with the satisfaction that they had been given a fair hearing and that a just decision had been reached.

Despite their knowledge of the jury's many weaknesses, most of which strike at the very heart of justice, a large number of judges still maintain quite firmly—even in the privacy of their own chambers—that the citizen decider of facts is basic in a system of justice and should not be eliminated. Their reasons are interesting and most enlightening.

One judge said that with a jury he could himself avoid making unpopular rulings in widely publicized cases. Thus, he felt, he could avoid criticism of himself. The jury had made the decision, not he. The jury was supposedly composed of a cross section of society and, evidently, that ruling was the wish of society. The judge admitted he was being purposely naïve in his idea that the jury's decision reflected the wishes of society, but felt it was a good way to get out of a hot spot.

Another judge concluded a lengthy discourse on the jury as an active arm of democracy, allowing the average lay person to judge his fellow man, with the comment that jurors were picked only from registered voters. Here, he said, in the parade of voters was a valued chance to meet vast numbers of electors over the years. Multiply that by the relatives, friends, and neighbors with whom they might speak and the shores to which the ripples of the judge's name might reach was without limit.

This judge took the time to meet each juror personally and, needless to say, most pleasantly. He politely explained to them the process of the court, and incidentally mentioned his many years of experience and the important cases he had sat in. He was most considerate of their wants and deeply appreciated their stage fright. When a member of the panel was dropped from the prospective jury, the judge was most apologetic and embarrassed at the rules which forced him to do it. In the meantime, his bailiff was carefully taking down the names and addresses of all jurors from the roll call. These were placed on index cards and developed into an extensive mailing list around election time. To this judge the jury was a valued public relations vehicle, which he would never consider giving up; he was a many-times re-elected judge.

Another judge admitted a jury gave him a good chance to relax and let his mind wander. He had to take only casual interest in the proceedings, so that he could determine whether a question were objectionable or not. The rest of the time he could relax. He already knew most of the facts in the case from his reading of the petitions and his pretrial sessions with the lawyers. He knew enough of the case to make up his charge to the jury. In the actual proceedings, he had only a casual or academic interest; and this had been forced on him over the years by the role to which he had been relegated by the law : the less he interfered, the better off he was.

One judge told me his biggest problem was to keep from the jury any sign of his attitude about various aspects of the case either by expression on his face or the tone of his voice. He was afraid that if he gave any indication at all the lawyers might regard this as prejudicial to their case. He was proud that thus far he had kept himself completely out of trouble. He was as about important in his case as was the lamp on his desk.

How shocked would be the judges of England to learn the pride an American trial judge had in his nonentity!

Dean Roscoe Pound, emeritus professor of the Harvard School of Law bemoaned this sad sate of affairs with this comment :

The central point in our legal polity was the common law judge. He dominated the whole administration of justice. Towering over counsel, controlling the trial, he was the pivot of the legal system. We adopted the system, but we reduced the judge to the level of the practitioner in his court. By legislation, beginning in North Carolina in 1796, in most jurisdictions we tied him down by elaborate procedural legislation so as to prescribe in advance almost everything he should do and how he should do it.

Finally, veteran judges tend to become inured to the jury frailties which they encounter in their daily work. One such example is their reaction to the inequality displayed by jurors in assessing damages. At one time I became aware that no large verdicts had been awarded in Cleveland's civil courts for a long time. Indeed, an unusually large number of juries found no damages at all. In discussing this with some of the older judges, I was surprised to find their attitude was that this is nothing unusual. Jury verdicts seem to run in cycles, they said. For several months, without apparent reason, juries just will not pay, no matter what the injuries sustained by the plaintiff. Persons whose cases come up for trial at this time are just out of luck. Then, without any plausible reason, the cycle reverses: verdicts suddenly start climbing; cases which were thought to have no chance come out victorious.

What are the reasons? The veteran judges simply throw their hands in the air and shrug. The cycle has turned; that is the only explanation they can give. And, besides, what difference does it make what the reason can be. The jury is the decider of the facts and all we need do is simply accept what they say.

Thus it can be seen that the jury is a very weak link in this system we call "justice." It is as now constituted out of step with the time. It once served a great purpose of protection from despotism, which today is no longer needed. It stands in the way of more equitable justice and the modern pace of living — it is a sad reflection of modern morals. As Osborne wrote:

There is no part of the legal machinery that "creaks" more loudly than the jury system. Of course, as soon as the citizens of a progressive society realize these things with sufficient intensity the abuses will be ended, but it is a fact that but few of the general public know what goes on under that blindfolded statue of justice year after year. One would think that lawyers and judges in certain places would hang their heads in shame for being part of a clumsy system so out of harmony with progress.

It is a subject which cries for a long, hard look—with a calm eye to readjustment—not only by the legal profession, but by the general public. For the people, like it or not, will some day become intimately involved with it, either as a litigant or as an earnest juror honestly seeking this elusive thing called justice.

² *Mind of the Juror*, p. 19.

18

Reform! Reform!

ANY EFFORT TO BRING SLIGHT CHANGE TO JURIES RESULTS IN outcries and bickering. Even President Johnson's very modest plan to modernize jury selections—part of the 1966 civil rights package—brought criticism from Chief Justice Earl Warren that the bills "go a long way and would very radically change the relationship between our federal and state governments." New York Democratic Representative Emanuel Celler, head of the House Judiciary Committee, in turn criticized the chief justice, saying "it is unseemly for a Supreme Court justice to comment on legislation pending in Congress." So it is that the snapping starts when juries are threatened. (The bills were defeated.)

But use of juries in state courts cries for reform if any part of the system is to be preserved. Any thinking citizen, any person caught up in the confusion of a jury trial as litigant or juror, is aware of that, and many methods are available: they range from tightening up the system as it now exists in order to bring it more within the reality of present conditions, all the way up to complete elimination of jurors and having cases heard by the judges alone. As we have seen, it is possible even to eliminate the judge and have these matters handled by arbitrators, boards, or commissions sitting in their place.

Let us start with the least drastic changes, which can be put into effect immediately—and most easily—within the present legal framework. The easiest way to begin is simply by changing the conditions which bring about the obvious flaws recounted earlier. For example, simply by allowing jurors to take notes during a trial, we would remove the need for mental gymnastics, errors, and faulty memories in the gathering of facts and marshalling them for logical study. Simplifying the recital of laws to the jurors and relating them to things which jurors can understand would do much to bring needed light into this dark corner of jury trials where both judges and jurors are helpless under present rules.

CHANGING JURY SELECTION

One important way of elevating the quality of juries is by changing the method of selecting the persons who sit on the panels; this is widely recognized and is already under way in some parts of the country. Several recommendations for sweeping changes, for example, were made in Baltimore after two years of study by the city's bar association. The aim of the recommendations is to make sure that a more intelligent and qualified cross-section of the community is called to jury service.

This bar association urged that a person serving as a juror should have at least an eighth-grade education and that the information requested from the prospective juror include data on his education and business interests. It asks also that the age of eligibility for jury service be reduced from twenty-five to twenty-one years. Most interesting are recommendations for a great many changes in exemptions in order to bring into the jury box a great many persons whose special abilities to serve have, surprising though it may seem, been the very things that kept them out. Thus, it was urged, exemptions should be eliminated for such persons as judges and clerks of election; city, state, and federal employees (unless they are elected officials), school teachers, other employees of the school board and wives of physicians.

This would appear to be the very minimum of what should be done : only a modest beginning on a major job. But at least it becomes evident that some of the short-comings of juries are being recognized. Unfortunately, however, the suggestions for reform are in large part timid and make only minor movement in the direction of what must eventually be done if greater justice is to be achieved in the courtroom.

GIVE JUDGES POWER

It is highly important that judges in state courts be given a great deal more power in the running of their own trials. The judge should in truth be made the master of his courtroom. The selection of the jury, for example, should be placed entirely into the hands of the judge. The too-often shameful spectacle of lawyers badgering and browbeating jurors, arbitrarily tossing out those they feel cannot be influenced or pressured, should be completely erased. The judge should question the jury himself; he alone should decide when a capable and unbiased jury has been seated. This should be done without interference from the lawyers on either side of the trial table. The seating of a jury should be done with dispatch and trial of the case should proceed at once.

When the trial is completed and the judge is giving instructions to the jury, he should be free to comment in any way he wishes on the evidence which has been presented. He may wish, for example, to point out which witnesses are to be believed — and why — as well as which are of doubtful value. Does this sound daring and revolutionary? It hardly is. This is the method which has long been in use in England. It proved exceedingly successful there. It has also been used to a somewhat lesser extent in our federal courts. Thus, it is hardly beating a path through virgin territory to suggest such a change. But it is certain to arouse cries of anguish from lawyers who may fear their power to win high verdicts — or very low ones — will be hampered by their loss of control over juries. It may, indeed, make the entire value of the democratic jury system suddenly seem less appealing to many who now shout loudest for its preservation. And it may, to the benefit of justice, even convince them that juries over which they have lost control are no longer necessary and might as well be waived altogether. In this they would again be following in the footsteps of England. Also, in this connection, the judges themselves would be performing a valued service to their courts if they would encourage the waiving of juries altogether or, failing that, urge that they be comprised of a smaller number of members, so they may be handled much more efficiently.

HELP THE JURORS

If the jury system must be retained, the courts have a gigantic task in devising methods to help jurors perform their obligations. This job is largely educational. Several suggestions have already been put into practice but, unfortunately, none of them has shown any marked degree of success. One, for example, is the printing of handbooks that jurors may read before beginning their service. This, in effect, would attempt to be a do-it-yourself quickie course in law and trial procedure. Unfortunately, the usual result of this is to confuse jurors even more than they normally would be, as can be testified to by any lawyer who can remember cramming for an examination in law school.

Another much-suggested help to jurors could be a short educational course given by a judge in the courthouse. Of course, this would take time of a valuable judge away from his important judicial duties; and it would be highly repetitive, the same lectures having to be given over and over again to new batches of jurors. What is more, its results would be highly inconclusive, since no one would know how much of the lectures were being absorbed by the involuntary and restless students. But this would be slightly better than on-the-job training at the expense of a defendant's liberty or at the cost of having to pay a mistaken judgment. A way of determining the value of this special training would be to require all juries to put their findings of fact into writing. They would indicate what facts they considered and what influenced them in reaching their conclusions. In this would be reflected whatever it was the jurors had absorbed in their short training course and it could be seen where they failed.

Still another help—and this would be a major improvement—would be to select jurors especially qualified to handle the case they would be hearing. For example, a case involving the evaluation of land to be appropriated by the government would be heard by a panel of real estate experts; a case involving personal injuries would be heard by a jury of doctors, nurses, or other medical personnel; a case involving contracts over machinery would be heard by engineers.

Loud opposition to this could be expected among some lawyers, who would argue that these people do not come to the matter with an open mind; that they are prejudiced by their own training. What they really mean is that these jurors cannot be influenced by emotional arguments which may have no bearing on the case and, since they cannot be pressured, are of no value in helping the lawyer win his case however meager its merit.

It should be noted that however much an improvement these suggestions may be, they still fall short of resolving the basic troubles with juries : they will still be juries composed of persons without sufficient training or experience in a trial to see through façades hastily thrown up by skilled lawyers. In brief, they may be able to pierce more often than at present the veil of oratory woven by legal counsel; but the veil will still remain, at times hiding important information from juries expert in their vocations but naïve in the ways of law.

THE TROUBLE WITH JUDGES

The most simple and direct reform would be to abolish the jury entirely. This would place the complete handling of trials in the hands of the judges alone, which on the surface would seem to be the most ideal method. He already has the required training in law, and by simple experience the judge gradually becomes an expert in ferreting out facts and learning what is a truthful claim and what is simply a smokescreen that contains nothing of value. He can give a decision in short order that would cover both the facts of the case and the law that is supposed to govern his ruling.

Of course, many judges would be reluctant to take on this added responsibility. Why should they be eager to accept it when they have gotten along until now without having to assume it, along with all the unpopular decisions it might entail. But this is a minor hurdle. If men ambitious of being judges are aware that it carries with it those responsibilities, they will assume them without argument as part of their job. They already do this in cases where there are no juries present.

The real problem here is not whether the judges would be willing to accept such obligations, or whether they would have the capacity to handle them properly. Everything tends to indicate an affirmative answer to both. The actual problem is the question of how they would react to political pressures in the search for justice, because there is no question that those pressures will be there in a very large degree. They will come from newspapers in cases of great public interest or over which the editors are conducting a crusade; they will come from political leaders who feel the judges owe them something for getting elected to this coveted position; and they will come from the general public, which, by casting votes to elect one judicial aspirant over another, feels it has a voice in directing how he shall administer justice.

The heart of this question, then, is how to take the judge out of politics, where he assuredly does not belong and which should have absolutely nothing to do with the weighing of facts and the determination of justice. One plan that is hoped will accomplish this has been carefully studied in Ohio with the encouragement of the Ohio State Bar Association. This proposal, the *appointive* system of selecting judges, provides for the nomination of judicial aspirants by a state-wide nominating commission. The actual appointment would be by the governor. Term of the judge thus selected would probably be for six years as at present and at the end of his term the incumbent would have to run for re-election. But he would have no opposition on the ballot. The question before the voters would only be whether or not he should be retained in office on the basis of his past record. If the majority of the votes cast should be against him, he would be removed from office and a new selection made by the governor. Under the proposed plan, the nominating commission would be composed of ten members, half Democrats and half Republicans. Half would be lawyers and half laymen, drawn from all sections of the state. In general, the plan would be similar to one already in operation in Missouri, after which it is patterned.

As is to be expected, the Ohio plan stirred up a great deal of opposition. Much of it has come from men already on the bench who appear to enjoy the vigor of a political contest and the ego satisfaction of having their names approved by the voters, most of whom do not even know the candidate's qualifications, and in reality are voting for nothing more than a popular name or a party affiliation.

Opposition of the jurists, however, is based on the argument that an appointive system would benefit largely the wealthy lawyer, the "silk-stocking crowd" with friends in the right places and would shut out the poor lads who had to work their way through night law school as well as members of minority groups in race or religion. They see it, thus, as a controlled super-political plan and in opposition to democracy. Areas which have appointive systems, however, report this has not happened.

Another effort at removing judges from the common cockpit of politics is the Cleveland Bar Association program of conducting a poll among lawyers on those seeking the bench and extending the association's endorsement on the basis of the results. This endorsement includes an advertising campaign on behalf of the fortunate candidates who have received approval and efforts to discourage less worthy opponents.

That politics too often plays a role in judicial attitudes cannot be over emphasized. This can be illustrated by an incident in which this writer participated : The Cuyahoga County (Ohio) Common Pleas Court for many years had built up a lucrative system of patronage in the assigning of criminal cases to private lawyers. These were the cases of indigent defendants too poor to afford attorneys to defend them. These assignments paid up to $300 to the attorney assigned for ordinary felonies and $3,500 plus expenses in homicides. The method of assignment was simple. The judge or his bailiff just picked up his telephone and offered the case to a lawyer. Often the lawyer had nothing to do but plead his charity case guilty and collect his fee, which was paid from taxes. Sometimes this lawyer worked hard for his fee, but many times he did not. The competition for these political plums was strong and many dozens of lawyers gave their calling cards to the presiding criminal judge for the term in hopes of being called. A glance at the names of lawyers assigned to these cases during a term showed many belonging to well-known political figures and friends of the judges. Finally, however, the local Legal Aid Society, after lengthy study, concluded that the defense of the poor could be greatly improved. In municipal courts, for example, where no tax-paid fees were available for lawyers, the defendant who happened to be so unfortunate as to have no money was without any legal representation at all. There were no legal calling cards waiting where there was no money to be had.

In view of all this, the much-respected Legal Aid Society established an office of Public Defender with the aid of a charitable grant of $100,000 from the Cleveland Foundation. It was set up with a staff of three outstanding criminal lawyers and a full-time investigator. It provided a concentration of service for improved justice that no single lawyer could match. Its record of acquittals was awesome and it won the whole-hearted support of the Cleveland Welfare Federation as well as the Cleveland and American Bar Associations. This giant step toward greater equality of justice for all was saluted by the city's newspapers and television stations. It won favor from everybody immediately — except a small band of trial judges and a minor group of political lawyers who wanted the fees. These judges rejected efforts of the Public Defender's office to get assignments of penniless prisoners in any worthwhile numbers. Some assignments were made, it is true, but far from enough to keep the office alive. The judges, with minor exceptions, fought to preserve their patronage, their political gifts, and shut their eyes to the achievements and public service promise of this new office. Specious arguments were made that the court owed no obligation to the Defender, that they should not spend "their" money—in reality that of the taxpayers—to keep an office going that would also defend the poor in the lower municipal courts, as though justice in other courts was none of the judges' business. While the Legal Aid Society cried that the Defender's office was being starved out of business, the judges continued to pass their assignments, and the fees from taxpayers, to their political friends. It took a long time before public pressures persuaded them to change their view and accept the Defender.

This is the type of situation engendered by having political judges on the bench. Here it was in the open and obvious to the public through newspaper reports. How many other decisions and activities across the country are also influenced by politics is hard to know. They are neither so blatant nor so publicized.

That is why it is important to take judges out of politics if they are to be entrusted with the sole conduct of a trial without the protection of a jury for the parties. Judges must be made to be above reproach if they are to have the confidence of litigants who appear before them. The display of Cleveland's judges toward the Defender's offices in its early years could hardly breed confidence in judges who acted that way. The men on the bench were, in effect, harming their own prestige and power by hewing strictly to the line of politics when the moment of decision arrived. Veteran members of the bar, however, just smiled knowingly and said that was the way of the world.

So it is that the most ideal method of eliminating the jury problem—the use of judges alone who could speed trials and make justice more nearly equal—rests on a preliminary step of securing judges who would enjoy a higher standard of confidence from both the public and the lawyers who practice before them. ·It is common knowledge that British judges, for example, enjoy a much higher reputation than do their American counterparts. Barristers there feel more secure in presenting their cases, because they have the assurance that politics, at least, will not color the final results. That American judges are fully capable of doing the same is seen in the very many instances where they serve without benefit of a jury's assistance. Good examples of this are the United States tax courts and the Federal Torts Act as previously noted. These are in Federal courts, and it should be noted that the judges there are somewhat separated from the political arena. Selection of the Federal judge is, of course, highly political in nature, depending all too often on the party to which they belong and how active they have been in it. But once appointed, they are there for life.

Thus divorced from the need for further campaigns, backslapping, maintaining good political relations, and all the other paraphernalia that goes with elective office, they can devote more of their time to dispensing justice regardless of influence. And that, after all, is their primary function and should remain their basic concern in this most sensitive post.

LIMITING JURY USE . . .

Another suggestion worth considering might be called a compromise. It stems from a recognition of the many frailties with which jurors come to their tasks. In this plan, while the possibilities of juries are retained, qualifications are placed on the absolute right to a trial by jury. In this respect it would be somewhat similar to the English system : applications would be addressed to the judge for the impaneling of a jury and the decision of whether this would be done would remain with him. Thus, it would reverse the present procedure which provides for a jury unless specifically waived and change it to one in which juries are not available unless specifically granted.

The reasoning behind such a program stems from the fact that there are many situations in which juries are absolutely worthless, yet judges are nevertheless saddled with their use. A complicated suit over breach of contract where a certain amount of damages is sought for failure to exactly meet specifications of a job, for example, would hardly benefit from a lay jury completely unacquainted with the technological problems involved.

. . . OR A LIMITED JURY

An offshoot of the suggestion to limit the types of cases in which juries may be used is the idea of limiting the jury itself. There is no absolute necessity to have a jury composed of twelve uninformed lay persons. It could much better be a jury of two persons exceptionally well informed on the subject of the case at hand and who would work together with the judge on the verdict. For example, if a personal injury case were before the court, the jury, or fact-finding panel, could consist of two doctors. They would sit on the bench, one on each side of the judge, and listen carefully to all the evidence. At the conclusion of the trial, the three would deliberate together. The jury experts would discuss the facts and evaluate the medical testimony which had been presented. The judge would advise them on the law applicable to the particular case as they proceed with the deliberations. Should their attention be drawn to improper evidence, the judge could warn them of the danger and bring them back to the legal channel.

The type of jury, therefore, can vary with the type of case. Engineers would sit in judgment upon technological disputes; hair experts would consider a case where the plaintiff claimed a faulty preparation had ruined her hair. This type of juror would tend less to be influenced by dramatic but meaningless evidence. They would know what is most meaningful.

The verdict would come by a majority vote. Thus, the expert jurors could overcome a prejudiced, biased, or politically inclined judge if that is what lawyers fear. The protection against an overbearing judge would be preserved if lawyers think it should be, and the public would continue to have its hand in the administration of justice; but in a more intelligent way than can be achieved under present circumstances. The panel would, in far greater degree than now, be aimed at finding facts rather than at weighing dramatic abilities of lawyers competing for their favor. Their members would be in the tradition of fact-finding bodies used by the government in attempting to resolve labor disputes in essential industries. They would relieve the tragi-comic note of helplessness prevalent in present juries, which is the cause of such great amusement among court observers.

Critics of this suggestion have said it would be practically impossible to find experts willing to give of their precious time to sit on such panels for any considerable period. The answer to this is obvious: if the cause of justice is so important that ordinary citizens are drawn from their normal pursuits to sit on juries, as is done now, it should surely be important enough to draw experts who are in reality simply ordinary persons with specialized training.

Another answer, too, would soon appear in the fact that attorneys, once deprived of uninformed juries who they would hope to convince to their cause, would more and more tend to waive these specialized juries and place their cases into the hands of the courts alone. For those particularly complicated matters which would continue to require the services of juries, the professional societies would be called upon to furnish these experts as an obligation to the communities from which they draw their livelihood. And not to be overlooked are those retired engineers, doctors, contractors, and others, who would like to retain an active hand in their fields and be willing to serve repeatedly on these fact-finding panels in instances where their particular skills are needed to resolve difficulties.

The argument for such specialized jurors relates to the logic of everyday transactions in the business world. The head of a commercial enterprise with a problem of increasing sales surely does not turn it over to a stranger he plucks from the street; he seeks a merchandising expert who is trained in the problem to be solved. It is common sense to do the same in the all-important search for greater justice in the community.

How sensible, in contrast, is the present system of calling top-flight experts to the witness stand to give their highly specialized opinions to a jury that cannot understand what is being discussed? How much better would it be to have a skilled neurosurgeon give his opinion to a panel of jurors who at least understand his language and the point he is trying to make.

Refusal of lawyers to realize that their clients prefer to have their disputes heard by experts is contributing to the hastening flight away from the traditional courts and toward arbitration and specialized commissions and boards. Clients would be much put out if they learned that their lawyers in their private offices, unable to reach agreement over differences by way of negotiations, went out into the street and rounded up twelve pedestrians to come up and settle the question. Yet that is what they are doing every day in court. They are putting matters of great importance into the hands of persons who do not have the training or abilities of the competing lawyers or the judge.

ARBITRATION AS A SUPPLEMENT

Some lawyers, distressed at the present situation in courts clogged by cumbersome, inadequate juries, have suggested help outside the courtroom by means of arbitrators agreed upon by the opposing parties. In a New York speech at an arbitration conference, Federal Judge Harold R. Medina said:

Every day, controversies are being resolved speedily and fairly by impartial members of the business community. It doesn't compete with our performance of the judicial function. It supplements it. There are many fields of controversy where it is the most efficient, the speediest, the most economical, and most plausible means of resolving disputes. It can lift the wearing uncertainties and the apprehensions that often play on the minds of businessmen who are engaged in bitterly fought and long-extended litigations. The courts have more business than they can keep up with. Every expansion of the use of arbitration contributes to the goal of speedy, impartial, and responsible administration of justice. That does not mean the courts are ousted. For in the final analysis, checks upon the system rest with the courts.

Its supporters say arbitration has many advantages over the tedious process of a trial by jury. The hearing can be promptly scheduled at the convenience of all concerned. The parties choose their own "judge," who may be selected on the basis of his integrity and particular knowledge in the field in which the dispute is concerned. The parties know in advance the exact day, time, and place of the hearing and the harassing experience of waiting for a case to be called is avoided. The award, or decision, is rendered promptly after the hearing is concluded, and can be made subject to judicial review.

An award rendered by an arbitrator, who is chosen for his experience, ability, and impartiality is consonant with sound legal practice. The informality which prevails at the hearing tends to conserve the time and energy of both the lawyer and the litigant, and results in decreased costs and expense. Laws can be so framed as to confer upon parties the legal right to arbitration and to bring the courts to their aid in enforcing their arbitration agreements and awards.

The trial of criminal cases has clearly not kept up with the sociological and scientific advances made in the area of crime. It is commonplace to find precise scientific proof going completely over the heads of jurors, who have never heard of the new techniques and have not the faintest notion of how to interpret their results. It is often, indeed, that the wisest criminal lawyer will abandon, or ridicule, the newest crime detection methods in order to reach the jurors at their own level. This simple rapport of the street is a hundredfold more effective in winning the jury mind—and its approval—than the language of the scientist of whom the jurors always have a little suspicion, born of lack of understanding.

The new advances of science in this field, therefore, would seem of themselves to call for a new type of juror, one with an understanding of their meaning if their value is to be fully utilized. In the social sciences, experts in such fields as psychology and racial relations deplore the narrow and stilted reactions from lay jurors. The greatest advances in thinking are least applied where they are most needed. Highly developed ideas of criminology, strangely enough, appear to have no place in a criminal court. Here the only method of handling major social problems is a vague rule-of-thumb emotional system that serves to create its own injustices and resentment which, in turn, serve to foster further crimes.

A wrongdoer who receives the harshest of sentences, but sees another man equally guilty freed on emotional appeal of a wily lawyer, can hardly be expected to have a fondness for modern justice or an appreciation of just punishment. It is clear that here the fate of a man, multiplied by all the other men he will brush up against, deserves much more care than the hap-hazard type of justice meted out by an uninformed jury of ordinary citizens. Yet it is in exactly this area that the hue and cry to retain the jury system as a form of unreasoning "protection" is the loudest.

If it should be true that an innocent accused needs a barrier against a particularly vicious or unfeeling judge, let it be by a trained two-man fact-finding team which will sit on the bench with the judge and deliberate with him, a majority of this three-man tribunal being needed for a verdict. The constant advice of a judge learned in the law would eliminate the gross inequities that come from simple lack of understanding of its meaning.

In the majority of routine cases, however, a single judge to hear the facts and decide them, as well as to apply the law, would be enough. In extremely serious cases, or those which might carry the death penalty, it would be wise to have a panel of three judges as is the case now where the jury has been waived. There is surely nothing new about this and it has been successful.

What would such reforms in criminal juries accomplish? It would bring a consistency to criminal verdicts for one thing. A young defendant who threw a rock through a window would be practically certain that he would be found guilty of that specific crime and not have the law bent to fit the concept of justice arising in the neighborhoods from which the jurors were summoned. The lawmakers who passed an act banning a specific action would know it would be enforced as equally as possible in all situations. The young lawbreaker, intending to perform the crime, would know well beforehand that it was going to be strictly enforced without the ameliorating effect of a lenient jury of citizens. Thus, this system would bring justice based on logic rather than the emotions of a jury, or their desire to be freed as soon as possible from the discomfort of a stuffy courthouse, or their desire for a peaceful and anonymous lunch. It would eliminate such sights as quarreling or vengeful jurors spitefully transferring their anger at their colleagues' obstinacy to the defendant. It would cut out a great deal of the community revenge, once described as a legal lynching by jurors, and promote the possibility of bringing in an outside judge from a distant part of the state to sit in cool detachment on the facts, a man who could ignore the emotional frenzy whipped up at the trial site by injudicious newspapers or other communications media such as radio and television as happened in the Sam Sheppard trials previously described.

If only part of the above results were to be achieved through modification of the present jury system, it would be more than worth the effort needed to bring it about. It would be a giant step in the direction of greater justice, and far from being opposed by the citizens, would instead win great applause as a forward-looking move.

It should be understood that many citizens do not look forward to serving on a criminal jury. Most of them do so with great reluctance, and where the death penalty is possible many of the most capable citizens, who would make the most able criminal jurors, bluntly refuse. The result, all too often, is a jury composed of insensitive, calloused, and inadequate individuals — far below the level that really should be used to decide something as important and meaningful as a man's freedom.

In a criminal trial, too, speed in coming to court is essential. Those too poor to post bonds, or those accused of serious crimes, must sit in a jail until the case comes up for hearing. If found innocent, every day confined is a monstrous deprivation of basic freedom. I personally covered a story in which a penniless, almost illiterate, Negro spent four months in a county jail cell. When he finally came to trial, it was found there was really no case against him. The judge himself took the matter from the jury and dismissed it of his own volition. The accused was happy to be freed, but behind him were those months of being locked away from society for no good reason. That is why it is of great importance to have prompt trials in such cases. And that is why elimination of cumbersome and time-consuming juries, or limiting them in a large degree, would prove of such value to the administration of this branch of justice.

CONCLUSION

It can be seen from all that has been said here that the jury system has created a great problem in the search for justice that is someday going to have to be resolved. In many ways, it has been shown, it is already being taken care of by the increasing flight from juries wherever that is possible. It could well be that the entire problem will thus ultimately be disposed of through a gradual change to new methods. It would appear, under this reasoning, that a natural law — pushing out the bad through increased use of the good — would make this inevitable.

Yet it appears clear that unless deliberate steps are taken, even these changes will not come into reality for a long time. The comfort of inertia is too pleasant for those not directly involved in the problems of justice to wish to arouse themselves into some form of action. The comfortable feeling too often exists among those who have not been pulled into litigation, or who have not served on juries, that this problem is too distant to concern them. They like to feel that the victim of jury-made injustice in criminal court, or of atrocious money verdicts in the civil branch, will not affect them.

This is a pleasant feeling of insulation that is inconsistent with the realities of life. When that smug and secure individual suddenly comes into contact with the confusions of court — and it can happen any moment by way of the unexpected rear-end collision at the next traffic light, the slip and fall on ice, the dispute over a bill, mistaken identification in a crime, or the summons from court to be on a jury—he comes awake with a start wondering why something has not been done about it long before this. When one is suddenly drawn into the full force of the hurricane and begins to feel its power intimately, he wonders how others sit so calmly just outside its perimeter and never lift a finger, although fully informed of its dangers.

Some may feel constrained to say that this is really not the business of the layman, any more than would be interference with the procedures of a hospital operating room. But here they tend to forget that the courts of law are really the courts of the people, and that judges in actuality sit there to administer the laws of the people, which were enacted by their elected representatives in legislatures. They forget that liberty, justice, and equality is the business of everyone, and its denial has been the cause more than once for the revolt of the people who fight to regain it. They tend to forget that the professional law-handlers also like the comforting security of a routine, that to many of them maintaining the present confusion and inefficiency is just fine.

Those lawyers who have piled up a long string of lucrative victories resting on the most notorious emotional weaknesses of the jurors will do all in their power to keep the situation as it now is; judges who have come to rely on juries to carry the greater part of the burden which should properly be theirs —those judges who regard the jurors as " such a comfort " in making difficult decisions—can hardly be expected to call for removal of this inept crutch of the law.

Thus it is that the very persons to whom the general community would look for reform are the ones who would be most reluctant to bring about change without a push from the outside. They are the ones who most often become angered when told of the deficiencies of the courts, and they resent suggestions for needed improvements. They speak in generalities of the

"great proud heritage of the jury system," and blissfully over-
look the difficulties it encounters today. They try to make the
citizen juror a sacred symbol of something which they themselves do not fully understand, although they freely admit that
there are many faults in the system. It is this emotional defense
of the jury trial—coupled with the utter lack of knowledge
about its operations by the many who have never personally
participated in the procedure—that makes any proposal to
reform, or to abolish, juries something that seems shocking to
the degree of being almost scandalous. But this book should
have made clear that the problem has been too long ignored;
that the challenge to a long-revered institution must have
attention.

There are those who feel that reform means one thing:
complete abolition of the jury system. They argue that previous
modifications of the jury, such as reducing the number of persons required to sit on a panel or making a vote less than
unanimous sufficient to reach a verdict in a civil case, has not
been enough. This, they say, has served to slightly ameliorate
the problems faced by juries, but it has not eliminated them.
As long as any part of the jury remains, it carries with it its
own seeds of inefficient operation and injustice. To cut out the
roots of the difficulty, they say, it is important to cut out the
jury system altogether. Others feel that the law would never
stand for so drastic a move, and that the change must be slow
and by degrees. They say that as juries and their powers fade
more and more, the emotional concern for them will also
gradually disappear until, when the time comes for complete
elimination, it will create fewer difficulties. Both of these points
of view evidently have the same goal; the only differences lie
in their methods of attaining it. But most evidently agree
—especially those who have observed the jury closely—that
something should be done and a beginning made soon.

That beginning is the province of the aroused lay person as well as the legal practitioner. If a jury, at the conclusion of a trial, were to announce with the utmost truthfulness that the matter for decision was completely beyond its ability, a startled legal profession would surely take notice. If increasing numbers of clients were to tell their attorneys to either waive juries or turn to arbitration for settlement—if through these efforts juries increasingly became a rarity—their practical elimination would be only a matter of time.

The path toward this has long been pointed out by other leading countries: England, France, Germany, India, Israel. This strange problem of justice, the jury, is indeed dying on all sides, yet holding firm at its heart in America.

But why should you, the reader, be concerned with this situation?

It may be due to your interest in justice generally; or it may be that you are concerned with the well-being of your fellow man and the society in which you live and are an integral part. The failure of any jury to convict a guilty accused, or to free a man really innocent, is a reflection upon you. The jury is chosen to represent *you* and to speak in *your* behalf.

Or—it may very well be—that the next victim of a confused and fumbling jury could, without too much need for coincidence, be you.

Appendix

Anatomy of a Civil Jury Trial: The $625,000 Bug-Bite Case

IT WAS A HOT DAY IN MID-SUMMER WHEN THE CASE OF James T. Gallick vs. the Baltimore & Ohio Railroad came to trial. Common Pleas Judge Victor Cohen asked his bailiff, Michael Volin, to draw the venetian blinds against the bright summer sunshine that usually poured into his courtroom on the south side of Cleveland's old, sprawling, grey-stone courthouse. It gave the room a quietly dim air and made it seem cooler.

Judge Cohen shuffled nervously through the legal papers on the high bench before him. He was a comparative newcomer as a trial judge, having been recently appointed by the governor after service on the Cleveland Transit System board and as a private lawyer. The case before him was a little frightening. It sought $750,000 and involved a complicated federal law — the Federal Employers' Liability Act — transplanted into the state court.

Before the judge, too, were two teams of the community's
top trial lawyers. On the side of Gallick, the injured railroader,
was Abe H. Dudnik and his expert on legal research, Marshall
I. Nurenberg. Dudnik had a long-standing reputation as a
colorful winning trial lawyer whose down-to-earth dramatics
and intuition of jurors established an amazing rapport. He was
in his early fifties, grey-haired, broad-shouldered, and with
a rich, booming voice that carried to every corner of the courtroom. Nurenberg, in his thirties, had won fame as the "brains
of the Dudnik office." He was slender, pale-faced, and wore
shell-rimmed glasses: the perfect picture of the studious intellectual. In the background supporting the pair were Dudnik's
partner, Sam Komito, and the lawyer who had referred the
case to them, Meyer Cook. Opposing them on the other side
of the trial table were the lawyers for the railroad, Russell E.
Leasure — tall, polished and of calm, logical temperament —
with his young assistant, Alexander H. Hadden, who carried
with him the aura of an ivy-league college graduate.

The center of attention, however, was the plaintiff himself:
fifty-eight-year old James T. Gallick, a former laborer and
railroad worker who had never, even in his best days, earned
over $5,000 a year. He lay on a crisp white hospital cart placed
just inside the courtroom gate: his bald head was showing; his
luminous eyes stared unwaveringly into the jury-box; the white
sheet he was covered with looked agonizingly flat from the
waist down — where his legs should have been.

Finally, the proceedings were ready to start. The first panel
of prospective jurors filed into the box and the questioning
began. It took two days of probing, questioning, dismissing,
and re-questioning before the full jury was seated to the satisfaction of the opposing parties.

Then they went to visit the scene of the incident: an
ordinary-appearing area in Cleveland's industrial valley, along
the Cuyahoga River not far from Lake Erie. Overhead was

the tangle of bridges connecting the city's East and West Sides, and surrounding the visiting jurors were the dirty large steel mills, the rickety old warehouses, and the miles of criss-crossing railroad tracks and spurs where cars are shunted to the various buildings to be unloaded. Special attention was given to a single track under the Columbus Road bridge and to a rain-made pond nearby. It was here that the incident was alleged to have happened: on the property of the Baltimore and Ohio Railroad Company.

Finally, the trial proper was under way. The jury of six men and six women settled into its seats. Ready to hear the complicated evidence involving three-quarters of a million dollars were three housewives, a divorced custard-stand operator, a charging-machine operator, a machinist, an assembler, a plumber, a stenographer, an unemployed widow, a technical translator, and a stationary engineer for a brewery.

First came the usual opening statements. Dudnik said he would show that the railroad had negligently allowed the pond of rainwater to accumulate for years near the track where the men worked. He said this pond at various times contained the bodies of rats and pigeons, which attracted vermin and various insects. These, Dudnik said, fed on the poisons in the pond, and one day in August, 1954, bit Gallick while at work for the railroad and poisoned his blood, leading to amputations and worse. In answer to this, Leasure said that the case was really a mystery. He said no one really knew what had infected Gallick's body and caused the festering sores that would not respond to treatment. No disease had been diagnosed, he said; no insect identified as a carrier; there was no proof that this terrible insect — if such an insect existed that could bring such appalling damage — came from the specific pond on the railroad's property. It might have flown in from elsewhere.

Then the nine-day parade of witnesses began. While Judge Cohen and the lawyers around the trial table hastily scribbled copious notes, the jurors sat with folded hands, or squirmed in their chairs, as the testimony went on and on.

The first witnesses called by Dudnik were fellow employees of Gallick on the railroad, summoned for cross-examination. Their testimony was routine and told of the plaintiff's work habits. They drove home again and again in the jury's mind the condition of the area around the track. William Molnar, a brakeman with the railroad for 14 years, said "Gallick was a hustler . . . a good, steady worker." He described the standard switching crew of three men with the oldest, Gallick, as the foreman. He remembered the pond near the track and said he often saw dead rats and pigeons in the swamp. His testimony was bolstered by other railroad employees, Walter Rady, a yard foreman, and William Clason, another yard foreman.

Next, the victim's wife was called to the stand. Mary Gallick, at 52, was a plain-looking, simple woman. She was employed as a waitress in a local restaurant: the same type of work she had done before her marriage in 1926. No, she testified, her husband had never had any skin trouble before that fateful August of 1954. He had, in fact, never even had any serious illness before the accident. Once, she remembered, he had pulled some ligaments and another time had injured an ankle in stepping off a railroad car into a hole. But nothing serious.

Mrs. Gallick was a good witness on the course of the disease, although she could tell nothing from her own knowledge about how it had started. She said that her husband asked her to look at the back of his left leg above the knee one August night after work. She said she saw there a welt about the size of a half fingernail. She saw it again the next morning, and the color was now a deeper pink. Her husband continued to go to work and each day the welt got redder and larger. Finally, she said, she got her husband to see a doctor, Jacob R. Heller, who treated him and then sent him to Dr. Victor D. Ippolito. The latter ordered Gallick to the hospital. The wife softly testified that her husband was sent into surgery, and then sent in again. He was in the hospital from September 18 to December 8, 1954, she said, and added that she saw no other marks on his body than the original welt.

When Gallick came home, she testified, he was very sick and appeared in great pain. Then she noticed sores breaking out on other parts of his body, on his ankle, under his arm, and other places. She described the whole process of draining the wounds, his pain, and the dressing of the injuries. He returned to the hospital for more treatment and then was sent home again. Afterwards, he returned to the hospital again and again, she said—adding that "After each operation he looked worse." Then, on May 21, 1958, almost four years after the "bite," Gallick's left leg was amputated. Three weeks later the right leg was taken off.

The next witness was not required to take the stand : it was Gallick himself. While he testified in a faltering voice from his cot, every ear in the jury box strained to hear his softest whisper and every eye was glued to him. He told how he had gone to the eighth grade in Minnesota schools and then worked at a succession of jobs : grocery clerk, truck driver, laborer for the Great Northern Railroad. He came to Cleveland in 1932 and worked as a laborer and labor foreman for a construction company. Then he went to work for the railroad.

Tension began to tighten in the courtroom as he told of the day in August when he went to work as usual at 2 :00 P.M. At 2:45, he said, he got his orders for the day and went to the spur track assigned to him. He said he stopped under the bridge to see if the engine was coming on the track. He had just started to walk when he felt the sting of a bite on his left leg. He testified carefully that he reached down and squeezed something between his thumb and first three fingers, felt it pop and then felt something roll down his pants leg. No, he never got a look at it because just then his engine came along and he swung aboard. He could not describe the "insect."

He repeated the story told by his wife of washing the sore, his gradually becoming worried and going to the doctors, and finally his trips to the hospital for surgery and grafts on the wound, which failed to take. Then, he said, the sores spread across his body and began running, accompanied by a "terrible odor." Finally, he came to the part where his legs were amputated. Dudnik's softness of voice matched Gallick's as he asked: "How do you feel about that, Jim?" The air hung tense. Gallick turned his face to the left and wept, a handkerchief to his face. The courtroom was in absolute silence; the jury stared at Gallick as though entranced.

Suddenly the spell broke; Mrs. Gallick rushed to her husband's side from her seat in the rear of the room. She wiped his face and offered him a glass of water. Judge Cohen suggested that the case be recessed briefly. But Dudnik and Gallick said they wanted to go on.

Dudnik's voice dropped even lower until it sounded like a hoarse whisper: "Do you want to live, Jim?"

In a voice so soft it was more felt than heard, the answer came: "Yes."

With a deep breath, Dudnik returned to his more normal voice. He drew from Gallick that the stump of one leg had healed. Gallick said he had once been a narcotics addict because of the unbearable pain but that he no longer was, although he still took "things for the pain."

The color had almost all returned to the faces of jurors when the next shocker came. Dudnik had asked Gallick to describe the sores. Then, in sudden drama, the lawyer stepped forward and peeled a bandage from the victim's right arm. A gasp could almost be heard from the jury as the angry, oozing wound sprang into view.

Cross-examination of the helpless victim was a weak effort.

The attorney, Hadden, drew from him that he had done work around the house—around the yard, the garage, the lawn—in that summer. But Gallick denied that he had worked in shorts outdoors. He agreed that he had gone through the industrial valley practically every day and said he wore shirt, khaki trousers down to his ankles, 10-inch-high shoes and 12-inch socks. The point here was obvious. Could the insect have been picked up—if such an insect indeed existed—someplace other than on the property of the railroad? The jury scarcely heard the questioning.

Again Gallick told how he arrived at work that day. There was some question raised by Hadden over the exact time of the arrival, and the story was repeated of the pause to look for the engine, the feeling of the bite, the squeezing of the unseen insect that Gallick described as being as big as his little finger. He said he had worked under that same bridge "off and on for about ten years" and that for the last four years he had been there at least twice a day every working day.

The next witness, called out of order for his convenience, was the Dr. Heller who had first seen Gallick. The doctor gave Gallick's previous medical history: treatment at one time for a back disorder, a bruise once of the right thigh. And then he told of treating a boil-like infection with drainage on August 26, 1954. He said he applied heat and gave a penicillin injection. He saw him several times later, but the infection did not respond to the treatments and he recommended hospitalizing the victim. He added that Gallick never returned to him.

On cross-examination, Dr. Heller said the wound had the appearance of a typical boil with discharge and tenderness of feeling, but that it did not act like an ordinary boil, because it was not responding to treatment. He said it was not apparent that the victim was suffering from an insect toxin or infection because the symptoms appeared purely local.

Another doctor to take the witness stand was the one to

whom Gallick had gone next : Dr. Victor D. Ippolito. He spoke angrily from the witness stand and repeated again and again "that was a dirty, filthy place with dead rats and pigeons." He again showed a fiery temper when the defense attorney, Leasure, tried to prod from him a reason for tying the insect to the particular pond on railroad property. In response to Leasure's question : "Doctor, do you really know that insect came from that pond?" he replied : "It is my professional opinion that they could have come from nowhere else, so it must have been from that pond. That is my professional opinion."

Dr. Ippolito next told how he tested the victim for such diseases as diabetes, cancer, Burger's disease, systemic diseases, syphilis, ulcerated cholitis, and found he had none of these. He told of taking biopsies of other lesions and finding none of them cancerous. Then he told of taking various biopsies, attempting skin grafts which ultimately broke down, repeated surgery for other swellings, and the constantly worsening condition of the patient. All this brought no hint of the origin of the problems. He described the pain of the patient, and said the last time he saw him professionally was some three years before the trial. He added that at the request of counsel he had examined the patient that morning and found a lot of scar tissues as well as an ulcerated condition. He said the arm was about the same as previous ulcer conditions and that his prognosis was that the arm might need to be amputated.

A high point in the questioning of Dr. Ippolito came with an exceedingly long hypothetical question by Dudnik. Told a great many facts, the doctor was asked, in essence, if he found a direct causal relationship between the condition of the area, the bite, and the ultimate condition of the patient. This, obviously, was a crucial point in the trial. The seriousness of the disease that had afflicted Gallick was evident; the condition of the pond was equally clear. But the great problem, which caused veteran lawyers to wince, was the practical impossibility of a clear connection between those two: could it be certain the "insect," if there really was one, had come specifically from that pond for which the railroad was liable—or had it come winging in from the nearby Cuyahoga River, or Lake Erie, or any other of the filth-ridden lots in the industrial area. The plaintiff had the obligation to prove that it came from the railroad's negligence. Dudnik felt secure. To him, under the broad interpretations of Federal law, all he need do was prove —*to the satisfaction of the jury*—that the railroad had not provided a safe place to work.

Leasure objected strenuously to the hypothetical question. He argued that it contained excessive facts, that some facts assumed were contrary to the evidence, that it assumed good health and no allergies, that it assumed the plaintiff was not improving when, Leasure said, the evidence showed that he was improving, and so on. He concluded that there was an assumption in the question that the "insect" was in contact with the pond. Nurenberg answered that under Federal law, the plaintiff did not have to prove that it came from the pond but only had "to prove a reasonable probability that it came from there."

Judge Cohen took great care with this question. He had the court stenographer type it up and he studied it overnight with the assistance of a law researcher. He finally ruled out parts of the question he felt were objectionable, but let most of it stand. Allowed to answer, Dr. Ippolito, of course, testified in the affirmative. However, under cross examination by Leasure, the doctor said he was a specialist in general surgery but was not an expert in dermatology and internal medicine and that he had no knowledge of insects.

Another medical witness for the plaintiff, Dr. Robin Anderson, told of the treatment that Gallick underwent, including 26 operative procedures, among which were 9 skin grafts, 2 amputations and 15 cleanings and debridements under anesthetics.

In answer to the hypothetical question, he, too, said he thought there was a causal relationship, even though he had not been present at the time of the alleged "insect bite." His records showed Gallick had chronic ulcerations but that no one knew the immediate cause; there was no proof of why ulcers appeared on other parts of the body.

At the conclusion of the plaintiff's case, Leasure offered a motion for a directed verdict. In asking that the court throw out the case, he argued that it had not been proven. Judge Cohen overruled the motion. This act was later to raise serious questions in the Court of Appeals.

First witness put on by the defense was William Clason, a yard foreman for the railroad. He testified that the area's water usually consisted of a puddle about two or three inches deep, which grew to a foot in depth after heavy rains. He said he never saw more than one dead rat or two dead pigeons at one time and never saw any extraordinary bugs. Clason testified that he had worked in the questioned area for ten years and had at times received mosquito bites, but nothing more serious.

The next witness was Joseph P. Corrigan, a trainman with the B & O since 1941. He testified that he knew Gallick and had worked with him many times. He said standing water was in the area as long as he had worked there. Yes, he said, he had seen a few dead rats or pigeons in the water, but the flies and mosquitoes were not any more numerous than in the industrial area generally. He also told of safety meetings held about once a month by representatives of different branches of the B & O for the purpose of reporting unsafe conditions.

The first expert witness called by the defense was Louis A. Stearts of Delaware. He was qualified as a medical and economic entomologist, an expert concerned with the habits of insects. In his opinion, the only insect to be found in that area would be the mosquito. He said he knew of no insect, as in this case, that could possibly attack a man. On cross-examination he said there were such things as water bugs, usually about three-quarters of an inch long and rarely over one and one-half inches. Some, he added, were hard-shelled; and one type, a giant water bug, could bite on provocation. But, he said later, it would be almost impossible for a giant water bug to climb up a pant leg.

Another witness, Ensel Richardson, a city engineer, testified that all waste and sewage of the industrial valley went into the nearby Cuyahoga River, and that creeks also emptied into the river. Thus, he implied, such an insect could have come from an area not on the railroad's property.

Dr. John H. Davis, who had also examined Gallick, testified bluntly that the basic cause of the victim's disease had never been found. He said that area conditions had nothing to do with Gallick's condition, that disease primarily came from living animals — and there was no history of disease from insect bites in northern Ohio. He said he saw other patients with similar lesions, but never saw one like this from an insect bite.

Finally, all the evidence was before the jury. Each side gave its closing arguments and Judge Cohen read a lengthy statement of the law which applied in this case. In an unusual move, special interrogatories were submitted to the jury. It was to take these questions with it into deliberations and answer each one to indicate how the conclusion had been reached. Here are the questions and the answers the jurors gave:

1) Did a pool of stagnant water exist under the Columbus Road Bridge during the entire early part of August, 1954?— YES.

2) Was the pool of stagnant water on the premises of the defendant B & O?—YES.

3) If the answer to 2 is yes, was the defendant B & O in

possession of the premises under the Columbus Road Bridge whereon the stagnant water stood?—YES.

4) Did the defendant B & O have under its control the premises under the Columbus Road Bridge wherein the stagnant water stood?—YES.

5) If the answer to question 2 is yes, did dead pigeons accumulate under the bridge in the stagnant water?—YES.

6) If the answer to 2 is yes, did dead rats accumulate under the bridge in the stagnant water?—YES.

7) If the answer to 2 is yes, did vermin accumulate under the bridge in the stagnant water?—YES.

8) If the answer to 2 is yes, did bugs accumulate under the bridge in the stagnant water?—YES.

9) Was the plaintiff required to perform his work duties in close proximity to the area referred to in question 1?—YES.

10) On approximately August 10, 1954, was plaintiff bitten by an insect?—YES.

11) If the answer to question 10 is yes, was he bitten while performing his usual and customary work duties?—YES.

12) If the answer to 10 is yes, was he bitten near or about the Columbus Road Bridge?—YES.

13) Did the defendant, B & O, provide the plaintiff, Mr. Gallick, a reasonably safe place to work under the facts and circumstances existing at the time?—THE JURY CAN'T DECIDE ON THIS QUESTION.

14) If the answer to question 1 is yes, did the defendant B & O know that by permitting the accumulation of said pool of stagnant water, pigeons, rats, bugs, and vermin would be attracted to said area?—YES. (*Only ten jurors signed this answer.*)

15) If the answer to 14 is yes, did the defendant B & O know that its employees would have to work in this area?—YES. (*The same ten jurors signed again.*)

16) Was the defendant negligent in one or more of the particulars alleged in the petition?—YES.

17) If the answer to 16 is yes, indicate in the words of the

petition the acts or omissions which constitute defendant's
negligence—"THERE EXISTED A POOL OF STAGNANT WATER ON
PREMISES IN THE POSSESSION OF AND UNDER THE CONTROL OF THE
DEFENDANT INTO WHICH WAS ACCUMULATED DEAD PIGEONS, RATS,
AND VARIOUS FORMS OF BUGS AND VERMIN." *(Ten jurors signed
this.)*

18) Was the illness or disease from which Mr. Gallick now
suffers caused in whole or in part by an insect bite sustained by
him on defendant B & O's premises?—YES.

19) Were the injuries to the plaintiff proximately caused in any
part, even the slightest, by one or more acts or omissions of the
defendant?—YES.

20) If the answers to any one of the questions numbered
1, 5, 6, 7, and 8 is yes, was there any reason for the defendant
B & O to anticipate that such would or might probably result
in a mishap or injury?—NO. *(Ten jurors signed.)*

21) Was there a proximate, causal relationship to the stagnant
water, the dead rats, the dead pigeons, the insect bite and the
present physical condition of the plaintiff?—YES.

22) If the answer to question 21 is yes, was it within the
realm of reasonable probability or foreseeability of the B & O
to appreciate this proximate causal relationship between the
stagnant water, the dead rats, the dead pigeons, the insect bite,
and the present physical condition of the plaintiff?—NO.

23) What amount of money will compensate the plaintiff,
James T. Gallick, for his injuries and damages, if any, resulting
proximately from this accident?—$625,000.

All six men and six women of the jury had agreed on this
figure, more than twice the previous highest verdict ever
awarded in the state. The jury had deliberated for two full
days. It returned to court at 4:56 P.M. and gave Judge Cohen
the written answers. The judge met with attorneys of both
sides, then sent the jury out to dinner, saying certain legal problems still had to be resolved. The verdict finally was delivered

at 8:22 P.M. Leasure asked the judge to poll the jury. Each member stood up and gave the $625,000 figure.

Judge Cohen called it an "important, well-thought case," and commended the jury. It was to be the last commendation that panel received, for around its decision burst a storm of disapproval and protest that ranged from the Academy of Medicine of Cleveland to informal meetings of lawyers to a later ruling by a Court of Appeals which bluntly reversed the decision and mapped the path to the United States Supreme Court.

Soon after the trial had concluded, an editorial appeared in the August, 1959, issue of the *Bulletin of the Academy of Medicine of Cleveland*. It said, in part:

A recent verdict in the amount of $625,000 against a railroad for forcing a man to work near a pool of stagnant water associated with "poisonous insects and vermin" again raises the question of whether courts are receiving competent medical advice.

Such verdicts are anachronistic. They smack of miasma and witchcraft, and reflect sadly on juror and jurist. That jurors and jurists are capable of precedent-making decisions based upon mysticism and fantasy is a terrifying prospect in this "enlightened" age.

In a brief filed with the Court of Appeals some time later, Leasure and Hadden listed 16 points of alleged error in the trial, among which was the argument that "damages assessed by the jury are excessive and appear to have been given under the influences of passion and prejudice." The brief went on to argue that Gallick, who had never earned more than $5,000 a year was awarded an amount equal to $125,000 a year tax-free for pain and suffering alone. It added that actual costs shown at the trial was $129,836 for hospitalization, medical expenses, lost wages, and similar expenses: "Almost half a million dollars is left to be accounted for in terms of pain and suffering," the lawyers said. "The $500,000 invested at four per cent would return $20,000 a year without reducing the principal one penny. Using principal and interest for the life expectancy, the verdict gives the plaintiff over $120,000 for pain and suffering alone, tax free. This is tantamount to over one million dollars per year taxable income."

The appellate brief added that the trial judge was in error for "limiting the jury's view of the premises to a very small part of the area involved" under the Columbus Road Bridge near the Cuyahoga River. (A jury can be challenged only for acting under "passion and prejudice," as was done above. All other challenges must be against the trial judge for doing, or failing to do, certain things.)

The brief added that no credible proof had been submitted at the trial "of a source on defendant's premises of the plaintiff's particular disease" or proof of the transmission of a disease from the pond to Gallick's person. It noted that the kind of insect involved was unknown and that the plaintiff had not been in contact with the pool.

In the spring of 1961, the Court of Appeals returned a unanimous decision : it did not find simple error and return the case to the trial court for a new hearing as is usual in such proceedings, but instead went further and bluntly reversed the judgment on the ground that it was contrary to law and entered a final judgment for the railroad, wiping out the entire $625,000 verdict to Gallick. I was the first newspaper reporter to get the verdict and I reported it to Dudnik, at that time in the midst of another personal injury trial. Dudnik was obviously disappointed, but said cheerily he expected to have the verdict reinstated by the top court.

Here is how the opinion written by Judge Oscar Hunsicker and concurred in by Judge Arthur W. Doyle (both of Akron,

Ohio) and by Judge Lynn B. Griffith of Warren, Ohio, reached this reversal :

We do not believe it necessary to discuss in detail each of the assigned errors, but, since this matter is brought under the Federal Employes' Liability Act, our consideration of the problem posed by these assignments of error must be controlled by the interpretation of such act by the Supreme Court of the United States. Under this statute, the test of a jury case is simply whether the proofs justify with reason the conclusion that employer negligence played any part, even the slightest, in producing the injury or death for which damages are sought.

Thus, the court noted, it must put aside the usual concept of causes of injuries as defined in Ohio law and apply instead the more liberal view of the Federal courts in such situations. Accepting this, the state court went on :

There are inconsistencies in the answers to the special verdict and the interrogatories made by the jury in the instant case. They did find, however, that the Baltimore and Ohio Railroad Company was negligent in maintaining the stagnant pool by the side of its track. Although the jurors stated that they could not answer the question as to Mr. Gallick being furnished a safe place to work, they did find a cause and effect relationship between the stagnant pool and the bug bite suffered by Mr. Gallick. After its affirmative answer to the proximate causal relationship between the stagnant water, the dead rats, the dead pigeons, the insect bite, and the present physical condition of the plaintiff, the jury found no reasonable probability or foreseeability of the Baltimore and Ohio to appreciate this proximate causal relationship between the stagnant water and other conditions leading to the present physical condition of Mr. Gallick.

The court then cited a great number of Federal cases and

asserted that "through all these cases there runs the underlying general principle that, before a plaintiff may recover damages, there must be proof of some causal relationship between the employer negligence and the injury or death of the workman."

Having set forth the rules it had gleaned from these cases which it intended to follow, the reviewing court then went into an analysis of the facts.

We do know by overwhelming testimony that the pool of stagnant, vermin-infested water was alongside the Baltimore and Ohio tracks for many years prior to the alleged "bite" suffered by Mr. Gallick. We know, by definite evidence, that insects were in and about this stagnant pool. There is a conflict in the testimony (resolved against Baltimore and Ohio) as to whether any insect of the size described by the injured employee might infest this pool, and which insect might "bite" a man.

We have sufficient credible evidence to conclude, as did the jury, that Mr. Gallick suffered a "bite" on railroad property by some insect while working for that railroad. We have an abundance of testimony that from such "bite" severe consequences to Mr. Gallick have ensued.

We can, with reason, say that, to maintain for a period of years a stagnant, vermin-infested pool of water on and over which insects gather, on property where its employees are required to work, could furnish the gravamen of an offense under the Federal Employers' Liability Act.

No similar "bite" or other insect bites were ever complained about, although complaint about the general unsanitary condition at the location of the pool was made to the railroad.

Throughout all the cases involving employer liability, in cases such as we have before us, the United States Supreme Court has held that a right to recover is established if, from the facts proved, negligence and its causal relationship to the injury and damage may reasonably be inferred; a jury question is presented if, with reason, the "conclusion may be drawn that negligence of the employer played any part at all in the injury."

From the facts heretofore set forth, it is obvious that the plaintiff's case, if it is to be sustained, must rest upon inferences to be drawn from the evidence.

There is no direct evidence that the existence of the unidentified bug at the time and place had any connection with the stagnant and infested pool.

We observe that proof is the effect of evidence—the establishment of a fact by evidence—and in litigation there may be evidence which does not amount to proof. Where there is neither direct evidence, nor reasonable inferences to be drawn from evidence, whether direct or circumstantial, a conclusion based upon such absence of evidence or reasonable inference is mere conjecture, and the drawing of a further inference from conjecture does not amount to proof. In proving a defendant's culpability, the proof must show that the tort is distinctly traceable as one of the efficient antecedents of the damages, and has a share in subjecting plaintiff to injury.

The observation made above refers only to legal cause. We are not here concerned with cause in the so-called "philosophic sense," for the reason that the causes of causes are infinite.

If the plaintiff's case is to be sustained, we must infer that this undescribed (except as to size and biting qualities) insect or bug had been attracted to the area in which the plaintiff was hurt by the stagnant pool, and that its bite caused the plaintiff's condition; that the pool created conditions and influences which helped to incubate or furnish an environment for the bug, whose bite was poisonous to the plaintiff; or, that the insect, having traveled from other areas, became contaminated or infected by the pool with a substance injurious to man, and that this substance infected the plaintiff when bitten.

The law is plain that, before the question of causation can be submitted to a jury, the trial judge must decide a preliminary question—i.e., whether from the evidence a jury could reasonably find the existence of a causal relation. If the judge decides in the affirmative, it will then be for the jury to say whether they do find. In other words, the judge must say whether on the evidence, a causal relation may be reasonably inferred. If the judge rules that it may be so inferred, the jurors then must say whether, from the evidence, the causal relation is inferred by them.

The question of causation should not get to the jury, and the judge should direct a verdict for the defendant, unless the court is of the opinion that a jury can reasonably find that the defendant's tort was an efficient cause of the damage to the plaintiff *and not a mere antecedent fact.*

As we view the record before us, we have a chain of possibilities that the negligence of the defendant might have shared in subjecting the plaintiff to damage and injury, but the proof of a legal causal connection between the negligence and the damage falls short of that required for the consideration of a jury.

Whether the insect causing the damage had any connection with the pool of stagnant water on the defendant's premises, or whether it came from the nearby putrid mouth of the Cuyahoga River, or from weeds, or unsanitary places situated on property not owned or controlled by the railroad, presents only a series of guesses and speculations, which speculations make a chain of causation too tenuous to support a conclusion of liability on the part of the railroad.

We determine, therefore, that where there is, as here, only a guess of speculation of a causal connection between the negligence of the employer and the injury of an employee, no liability attaches, and a judgment based upon such speculation cannot be sustained.

All other claimed errors have been examined, and we find none prejudicial to the rights of the appellant. The judgment herein is reversed as contrary to law, and final judgment will be entered for the railroad-appellant.

The road was long for both Ohio's famed bug-bite case and for the jury which thought it, too, would fade back into anonymity as others had done. Rejection of the jury's decision was upheld by the Ohio Supreme Court, in effect, when it refused to take the case under consideration. This supposedly ended the case in the state. Preparations were under way to take it to the United States Supreme Court—on the basis of the Federal law which was involved—when it suddenly exploded into violent headlines because of the jury.

One of the jurors, a forty-four-year-old widow, Mrs. Eleanora Stewart, gave a statement to police. She said that an employee at the restaurant across the street from the courthouse, a restaurant where jurors frequently ate, had tried to bribe her to influence the jury. Mrs. Stewart said that Ernest Constantine had offered her $2,500 "if you swing the Gallick case . . . for Gallick." She said that she had refused Constantine's request to "persuade some of the jurors, and to do all that I could to swing the case for Gallick." But, she said, the day after Gallick had won the gigantic verdict, Constantine came out to her home and gave her daughter $50 and gave her $200 "because the case closed like it did." Later she had several dates with Constantine.

She emphasized that she had not attempted to sway the jury.

Constantine at first said he had been approached to contact jurors and win favor for Gallick. Attorney Dudnik, victor in the case, emphatically denied that he or any one in his office had made such an offer. He told me, instead, that Constantine had come to him with a demand for money and a threat to reveal such a story if he were not paid off. After several days of headlines on the "jury scandal," Constantine suddenly repudiated his story. He was arrested and charged with both extortion—in trying to get money from Dudnik—and jury tampering. He was held for trial.

After public excitement of the "jury fix" case had died away and newpaper attention had turned to other matters, it was suddenly announced that Constantine had pleaded guilty to extortion, that the jury tampering charge had been dropped, and that he was on his way to the penitentiary. Again, the bug-bite jury faded away—for awhile.

In April, 1962, the United States Supreme Court decided to admit the case for full hearing. Preparations went into full swing among the lawyers. A date for hearing was set for December 6.

Suddenly new tragedy struck. In November, it was discovered that Dudnik, who was to argue the case before the top court, was the victim of advanced incurable cancer. His days were numbered and the task of arguing the case went to his colleague, young Nurenberg. The Supreme Court took the matter under advisement in Washington and, while Dudnik's life ebbed away, studied the case. Then, with Dudnik on his death bed, the ruling came : Dudnik had won. The Supreme Court reinstated the original $625,000 verdict, plus interest which brought it to $750,000. Dudnik was aware that he had won his greatest victory.

A couple of weeks later—on March 16, 1963—Dudnik died. And four days later Gallick, center of the case, also died. The money, when finally paid, was to go to his estate, which in turn would go to his widow under his will. Apparently the matter was finally resolved.

Then a new twist came and the jury suddenly sprang into the spotlight again. The B & O Railroad, through its attorney, Leasure, filed motion for a new trial with the state Court of Appeals. Basis claimed for this new trial were the alleged efforts to tamper with the jury in the original trial nearly four years before A whole new round of battle seemed ready to start, bringing its own appeals and mountains of legal briefs. Then, again suddenly, a solution came. Both sides agreed to a settlement of the entire matter for $450,000. All appeals would be ended. No further contests would start. Thus, without a jury, with the simple expedient of agreement between opposing parties, the entire complicated situation was completely resolved.

Index